MW01116441

Multimodal Conduct in the Law

The study of language and law has seen explosive growth in the past twenty-five years. Research on police interrogations, trial examination, jury deliberation, plea bargains, and same-sex marriage, to name a few, has shown the central role of written and oral forms of language in the construction of legal meaning. However, there is another side of language that has rarely been analyzed in legal settings: the role of gesture and how it integrates with language in the law. This is the first book-length investigation of language and multimodal conduct in the legal context. Using videotapes from a famous rape trial, Matoesian and Gilbert examine legal identity and impression management in the sociocultural performance of precedent, expert testimony, closing argument, exhibits, reported speech, and trial examination. Drawing on insights from Jakobson and Silverstein, the authors show how the poetic function inheres not only in language but in multimodal conduct generally. Their analysis opens up new empirical territory for both forensic linguistics and gesture studies.

GREGORY MATOESIAN is a professor in the Department of Criminology, Law, and Justice at the University of Illinois at Chicago. He is the author of *Reproducing Rape: Domination through Talk in the Courtroom* (1993), *Law and the Language of Identity* (2001), and coeditor (with Elizabeth Mertz and William Ford) of *Translating the Social World for Law* (2016).

KRISTIN ENOLA GILBERT received her PhD from the Department of Criminology, Law, and Justice at the University of Illinois at Chicago. Her current work focuses on language and multimodal conduct in focus group interactions. She has published peer-reviewed articles on gestures in *Gesture, Multimodal Communication, Narrative Inquiry*, and *Discourse and Communication*.

Studies in Interactional Sociolinguistics

FOUNDING EDITOR
John J. Gumperz (1922–2013)

EDITORS
Paul Drew
Rebecca Clift
Lorenza Mondada
Marja-Leena Sorjonen

Books in the Series

Multimodal Conduct in the Law

Language, Gesture, and Materiality in Legal Interaction

Gregory Matoesian

University of Illinois at Chicago

Kristin Enola Gilbert

University of Illinois at Chicago

CAMBRIDGE
UNIVERSITY PRESS

CAMBRIDGE
UNIVERSITY PRESS

University Printing House, Cambridge CB2 8BS, United Kingdom

One Liberty Plaza, 20th Floor, New York, NY 10006, USA

477 Williamstown Road, Port Melbourne, VIC 3207, Australia

314–321, 3rd Floor, Plot 3, Splendor Forum, Jasola District Centre,
New Delhi – 110025, India

79 Anson Road, #06–04/06, Singapore 079906

Cambridge University Press is part of the University of Cambridge.

It furthers the University's mission by disseminating knowledge in the pursuit of
education, learning, and research at the highest international levels of excellence.

www.cambridge.org
Information on this title: www.cambridge.org/9781108416351
DOI: 10.1017/9781108236362

First published 2018

Printed in the United Kingdom by TJ International Ltd. Padstow Cornwall

A catalogue record for this publication is available from the British Library.

Library of Congress Cataloging-in-Publication Data
Names: Matoesian, Gregory M., author. | Gilbert, Kristin Enola, author.
Title: Multimodal conduct in the law : language, gesture and materiality in
    legal interaction / Gregory Matoesian, University of Illinois, Chicago,
    Kristin Enola Gilbert, University of Illinois, Chicago.
Description: New York : Cambridge University Press, 2018. |
    Includes bibliographical references and index.
Identifiers: LCCN 2018016882| ISBN 9781108416351 (hardback : alk. paper) |
    ISBN 9781108402866 (pbk. : alk. paper)
Subjects: LCSH: Law–Language. | Semantics (Law) | Sociological
    jurisprudence.
Classification: LCC K213 .M384 2018 | DDC 340/.14–dc23
    LC record available at https://lccn.loc.gov/2018016882

ISBN 978-1-108-41635-1 Hardback

After the battle of Borodino, the enemy occupation of Moscow and the burning of the city, the most important episode of the war of 1812, according to historians, was the movement of the Russian army across from the Ryazan to the Kaluga road and on to the camp at Tarutino, the so-called flanking manoeuvre beyond the river Krasnaya Pakhra. Historians credit a number of different people with this stroke of genius ... [but] students of history seem determined to ignore the possibility that this march cannot be attributed to any one individual; no one ever predicted it ... the ploy was, in fact, never fully worked out in advance by anybody. It came about step by step, incident by incident, moment by moment, emerging from an infinitely varied set of unimaginable circumstances.

Leo Tolstoy, *War and Peace*

Contents

Preface

In his historical overview of gesture studies, Adam Kendon (2017) notes how scholars studied gesture as a feature of persuasive oratory prior to the eighteenth century, in contrast to the modern era's emphasis on gesture as a psychological or cognitive phenomenon. In the spirit of the Tolstoy quote in the epigraph, we view the law in the former sense, as an interactive and improvisational performance. We view the integration of speech, gesture, and materiality – multimodal conduct – as a persuasive oratory unfolding moment by moment in the concrete details of situated action. As we demonstrate in vivid detail, multimodal conduct furnishes the communicative infrastructure of the legal order.

Ironically, while massively present in the performance of law, the study of gesture (as it integrates other modal forms) is conspicuously absent in language and law research. By the same token, the study of legal interaction is largely absent in the field of gesture studies. If law is such a fateful force in social life, especially (as Max Weber reminds us) for the historical evolution of Occidental modernity, then its multimodal infrastructure deserves more analytic consideration than it has been given thus far.

Acknowledgments

A number of friends and colleagues have helped over the years in various ways. Thanks to Michael Silverstein, Adam Kendon, Beth Mertz, Pam Hobbs, Susan Ehrlich, Robert Moore, Adam Jaworski, Jim Wilce, Matthew Lippman, Susan Gal, Michelle Aldridge, June Luchjenboers, Alison Johnson, Susan Goldin-Meadow, Stephanie Dressler, and Ronjon Paul. Lindsey Elizares and Caitlin Bosch worked their magic on the photos. Thank you Troy Elizares for the jacket design. David McNeill and Susan Duncan allowed the first author to hang out at their gesture workshops at the University of Chicago, so many thanks to them for the exciting sessions. We are deeply indebted to Jurgen Streeck for all his help and encouragement. We owe a special debt to Paul Drew, Helen Barton, and Sapphire Duveau at Cambridge University Press. Catherine Rae's superb copyediting greatly improved the finished manuscript. We would like to thank the following publishers for permission to use parts of previous articles and chapters: Sage, Oxford University Press, Routledge, John Benjamins, John Wiley, and Walter de Gruyter.

Transcription Conventions

Symbol	Meaning
(.)	short untimed pause
(1.5)	time pause in seconds and tenths of seconds
((head nod))	double parentheses for descriptions of events
[((gesture))	left bracket double parentheses for embodied action
word	italicizing for stress
lo:::ng	colon(s) for vowel extension
bold	bolding for louder than surrounding talk
=	equal sign for latched utterances with no pause
> <	more than / less than refers to sped up portions of speech
look-	dash for cutoff utterances
[	above and below brackets for overlapping speech/ gesture
	(beat gesture symbols in Chapters 8, 9, and 10)
vc	parallel vertical chop gesture
ig	interdigital gesture (tip of right index finger lands on and ascends up the fingers of the left hand)
^ig	intradigital gesture (right hand index finger latched onto little finger of the left hand where rhythm is beat out with latching motion)
fh	horizontal fist hitting gesture where the right hand fist hits the left hand grasping palm
rh	residual hitting gesture where the form of the last hitting beat is maintained to form two up-down vertical gestures in the hitting beat position
mmg	material mediated gesture with photo where there is up and down and/or forward movement of the photo; material mediated gesture with both hands holding the transcript and moving up and down.
dg	deictic gesture with left hand pointing to the top of the transcript held in the right hand

Introduction

Despite the recent spate of textbooks, monographs, and review essays on language and law or what is often referred to as forensic linguistics, researchers rarely, if ever, mention the role of multimodal conduct – gesture, gaze, posture, and physical objects, and how they work in concert with the verbal modality in legal settings. In fact, the first major textbook in the field, *Just Words*, is quite revealing in its title, representative of prevailing sentiments that legal discourse consists solely of verbal and/or written modes of language.

By the same token, despite the proliferation of gesture and multimodal studies over the past several decades, researchers rarely, if ever, mention their role in the legal institution. This omission is all the more glaring because the law touches virtually all aspects of social existence, from the most intimate moments in a personal relationship (as in *Obergefell* v. *Hodges*, *Loving* v. *Virginia*) to broad scale social changes like voting rights, desegregation, and, for Max Weber, the "rationalism of world mastery" in the Occident.[1] Indeed, the two-volume, 2,200-plus-page *Handbook on Multimodality in Human Interaction* (Müller et al. 2013 and 2014) with 172 chapters makes no mention of multimodal conduct in the law, a rather glaring neglect of this most crucial institution for organizing social life.[2]

In this book, we demonstrate that legal discourse involves much more than *just words,* and that language and other modal resources operate

---

[1] In this regard, we might consider Weber's statement that capitalism is the "most fateful force in our modern life" (1976: 17). As he goes on to note, since modern capitalism requires a formal rational system of law, an elective affinity exists between law and capitalism in which each feeds off the other to produce the uniqueness of Western civilization and its historical trajectory. If Weber is right that the law is "indispensable for a modern capitalist society" (Weber 1978: 682) then it might be more accurate to consider both formal rational law and modern capitalism as the "most fateful forces in modern life."

[2] To be more precise, while the *Handbook* includes a number of chapters on the role of multimodality in theater, politics, music, television, classrooms, industrial settings, language acquisition, robotics, dance, religion, and nonhuman primates, it omits the relevance of multimodality for the legal system.

together as co-expressive semiotic partners – as multimodal practices – in utterance construction, the production of meaning in legal interaction, and, from Goffman, in impression management.[3] Focusing on just words neglects the role of multimodal conduct in legal proceedings – how both language and other modal resources mutually contextualize one another in a reciprocal dialectic – and leaves the study of language and law with an incomplete understanding of legal discourse. Drawing on analytic and empirical inspiration from scholars in embodied interaction (Goodwin, Streeck), linguistic anthropology (Silverstein), gesture studies (McNeill, Kendon, Müller, and Goldin-Meadow), and material conduct (Heath et al.), and using audio-video data from a notorious (yet quite fascinating) criminal trial, this book demonstrates in concrete detail the relevance of multimodality for understanding legal discourse and how the law offers a dynamic institutional site for the sociocultural investigation of gesture and other modal resources. In so doing we illustrate the interactive and co-constructed social organization of this neglected yet crucial aspect of the legal order.[4]

Plan of the Book

The plan of the book is as follows. Chapter 1 will introduce the basics of multimodal conduct: gesture, gaze, posture, movement, and materiality. We begin with a review of the work of Kendon, McNeill, Goldin-Meadow, and Müller on different types of gesture and how ad hoc, co-speech gestures relate to language and speech more generally. We then move into the study of gaze, and review work by Goffman and Goodwin on the contribution of gaze and posture and how these modalities, in concert with speech and gesture, figure in various discursive activities like involvement and participation. The next section of Chapter 1 moves into

---

[3] The reader will soon see how indebted we are to Goffman, even beyond the universal emblems of dramaturgy and theater produced on the front cover. As he mentions (Goffman 1967: 3), "What minimal model of the actor is needed if we are to wind him up, stick him in amongst his fellows, and have an orderly traffic of behavior emerge? ... A psychology is necessarily involved, but one stripped and cramped to suit the sociological study of conversation, track meets, banquets, *jury trials* [our emphasis] and street loitering." We address how the "orderly traffic" of the trial emerges through multimodal conduct.

[4] Some may question or find problematic our use of the term *multimodal conduct* for the communicative practices we document in this book. In response, we can only offer the following. In a recent content analysis of the journal *Research on Language and Social Interaction*, Nevile (2015: 129) found "over 200 different forms of wording that seemed somehow to be used generally for the body in interaction ... nonverbal, embodied action, visible action, multimodal resources ..." etc. We find multimodal conduct sufficient for our purposes and offer no further justification other than that the term, for us, captures the active integration of gesture, gaze, physical objects, and posture/movement in concert with speech, to construct meaning in the law.

the role of material objects in court (such as exhibits, transcripts, and tape recordings), and reviews the conceptual resources that Heath and his colleagues have proposed for this taken-for-granted realm in the study of embodied action. In the last part of the chapter we will note how multimodal conduct possesses sociocultural resources for constructing identity, participation, and persuasive/charismatic speech in the law (referred to as the poetic function of language as found in the work of Jakobson, Bauman, and Silverstein). We also show how speakers in court can do things with multimodal conduct that is often prohibited in speech.

Part I examines how courtroom participants negotiate identity – who we are and what we are doing on a moment-by-moment basis – and participation, – the micro organization and projection of discursive roles in context – in multimodal conduct.[5] Chapter 2 demonstrates the co-construction of expert roles in court and how the prosecuting attorney attempts to impeach the credibility of an expert witness by claiming he is an "academic" rather than a "private" (hands-on) physician. In response, the physician employs specific types of facial expressions, lip protrusions, hand gestures, and headshakes in concert with speech to negotiate the status of his expertise and experience. In one fascinating segment, the expert recalibrates the prosecuting attorney's question and projects his own question to which his answer can be arguably heard through the use of gaze, head shakes, and open palms (that is, he recalibrates questioner and answerer roles through multimodal conduct).

Chapter 3 analyzes the intertextual construction of precedential identity in a pretrial motion to determine if a particular precedent applies to the facts of the case. We demonstrate how the prosecuting attorney brings multimodal resources and epistemic stance to bear on the constitution of legal evidence, identity, and sociocultural relationships in an intertextual and interdiscursive drive to shape a coherent, precedential narrative against the defendant. More explicitly, we show how a metaphoric gesture functions as an evidential practice in constructing the relevance of testimony from three other women who claimed that the defendant sexually assaulted them prior to the current victim.

Chapter 4 introduces a deviant case where the witness uses multimodal conduct like gaze and head nods to solicit a response from the defense attorney: a request to complete a spate of testimony from the previous day. In a stunning virtuosic response, the defense attorney evokes a metapragmatic

---

[5] According to Goodwin and Goodwin (2004: 222), "participation refers to actor's demonstration of involvement performed by parties within evolving structures of talk." Along similar lines, we conceptualize participation as the micro-organization of interactional roles in the courtroom – real or virtual – and their possible laminations or embeddings.

frame, or what Silverstein (1979) refers to as linguistic ideology (folk rationalizations about language) that shapes the epistemological criteria for
gauging the authenticity and truth of testimony. As the witness' utterance
progresses, we will see how her narrative and reported speech are signaled
through body torque, middle-distance or thinking face gaze, eyebrow flash,
and embedded parenthetical – multimodal conduct that, quite ironically,
confirms the defense attorney's suggestion that she is speaking from a prepared script produced in collusion with her attorneys from the prior evening.
Here we demonstrate in vivid detail how reported speech constitutes an
interactive and multimodal co-construction rather than a mere discursive
object that inheres in the grammatical and paralinguistic properties of an
isolated speaker's utterance. In Goffmanian terms, we show how a particular
footing and forms of participation emerge as a joint multimodal activity.

Part II focuses on how multimodal conduct figures in the prescriptive
culture of trial advocacy (or advice manuals and textbooks on "effective
trial techniques and tactics" Gaines 2016: 3): multimodal conduct in direct
and cross-examination and its relation to legal strategies like motivation,
control, and credibility. In Chapter 5, we study a specific type of hand
gesture, what is often referred to as a "beat," and investigate how this
understudied gesture is more complex and multifunctional than ortho-
doxly conceived. In an analysis of witness motivation and resistance, we
show how beat gestures do much more than beat out rhythm and foreground points of significance in speech. Looking at a witness (the victim)
in a rape trial, we reveal how she fuses accusatory metaphors and deictic
points with rhythmic beats to fragment legal recipiency into institutionally
emergent laminations of participation, keeping shifting alignments of
participation in play simultaneously through multimodal conduct.

Chapter 6 illustrates a questioning strategy in trial examination
designed to control an evasive witness, referred to in legal texts as "nailing
down an answer." In "nailing down" we show how question control
functions through the interactive contours of verbal and embodied conduct. The attorney punctuates the pace and rhythm of each phrase with a
series of forefinger gestures, moving up and down, that evoke a metaphoric imagery of "nailing" to enhance emphatic stance, and build a
dramatic tension into the questioning. What is also novel in this segment
is how the attorney uses postural shifts, facial expression, and gaze shift to
comment negatively on the witness' testimony without using any words,
enabling him to circumvent legal constraints on verbal evaluation. This
reveals the necessity of looking to multimodal conduct for a more comprehensive analysis of legal discourse.

Chapter 7 focuses on the art of impression management as it emerges in
the integration of exhibits, movement, and speech that deals with

previously inconsistent statements made by the witness. Here we explore how material objects and language reflexively animate one another and other modal resources, such as tape recordings of speech. We examine how disparate streams of multimodal resources converge in an incremental build-up of suspense, and intertextual escalation of evidence that circulate around a key piece of material evidence: an urn. The urn anchors shifting contexts of legal evidence as it transforms its own identity across current and historical discourses. We show that the urn is not so much relevant momentarily to a particular sequence of speech or utterance or lexical item, as it is to the incremental and progressive build-up of suspense about itself, within and between the narrative segments – retaining its physical presence even in the midst of significant evidential transformations. It indexes inconsistencies in the witness' statements and promotes an iconic representation of confusion not just in the current speech, but even more importantly, during the reported event as well.

The final part explores rhythmic gestures and the integration of gesture and material objects in closing argument. Chapter 8 investigates how the attorney's narrative integrates hand movements, material objects (transcripts and photos), and speech to reinforce significant points of evidence and reduce the social distance between himself and the jury: what we refer to as *material mediated gestures*. In particular, the attorney uses polyrhythmic patterns and laminations of multimodal conduct to transform a partisan and unilateral interpretation of evidence into a joint construction between him and the jury – bringing them into a state of deictic immediacy as a persuasive legal strategy. The chapter shows how material objects like photos and transcripts are used to gesture, and how the attorney uses them to point out significant pieces of evidence. We display how metaphoric gestures point to and beat out displacement of mind to transcript, giving it a corporeal quality that he can reference as an object.

Chapter 9 continues with an example from closing argument and demonstrates how movements of the hands and fingers can vary in form to invoke semantic content, and reference objects along with their rhythmic function. Such gestures engineer emergent forms of propositional imagery (or add to the propositional meaning in the utterance) in addition to, and simultaneously with, their more orthodox rhythmic function, producing a multifunctional dimension of meaning that cannot be conveyed as richly through speech alone. In so doing, we offer a critical perspective on gesture typologies and seek to anchor such conceptual taxonomies in a detailed analysis of naturally occurring data, making a contribution to the study of both courtroom interaction and gesture.

In the movie, *The Devil's Advocate,* Al Pacino's character, Satan, refers to the law as the "ultimate backstage pass," and lawyers as the "new priesthood," along with a thoroughly unveiled allusion about their (and his) power in society. To continue with the Goffmanian analogy, the law is not just part of the backstage region but a sacred front stage ritual, a sociocultural performance that permeates our modern and postmodern condition from the most intimate aspects of social life to the most impersonal contracts, accelerating the globalization of rationality, and channelling the powerful conflicts associated with and resolved through it. However, in sharp contrast to the current state of scholarship in the field of language and law, we demonstrate in concrete detail how the "new priests" (like the old priests), perform their rituals with quite more than just verbal and/or written modes of language. We offer this study as an empirical exercise, not only on how the study of language and law can draw on analytic resources from the field of gesture studies to generate a more comprehensive analysis of legal interaction, but also how the study of multimodality in the legal order can make distinct and novel contributions in its own right to the study of the gesture-speech relationship.

1   Multimodal Conduct

What Is It?

Since the groundbreaking works of Atkinson and Drew (1979) and O'Barr (1981), the study of language and law has become a dynamic fixture on the sociolinguistic landscape. A wealth of research has found that rather than being the passive vehicle for the imposition of legal variables, language use – either written or verbal or both – constitutes the interactional modality through which evidence, precedent, and identity are forged into legal relevance, anchoring the infrastructure of legal decision-making and integrating social context into the fabric of legal conduct. Indeed, modern linguists define the law as a "law of words" (Tiersma 1999: 4) and an "overwhelmingly linguistic institution" Gibbons 2003: 1).[1]

However, a fleeting glimpse into any courtroom will reveal participants engaged in much more than language use. Attorneys gaze at witnesses when addressing them, beat out the rhythm of their speech with distinct hand movements, and extend an open palm facing upward when posing a contrastive question to reveal an inconsistency in testimony. By the same token, witnesses raise their right hand when taking the oath (in the United States), spread both palms upward and horizontally as if pleading to "give me a break," and curl their fingers under the thumb while extending an arm and index finger to point out the accused among co-present participants. Judges may raise a spread, outward-facing palm while admonishing a witness to stop talking while they rule on a pending objection. Borrowing from Depperman and Streeck (forthcoming), we use terms like "multimodal conduct" and "multimodal resources" interchangeably when referring to the integration of speech, gesture, gaze, material artifacts, posture, and movement in courtroom performance and modal resource to "refer to a single modality."[2] We begin first with an overview of gesture studies,

---

[1] More historically, in ancient Rome lawyers were referred to as "orators" (Friedman 1977: 21), while in medieval England barristers were called "storytellers" (from the Latin "narrators," Simpson 1988: 149). Both terms highlight the legal value placed on verbal skills.

[2] Our definition of multimodality also fits closely with that of Mondada (2016: 338): "Within perspectives inspired by gesture studies and the study of social interaction ... the term is used to refer to the various resources mobilized by participants for organizing their

then gaze, and finally material objects, highlighting their relevance for legal interaction.

What Are Gestures?

The study of gestures goes back to Rome in the first century AD. Writing on legal and forensic oratory (or "delivery" as he calls it), Quintilian discussed how gestures, especially movement of the hands, synchronize with the voice to convey powerful meanings – emotions that "move" or persuade the judge. He notes (Quintilian, 2001 Book 11.3, p. 129): "As for the hands, without which delivery would be crippled and enfeebled it is almost impossible to say how many movements they possess [...] ." Although writing in a prescriptive vein, he still demonstrates a keen awareness of the fine-grained details of gesture used in concert with speech. "The left hand never rightly makes a gesture on its own, but it often lends support to the right, if we are either (1) telling off arguments on our fingers [...] or (3) making an objecting by thrusting them forward [...] . The use of two hands together produces more emotion [...] ." (Quintilian 2001, Book 11.3: 143–145). We will see the relevance of his work on voice and gesture in legal delivery throughout our study.

Centuries later, in his study on *The Natural Language of the Hand* and *The Art of Manual Rhetoric,* Bulwer (2003: 184–186) examined what he referred to as the "dialects of the fingers" and how they play a major role in rhetorical eloquence (see Wollock 2002, p. 244). Especially relevant to the current study is his analysis of how lawyers use the fingers of one hand to count off arguments on the other hand (Bulwer 2003: 86).[3]

In a more methodological vein, de Jorio's recommendations for conducting detailed analysis of gestures prior to conceptualization and theorizing constitute a major point of departure for our analyses. He argues for the "importance of being exact in recognizing and describing the physical part of the gesture." Failure to accurately describe the gesture's physical position, he notes, is to ignore how "exactness can influence the interpretation of the gesture" (de Jorio 2000: 59). We also agree that observing and describing gestures in concrete detail – as situated action – in natural settings represents the first step prior to classification (see Streeck 2008 for a similar position).

---

action – such as gesture, gaze, facial expression, body postures, body movements, and also prosody, lexis and grammar."

[3] Bulwer's classic studies *The Natural Language of the Hand* and *The Art of Manual Rhetoric* are contained in a single volume but they have different pagination. Page 86 refers to his second work.

More recently, Kendon (2004) and McNeill (1992, 2005, 2012, 2016) refer to gestures (or what they refer to as "gesticulations") as idiosyncratic or ad hoc hand movements that co-occur and synchronize with speech in the production of meaning and construction of utterances.[4] For both authors, the meaning of gesture is context-sensitive and emerges at the moment of speaking (McNeill 1992), a meaning bearing moment that is referred to as the gesture stroke.[5] This definition excludes gestures with language-like properties, such as sign language, homesign, emblems or quotable gestures (V for victory, etc.), and so on, which impart meaning independently of speech. Unlike the compositional, analytic, and conventional features of language, gesture or gesticulation is global (meaning of the part emerges from the whole), synthetic (a single image captures a particular meaning), and idiosyncratic (or constructed improvisationally in real time) (McNeill 2016: 22). Thus speech-synchronized gestures convey meaning instantaneously or "on the spot" as it were, and convey visuospatial images in co-temporal movements with speech. To illustrate, we will show in later chapters how speakers continually adjust and readjust what Kendon (2004) refers to as "speech-gesture ensembles" so that the gesture coordinates with its speech counterpart to achieve discursive balance and semantic coherence – coherent courses of improvisational action. Most importantly, gesture and speech are co-expressive – not redundant – semiotic systems that together produce a richer tapestry of meaning than either could convey alone. As McNeill (2013: 31) states, speech and gesture "convey the same elements of meaning: ... but each may express a different aspect of it." According to Goldin-Meadow (2003: 9), "gesture and speech never convey exactly the same meaning."[6] For example, in Chapter 9 we show how a motion verb (*collide*) describes the

[4] The fact that gestures consist of ad hoc hand movements is only generally not invariably the case. Facial gestures, for example, do more than express emotion and may function as stance markers (see the example from the Menendez Brothers Murder Trial shortly), performatives, and reference (such as "lip points" or "chin points"). Moreover, facial gestures often work together with hand gestures in the production of meaning. See Bavelas et al. (2014a, 2014b) for a more thorough discussion.
[5] According to Kendon (2004: 112) and McNeill (1992: 25), gesture production is organized around a *gesture phrase* or excursion consisting of optional and obligatory components: (1) a preparation or movement leading up to the (2) stroke or the meaningful (main) part of the gesture that is obligatory and (3) an optional post-stroke hold in which the stroke is suspended or prolonged for a brief moment, often to create emphasis. These gesture movements depart from the "home" or base position (Sacks and Schegloff 2002) and then return after completion of the excursion.
[6] As she (Goldin-Meadow 2003: 3) illustrates, "when a child utters 'chair' while pointing at the chair, the word labels and thus classifies (but doesn't locate) the object. Pointing, in contrast, indicates where the object is but not what it is." We reveal in microscopic detail how co-expression works in legal interaction.

manner of contact between two objects while the gesture visualizes the intensity, shape, and consequences of that collision, providing a more robust unity of meaning than either could provide independently. Thus speech-synchronized gestures are not the mere emotional and/or relational underbelly of speech, but an integral component of the message itself.

This sets aright the rather common misperception that gesture plays a subordinate role relative to speech. If gestures were minor embellishments of verbal action, then we could perhaps dispense with a description of their contribution to discourse on the grounds that they are mere redundant supplements to speech. However, gestures may be subordinate to speech on some occasions, superordinate on others, or may work equally – as in the previous example – on others (Norris 2004). Whatever the degree of interplay, speech-synchronized gestures rarely convey the same information as their lexical counterparts, often producing information not captured adequately or as vividly in speech. Because they perform meaning visually or imagistically, gestures add another dimension to speech: complementing or clarifying verbal messages, performing distinct speech acts, intensifying commitment to an assertion (functioning as stance markers), foregrounding information, coordinating the rhythm of speech – parsing it into significant segments – and pointing out objects in the world (Kendon 2004: 281–282). Perhaps most importantly, as we will see in Chapter 5, gesture works with other modalities to keep shifting participation alignments and discursive activities in play simultaneously.

These similarities are not meant to downplay significant differences between Kendon and McNeill in conceptualizing gesture. For the former, gesture and speech represent different yet compatible modalities that interact in utterance production and constitute sociocultural resources in the conduct of social interaction or "utterance as visible action." For the latter, gesture and speech consist of an underlying unity of thought that is called "language" and represent a window to the mind. As McNeill (1992:1) puts it, "we should regard the gesture and the spoken utterance as different sides of a single underlying mental process." The difference is significant for the current study, for we also conceptualize how social actors in a natural setting orchestrate gesture–speech ensembles (and integrate other modal resources) as units of social action a la Kendon in the interactive assembly of legal context. Rather than being separate or isolated sign systems, gesture and speech constitute dynamically fused multimodal signal streams that feed into utterance construction and the co-improvisational interplay of legal discourse.

Despite their differences, both McNeill and Kendon offer crucial insight into a rather misleading yet commonplace conceptualization of gesture: the nonverbal and verbal dichotomy. For both authors, these are inaccurate and misleading terms to conceptualize what is more accurately referred to as speech-gesture synchronization, in which both function as equal partners in the embodiment of meaning in utterance construction (Kendon) and language as a cognitive system (McNeill). Jones and LeBaron (2002: 499) capture this point forcefully when they state: "verbal and nonverbal messages have been studied separately, as though they were independent rather than co-occurring and interrelated phenomena."

McNeill's Gesture Classification Typology

Gesture researchers have developed a number of schemes for classifying the gestures that accompany speech. However, the system devised by McNeill is the most influential, and since his typology has been widely adopted by most gesture researchers, it will be our focus here. McNeill (2006: 60) sorts out gestures in terms of a typology of what he calls the "iconic, metaphoric, deictic and beat quartet." Iconic gestures present images of concrete entities that resemble their referent. Using our previous example of *collide,* the defense attorney uses a fist-shaped gesture on the right hand that hits the open palm of the left hand in a vertical movement at the precise moment he utters the motion verb to produce an iconic imagery of one object hitting another. Metaphoric gestures present an abstract image in which a concrete source domain is mapped onto an abstract target domain. For example, after the defense attorney reads the victim's negative sentiments toward men from a written transcript, he points to the transcript and tells the jurors to "look to see what is in her mind," displacing the abstract notion of "mind" to the concrete transcript as we will see in more detail in Chapter 8. According to Müller (2008:75), *in the mind* would be an instance of an ontological metaphor, in which "non-physical or abstract objects are containers."[7]

Unlike iconic and metaphoric gestures that depict, display, or represent some object, action, or movement, deictic and beat gesture are, according to McNeill, non-imagistic. Deictic gestures locate referents through pointing, as when the alleged victim on the stand states, "What he did to me was wrong," and simultaneously points to the defendant on the pronoun. But as we will see in Chapter 5, her finger does quite more than just project a vector in the direction of the defendant; it recruits other functions beyond the deictic as well. And, canonically, beats orchestrate the rhythms of speech and highlight significant information. Like an orchestra

---

[7] Müller (2008) and Cienki (2008: 8) argue that iconic and metaphoric gestures are both iconic, the former being a concrete reference, the latter an abstract reference.

conductor's baton, they land on stressed syllables and visually parse speech into prominent segments (Norris 2004; Streeck 2008). Using up and down movements of the index finger or hand or both hands, beats increase the perceived prominence of their lexical (or phrasal, clausal, etc.) partners compared to words or segments without them, a vivid proof that speech synchronized beats increase the persuasiveness of the message (Goldin-Meadow 2003: 8; Maricchiolo et al. 2009: 244; Broaders and Goldin-Meadow 2010). For example (as we will see in Chapter 8), while reading the alleged victim's words from the transcript, the defense attorney uses the transcript to beat out the lexical affiliates *didn't, feel, trust,* and *men* (in the quote *I didn't feel I could trust men*). The surprisingly intricate and multifunctional contours of this persuasive and pervasive yet relatively under-explored gesture in oratorical delivery occupies our interests in several chapters.

However, as Kendon (2004: 103; see also Streeck 2009: 11) mentions, "Although McNeill seems content with his categories, it is not hard to see ... the different types proposed are not nearly as easily differentiated from one another as they seem ... it is sometimes quite difficult to decide whether a given unit of hand action should be considered a 'beat' or a gesture with some imagistic features. Often it must be considered to be both." In this study, we also take a critical perspective on gesture typologies in general and the beat-iconic/metaphor dichotomy in particular, and seek to anchor such conceptual classifications in detailed analyses of naturally occurring data (see also Bavelas 1994; Bavelas et al. 1995 and Bavelas et al. 1992 who advocate a similar strategy). As we will demonstrate in some detail, a given gesture may, at certain moments, operate multifunctionally, conveying both imagistic and non-imagistic dimensions simultaneously when looked at in naturally occurring contexts of legal performance.

Gaze, Postural Orientation, and Movement

"Given the pain of being stared at, it is understandable that staring itself is widely used as a means of negative sanction, socially controlling all kinds of improper conduct ... it often constitutes the first warning an individual receives that he is 'out of line'" (Goffman 1963: 88). Gaze, posture, and movement represent more nebulous – less extensively studied – categories of multimodal conduct but still provide crucial components of co-constructing participation and degrees of engagement in legal context. Along with his study of the "hate stare," Goffman (1963: 83) illustrates the analytic value of examining gaze – the direction of the head and eyes – and gaze shifts in his classic chapter on "face engagements," and as we will see, gaze co-occurs with both gesture and speech to create multimodal laminations of meaning in legal performance.

Building on Goffman and laying the foundation for the study of gaze in social interaction from a conversation analytic point of view, Goodwin (1979) examines how gaze direction aids in the accomplishment of interactional tasks facing a speaker in the construction of a turn at talk. Both structural properties of an utterance and gaze deployment locate recipients and resolve interactive problems that may arise in the construction of a turn at talk, specifically when to negotiate a state of mutual gaze at certain moments in the interaction. For Goodwin (1979, 1981), gaze behavior is a resource to design (and redesign) unfolding courses of action in interaction, recruiting appropriate states of involvement between speaker and hearer.[8]

Although the study of gesture has received the most theoretical development in recent multimodal scholarship, gaze (and gaze and postural shifts) often coordinates with both speech and gesture in court to (1) select the recipient of an utterance, (2) create a focus of joint attention, (3) display engagement with or disengagement from select participants and courses of action, and (4) most importantly, contextualize emergent forms of participation in the temporally unfolding rhythms of situated activity, distributing multiple layers of multiparty involvement simultaneously based on institutional roles and responsibilities (as we will show in Chapter 5). In essence, gaze represents a generic cultural resource in the coordination of discourse and management of involvement and social control in co-present interaction.

For example, in Chapter 7, we show an instance of affective stance as the witness withdraws gaze and closes her eyes after an acutely face-threatening accusation from the attorney. In the two examples to come, the judge shifts gaze from the prosecuting attorney (Figure 1.1) to the defense attorney (Figure 1.2) after an especially egregious evidentiary violation contained in the former's question to the defendant on the stand, signaling the latter to object to the question (or at least to display an expectation of an objection), even though, formally, judges in the adversary system in the United States are neutral referees rather than active participants.

"Although an individual can stop talking, he cannot stop communicating through body idiom" (Goffman 1963: 34). By posture we refer to the orientation of the body and differentially positioned parts of the body – what Goffman calls "body idiom" – and how these communicate, in

---

[8] Goodwin found that when speakers do not find the expected gaze alignment from their interlocutor, they actively recruit that gaze through cutoffs, repairs, restarts, and other speech disfluencies.

Figure 1.1: Judge Lupo gazes at prosecuting attorney pre-objection.

Figure 1.2: Pre-objection gaze shift and open-mouth display with eyebrow flash to defense attorney.

concert with speech, gaze and gesture, different types of activity, and degrees of involvement in those activities for legal performance. According to Norris (2004: 24), "Posture is the study of the ways in which individuals position their bodies ... first, the form of the body position and, second, the postural direction that an individual takes up towards others." For example, in Chapter 5, we display how the alleged victim deploys gaze and postural orientation – in concert with talk and a pointing gesture – to distribute differential legal obligations to specific participants (the defendant, prosecuting attorney and jury) and assign their emergent relevance in her ongoing narration, revealing an improvisational density and flexibility in the interpenetration of multiple sign systems, especially during her "staring" gaze at the defendant (in a manner strikingly reminiscent of the aforementioned Goffman quote). In Chapter 4, we show how the witness's body torque (or as Schegloff 1998: 536 defines it, "divergent orientations of the body sectors above and below the waist, respectively") signals shifting laminations of engagement and fractures participation roles in her narrative performance. Yet this is not the product of a sole speaker's viewpoint.[9] Our concern is to show how her postural viewpoint unfolds sequentially as a multimodal and interactive co-construction rather than a product of an isolated speaker's cognitive process.

But bodies do not stay still; they are in movement, even in the courtroom. To illustrate, in Chapter 7, we show how the defense attorney, ostensibly under auspices of asking the witness to identify a piece of physical evidence, carries a rather unwieldy object – an urn – from one end of the courtroom to another, takes it out of a box, and places it on the witness stand directly in front of the witness. Why would the attorney engage such movement when he could have taken the object out of the box and asked the witness if it was the object referred to? The movement itself (and placement) offers a clue as to its impending significance. That he transports a rather heavy and unwieldy object from one end of the courtroom to another rather than merely taking it out of the box for a quick identification from the witness provides evidence that the movement itself augurs something much more important than determining referential identity.

In sum, gaze, positioning, and movement of the body (and orientation of parts of the body) work in concert with both speech and gesture to build variable laminations of participation and degrees of multimodal engagement in co-present activities in the courtroom.

Materiality

Any discussion of multimodality in the law would be incomplete without considering the role of materiality – or in more active terms *material conduct* – and how it integrates into the semiotic stream of embodied and verbal action: what Heath and Hindmarsh (2002: 117) refer to as the "local ecology of objects and artifacts." As they mention, although material objects appear in much research as passive features of the environment, their semiotic function emerges only *in the moment* as it actively contextualizes the environment in which it is embedded. They emphasize

---

[9] Kendon (1990: 212) also discusses "how the hierarchy of priorities and longer and shorter term commitments in the organization of the individual's attention is directly perceivable by the way in which the various segments of the body are oriented." Basically, body torque refers to a twisting of the neck and head (or upper torso) in a direction away from the body's stable/main position.

that when research conceptualizes material objects as mere stable and passive props of the physical environment, it ignores their dynamic role in constructing coherent courses of action and how participants utilize them to accomplish distinct interactional tasks. In a similar vein, Goodwin (2007: 196) refers to "environmentally coupled gestures . . . that encompass not only talk and gesture, but also objects in the world."

While relatively neglected in language and law research, material objects represent a crucial modal resource in the law, especially trials. We pose the question: How are material objects made meaningful at specific moments in particular contexts? For example, in the case of the urn mentioned previously, it not only takes on considerable testimonial intrigue and suspense via movement from one end of the courtroom to the other but also becomes an intertextual object of immense evidentiary significance in the defense attorney's handling and positioning of the exhibit. In several chapters, we demonstrate the intertextual role of exhibits, tape recordings, and photographic evidence in and as multimodal performance (and the linguistic ideologies that circulate around them): how speech, gesture, and material objects mutually elaborate one another.

Written and Verbal Language in Multimodal Conduct

One area that has received scrutiny in language and law studies is the use of written transcripts. In a recent issue of *Research in Language and Social Interaction* devoted exclusively to the relationship between talk and written language in legal settings, Komter (2006: 195) found that transcripts of police interviews were "considered as objective and factual accounts" of what happened. Komter (2006 and other contributors to the issue) demonstrated how written texts integrated with talk in court, such that each modality mutually elaborated the other. Most interestingly, she discovered that the interviewer's questions in the transcript were conspicuously "absent" in verbal discussion in court, fostering the impression that the witness produced a narrative account or monologue (Komter 2006: 197).

What is not conspicuously absent, as we will document in this study, is how the attorney uses the witness' words in the transcript to beat out the significance of her words as he is speaking them, using the transcript to enact beat and metaphoric gestures simultaneously for rhetorical and ideological effect. Although Komter illustrated in concrete detail the importance of the neglected relationship between written and verbal modalities in legal settings, she neglected the role of gesture, gaze, and posture and how these integrate with both talk and written materials in the production of a factual account, the hidden intertextual and metapragmatic processes that shape evidence and identity at specific moments in the legal proceeding. What is the interaction among the written police (and deposition) interview, current talk, and multimodal conduct in the legal proceedings?

Applied Implications of Multimodal Conduct for the Law

If, as we have indicated, legal interactions emerge from and consist of multi-modal conduct and if trial transcripts based on those interactions are sent to appellate courts for case review, then their omission may leave both the trial and appellate courts with an inaccurate depiction of those proceedings. Consider the following examples. Broaders and Goldin-Meadow (2010) demonstrate how consideration of only the spoken modality in legal interaction may provide an incomplete picture, especially given that gesture and other forms of embodied conduct do not appear in written transcripts of the proceedings. Consider the following exchange between an investigative interviewer and a child taken directly from Broaders and Goldin-Meadow (2010: 623).

(a) INTERVIEWER: "What was he wearing?"

    CHILD: "A music hat."

An investigator examining a written transcript of this exchange would assume that the new information – the hat – was the child's idea. Now consider a second exchange:

(b) INTERVIEWER: "What was he wearing?"

    CHILD: [silence]

    INTERVIEWER: "Was he wearing glasses?"

This time the investigator would assume that the new information – the glasses – was the interviewer's idea.

    Written transcripts are essential tools in legal interaction, but they may be misleading and incomplete. The aforementioned transcripts misrepresent what actually happened during the two interviews. In (a), the interviewer gestured "hat" (tipping fist to forehead as though donning a hat) while asking her question. In doing so, she silently encouraged the child to mention a hat when, in fact, no hat had been worn. In (b), the child gestured "glasses" (two O-shaped hands held to the eyes) during the silence. From the transcript, the glasses appear to be the interviewer's idea, but they were actually the child's idea. Moreover, and not addressed in their analysis, the tipping of the fist to the forehead encodes even more information than gesturing about an object. It is not just an iconic gesture of "hat" but a hat that has a brim, such as a baseball cap rather than, for example, a "beanie." This has implications for the accuracy of testimony and the ability of an interviewer to "steer" the interviewee in a particular direction.

Let us introduce a second example concerning evidentiary constraints in the adversary system in the United States. In the adversary trial, only answers from witnesses constitute evidence, not questions from attorneys (in a legal prescriptive sense only of course). Moreover attorneys cannot verbally comment on or evaluate the testimony of witnesses during questioning, such that comments like "Give me a break!" would be argumentative and thus inadmissible. However, consider the example to follow from the Menendez brother's murder trial in 1993 (held in Los Angeles, California).

In the *State of California* v. *Menendez*, two brothers were on trial for murdering their parents in 1989 (for a 15 million dollar inheritance). The police investigation failed to implicate the two brothers until they confessed to a psychiatrist, Dr. Oziel, who had his girlfriend and patient, Judalon Smyth, listen in from an adjacent room. She notified the police that she heard them confess, and they were subsequently arrested. However, after Dr. Oziel broke up with her she changed her testimony just before the trial, claiming that Dr. Oziel had given her memory implants and that she suffered from disassociation. The following is a one and a half-minute (edited) segment of Smyth's (JS=Judalon Smyth) cross-examination (PA=Prosecuting Attorney). Brackets followed by parentheses [(( )) below the utterance indicate the precise alignment and type of co-occurring embodied conduct.

```
PA:   And when you testifi:::ed in Jan- in June excuse me.
      July of 1990 did you understand you were testifying
      under penalty of perjury?
                          (1.9)
JS:   Yes
                           (.)
PA:   And when you testified did you tell the truth?
                          (0.4)
JS:   Yes. I told the truth as I- believed it and knew it
      at the time
                           (.)
PA:   Would you say your memory today u:::h (.) four
      years later is better than your memory was (.) in
      July of 1990?
                          (1.0)
JS:   In some aspects yes (.) because I now have my own
      memory not the memory Oziel planted in me
                            .
                            .
                            .
```

```
PA:   When you refer to disassociation what are you
      talking about?
                        (1.2)
JS:   U::m (1.0) apparently what I've learned (.) about that
      incident was u::::m (4.2) whe:::n (2.0) I::: came into
      what I perceived as a hostile environment (0.5) and
      something that was (0.6) u::m part of the:: (1.0) initial
      trauma that I had suffered, which was (1.3) coming and
      being in the room with the Menendez brothers (.) u::::m
      I:: did something whi::::ch (1.8) is called disassociating
      where I::: (.) somehow (.) separated (1.0) myself and
      (1.4) I was there and I answered questions from some
      element of my consciousness but (.) u:::::m
                        (1.5)
PA:   But you weren't really there?
      [((micro-expression of disbelief or disgust))
                                          .
                                          .
                                          .

PA:   ((cheek screw))
```

After the narrative from witness Judalon Smyth about "disassoci-ation," Pamela Bozanich, the prosecuting attorney, completes the wit-ness's testimony with a contrastive clause that occurs with two noticeably marked facial gestures (functioning as stance and a speech act): first, a micro-expression of disbelief (or disgust in Figure 1.4) that co-occurs with the clause (in which the upper eyelids and cheeks are raised, the nose is wrinkled and lines show up above and below the lower eyelid, see Rozin, Lowery, and Ebert, 1994; Ekman and Friesen 2003: 66–77) and, second and afterwards, a solo "cheek screw" gesture (using a pencil to make the gesture in Figure 1.5) that indicates the individual has a "screw loose" (it might also indicate "give me a break").[10] Although such gestures may have an effect on the jury they will never appear in the official record should the transcript be sent to an appellate court for review. Consequently, the appellate courts will not have a comprehensive and accurate representation of the trial proceedings to base their review of the case. We will see how the defense attorney in Chapter 6 produces similar evaluative gestures when commenting on the testimony of the witness.

---

[10] The cheek screw gesture here appears as a variation on the "temple screw" (Morris 1977).

Figure 1.3: Prosecuting attorney's "home" position.

Figure 1.4: Prosecuting attorney micro-expression of disgust/disbelief *(But you weren't really there?)*.

Figure 1.5: Prosecuting attorney using pen for "cheek screw" gesture.

Multimodal Conduct as Verbal Artistry in Court

Our concern involves more than demonstrating the relevance of multimodal conduct for the law. Throughout the ensuing chapters we pay close attention to the poetic performance of multimodal conduct and how speakers mobilize speech and other modal resources as a sociocultural vehicle of artistic expression designed for a strategic payoff: persuading the jury of the particular point at issue. Following Jakobson (1960) and Bauman (1986), we situate the study of multimodal conduct in what the former referred to as the poetic function of language or language as an aesthetic performance "above and beyond referential content" (Bauman 1986: 3) or denotation (Silverstein 2014).[11] For Jakobson, the poetic function (e.g., parallelism, Jakobson and Pomorska 1988: 99–108) foregrounds language form over content and draws attention to oratorical strategies rooted in the sociocultural performance of identities, participation, and intertextuality.[12] In a similar vein, Silverstein (1985) discusses how text-metrical forms of language like parallelism signal specific interpretive (or metapragmatic) strategies in both narrative and co-present interaction. That is, such linguistic forms channel and naturalize inferences through rhythmic cohesion in the metricalized text (see Lempert 2008, 2012; Fleming and Lempert 2014).

Yet there is no *a priori* reason to limit the poetic function to language or verbal artistry. In the forthcoming chapters we will explore how a multimodal fusillade of gesture, gaze, and materiality creates dense clusters of poetic harmony that work together to weave an overall picture of legal reality, a coordinated and co-improvisational ensemble designed to enhance the effectiveness of oratory and thus persuade the jury (Bauman 1986:). Indeed, the microcosmic infrastructure of the legal order emerges not only through the drama of spoken performance but theater of multimodal action as well.

The Data and a Methodological Note on Data from Courts

The data we use for this study consists of videotapes of the William Kennedy Smith rape trial, one of the most infamous and widely publicized trials of the last century, involving a member of the Kennedy family and the daughter of a wealthy industrialist in West Palm Beach, Florida. After giving Smith a ride home from a trendy nightclub, Patricia Bowman claimed that on March 30,1991 at around 3 am, he raped her on the lawn of the Kennedy estate. The trial took place from November to December

---

[11] And well before Jakobson, we have the work of Quintilian who wrote on emotional legal delivery in the form of gesture and speech. More recently and explicitly, Lempert (2012:184) defines the poetic function as the "cardinal arrangement of co-occurring signs, which appear metricalized, that is, measured out in countable, recurrent units."

[12] By intertextuality we refer to the decontextualization of some stretch of discourse and how it is recontextualized in the current speech event, typically for strategic purposes. We use intertextuality and interdiscursivity more or less interchangeably in this work.

1991 and pitted charismatic defense attorney, Roy Black, against prosecuting attorney Moira Lasch. After a brief deliberation, the jury acquitted Smith of second degree sexual assault.

But while we use the sexual assault trial as data, our unit of analysis is neither rape nor the rape trial, or even trials more generally but the multimodal resources court participants bring to bear on the co-construction of legal context and the co-improvisational interplay of such communicative tools for sociocultural performance.

Bearing these points in mind, the trial was filmed in its entirety and provided researchers unprecedented access to visual data that was previously available only on audiotape and/or in written transcripts. For the researcher, audio-visual data does not rely on memory, intuition or written-up field notes (and interpretations of ethnographic field researchers), nor does it depend on the court reporter's determination of what to include in the official transcript.[13] Researchers can view such data repeatedly to capture the delicate nuances of real-time interaction and thereby subject it to detailed scrutiny and systematic analysis, not just talk but gesture, gaze, objects, movements, body orientation, and other fine-grained features of the setting that might otherwise escape notice. Audio-video recordings of the trial, together with data transcripts, allow other researchers to check the validity of one's claims and possibly offer alternative explanations – the bedrock of scientific replication and falsification. Other researchers have access to the same data to falsify, modify, or accept the analysis (rather than having to rely on experiments and interviews) prior to the data being domesticated into *a priori* coding schemes and statistical design. Data can be stored, so that possible relevancies that may have been overlooked in prior analyses can be used to refine new dimensions and directions of study, often at much finer levels of granularity. Still, ethnographic data is often required for a more complete understanding of legal strategies and tactics, and we employ these when relevant.

However, audio-video data, like all data, is far from perfect, and a major methodological issue needs to be broached in any discussion of trial videotapes. While indeed valuable for enhancing the precision of empirical research, there are practical and logistical considerations that figure in the use of multimodal forms of data in legal settings like the courtroom. In their informative overview, Jones and LeBaron (2002) recommend that: "future studies of face-to-face interaction be grounded in visual records." While this would be an optimal scenario for studying courtroom interaction, it is often not feasible. Frequently, video recordings of the proceedings are not

---

[13] Official court transcripts include only language and hence bleach multimodal conduct from view, as well as other prosodic and paralinguistic features of speech.

permitted (at least not in the United States nor in the United Kingdom) and even in those cases where they are, it is quite different from videotaping everyday conversation where researchers can position the camera angle (or even deploy multiple cameras) to include the entire set of participants. Instead, researchers have to rely on third parties (like Court TV and other news sources), which means that the available visual record will be selective in what is recorded, and rarely will all engaged participants and relevant interactive contours of embodied conduct be captured on video. Such limitations apply to the current data also.[14] In Chapters 3 and 6, for example, much of the multimodal conduct is unavailable for inspection because the camera has switched angles or to a non-speaking participant and we are left only with the verbal component.

Even so (and with these limitations in mind), since multimodal interaction in the law in general and the adversary context in particular has never been the topic of systematic description and analysis, this study offers a first attempt to understand multimodal conduct in the legal context. In the chapters to follow we investigate how physical evidence, testimony, precedent, inconsistency, credibility, expertise, motives, affect, and reported speech emerge and take shape in the concrete details of multimodal conduct. In the process, we address how multimodal conduct builds the interactional and evidentiary infrastructure for discovering sexual assault in court and contributes to our understanding of the social co-construction of rape's legal facticity. Still more generally, we strive to articulate a robust integration of both multimodal conduct and the law without compromising the integrity of either.

In her classic work, *Hearing Gesture,* Goldwin-Meadow (2003: 3) writes: "To ignore gesture is to ignore part of the conversation." To revamp her proposition slightly, if conversation is multimodal then it follows that the study of legal discourse needs to incorporate a more comprehensive view of the communicative process in its sociocultural context: language use as the improvisational integration of verbal and embodied modes in the contextualization of sociolegal action. Ignoring this other half of the conversational equation leaves us with an incomplete understanding of the "new priesthood" and the sociocultural dynamics found in it. We start our analysis of that "other part of the conversation" by examining how the prosecuting attorney attacks the credibility of an expert witness through a novel impeachment strategy, and how the witness responds to her attack just as "creatively" through multimodal conduct.

---

[14] Needless to say, another aspect of the data – not necessarily a limitation – is that we can only claim that speakers *attempt* to persuade the jury. The data we use does not allow us to make claims about the actual effects of multimodal conduct on the audience.

Part I

Negotiating Legal Identity in Multimodal Conduct

2   Co-Constructing Expert Identity

Introduction

Expert testimony is one of the hot – perhaps revolutionary – topics in the field of law. Recent Supreme Court cases such as *Daubert* v. *Merrell Dow Pharmaceuticals*, *Kumho Tire Co.* v. *Carmichael*, and *General Electric* v. *Joiner*, as well as the use of experts in high-profile cases involving Rodney King, O. J. Simpson, Louise Woodward, and William Kennedy Smith have captivated the interests of legal scholars, the mass media, and the public. And it is not difficult to see why. While lay witness testimony is limited to the facts known to, or observed by them, experts may provide professional opinions and hypothetical explanations about the fact in issue based on their specialized training, qualifications, skill, education, and knowledge. Indeed, expert witnesses might be thought of as the new legal "superstars," for without their testimony, civil and criminal cases dealing with DNA, recovered abuse memories, cancer-causing properties of secondhand tobacco smoke, silicone breast implants, the biomechanics of head trauma (or shaken-impact syndrome), to mention but a few, would be impossible. Consequently, the gatekeeping role of law in terms of governing the scientific adequacy and thus admissibility of expert knowledge has emerged as a central issue in both legal scholarship and law and society research (Saks and Faigman 2005).

While the legal and scientific dimensions concerning the admissibility of evidence are indeed impressive, there is still a sociocultural aspect of expert testimony just as, or even more relevant to trial practice and outcome. Regardless of how the United States Federal Rules of Evidence, the *Daubert* trilogy of Supreme Court cases, or any of the myriad legal principles governing expert testimony are logically applied and variably interpreted, and whatever the legal outcome of that process, there is still the mundane task of constructing expert identity – whether in judicial decisions to admit the testimony, juror evaluations of the testimony, appellate review of that testimony, (or all of these).[1] That identity (and the incontrovertible scientific or junk evidence offered through it) is constituted through our contextually situated communicative practices (Cotterill 2003). As Carr (2010: 26–7) puts it, "expertize is not something one has but something one does ... expertize is enacted in the real-time course of communicative practice." Following her lead we ask: How do attorneys and experts make, challenge, and negotiate claims to expertise in and through the law in multimodal conduct, the law not as abstract theorizing, but as it actually happens?

In the Kennedy Smith trial, a crucial part of the case involved a police statement from the victim in which she stated that during the act of penetration the defendant held one arm down, pinned her other arm between their chests, pulled her dress up, pushed her underwear to the side of the crotch area, and then entered her with only a partially erect penis as she was struggling. The defense team called an internationally renowned psychiatrist and gynecologist in the field of human sexual dysfunction, Dr. Raphael Good, to provide an opinion on a hypothetical scenario based closely on the victim's statement. Hypothetical statements allow the defense to invite inferences about the ultimate fact in the case without presenting any evidence or interviewing any of the witnesses (such as the victim). In the case here, it is inferred that she must have assisted the defendant in some way for sexual intercourse to have occurred, and that it was therefore consensual sex rather than second degree sexual assault. As seen in Excerpt 1 , Dr. Good testifies not to the ultimate fact at issue, whether rape or even penetration occurred, but to a hypothetical question containing facts.

Excerpt 1 (edited) (DA = defense attorney; RG = Dr. Good; PA = Prosecuting Attorney)

```
DA:   Doctor I would like you to listen carefully to the
      following hypothetical please. Assume that a twenty-nine
      year old female ... is struggling, twisting, arching her
      back and is doing everything possible to prevent the male
      from entering her vagina ... Assume that the woman claims
      that in this particular uh- situation, this hypothetical,
```

[1] In the Daubert trilogy, the US Supreme Court ruled on the admissibility of expert testimony in terms of reliability standards in addition to legal relevance. Is the work accepted by the scientific community? Is the expert's theory testable? Has the theory been subjected to peer-reviewed publications? Is the testing procedure reliable, and if so what is the rate of error? Keep in mind that the stated criteria do not constitute a definitive "check list" of necessary conditions, and whether Daubert has resulted in marked changes in legal practice is questionable (see Saks and Faigman 2005).

the male is only partially erect and that she claims that he
pushes the crotch of her panties aside and penetrates her
with his partially erect penis ... Do you have an opinion
within a reasonable degree of medical certainty as to
whether penetration under those circumstances is likely
or unlikely?

RG: Mr. Seiden under the scenario that you just painted I would
be- conclude that it is highly unlikely, very, very
unlikely for penetration to occur.

In cross-examination, prosecuting attorney Ellen Roberts challenged
neither the scientific adequacy of Dr. Good's physiological theory nor
even his damaging opinion on the hypothetical. Instead, she attacked his
competency and qualifications by making an invidious comparison
between a private practitioner, who deals solely and closely with patients,
and a *detached* academic physician, who possesses numerous administrative, research, service, and teaching roles in addition to seeing patients. In
so doing, she attempted to project a role strain or ambivalence in the
fulfillment of professional demands as a technique for impeaching his
credibility, hence undermining his authority to make definitive claims.

In what follows, we examine the epistemological grounding of claims to
expertise and how a represented role conflict emerges in the improvisational moments of multimodal practice.[2] We examine the multimodal

---

[2] In a theoretical sense, the prosecuting attorney's strategy is reminiscent of Robert Merton's
concepts of role set and sociological ambivalence. Merton (1957) expanded Linton's simple
conception of role theory – a single role attached to a single status – to encompass a
complex network of role relationships linked to a single status, which in their entirety
represent social structure. The status of professor, to use one of Merton's examples,
includes not a single role but first, an array of roles such as teacher, advisor, researcher,
administrator, and colleague, each relating to other statuses, and, second, bundles of sub
roles nested in these, such as teacher being both sponsor and evaluator in relation to
graduate students (Merton 1957; Hilbert 1990). Because each member of the role set is
differentially situated in social structure, there is no guarantee that members of each set will
possess the same expectations of other role occupants. For Merton (1976), sociological
ambivalence or conflicting expectations, rather than consensus or conformity to internal-
ized norms, is systemic, built in to the structure of the role set, even within a single role in
the set (Handel 1979; Crothers 1987; Hilbert 1990). For instance, the teaching role of
university professor may not only conflict with the researcher role, an inter-role conflict.
It may also exhibit contradictory norms because the teacher must be both sponsor and
evaluator of graduate student work, a case of intra-role conflict. To use another of Merton's
examples, one relevant to the current study specifically, the physician should have a degree
of affective detachment from the patient on the one hand, yet a sense of compassionate
concern for him/her on the other (Merton 1976). Yet we depart from Merton in the
following way: Rather than consider ambivalence as a factual social order or static social
category, we show how participants display an orientation to ambivalent norms and
counternorms in the situated details of embodied practice.

resources that shape the fragmentation of identity, competence, and expertise as both participants circulate beliefs about the relationship between medical and academic practice through an orientation to ambivalent norms in the role set. As we will see, the prosecution's task is to modify expert identity, transform it into an academic role distinct from private practice, and then dissect that role into a series of ambivalent sub roles. On the other hand, the expert's task is to minimize the strain of such conflict, displace the ambivalence, and maximize expert identity as the primary interpretive frame for calibrating his authority – to stress continuity among teaching, research, and medical practice. In the process, we will also see how a multimodal conflict is superimposed upon the represented conflict as it simultaneously mediates and projects role relationships into interpretive prominence. That is to say, the representation of role conflict parallels an array of multimodal ambivalences or dilemmas organizing the exchange between the prosecutor and expert as they strive to articulate disturbances in the projected role set. We examine not only how the prosecutor attacks the expert along the fault lines of this represented conflict, but also how both participants calibrate and recalibrate the criteria for judging expertise and grounds the adequacy of cultural beliefs about scientific knowledge in the multimodal particulars of legal interaction – how ambivalent identity emerges as a sociocultural practice through multimodal conduct.

The chapter is organized as follows. The first section discusses the primary, hierarchical opposition between private practitioner on the one hand, and academic physician on the other. The ensuing sections analyze how the prosecutor and expert negotiate academic conflicts among administrator, teacher, service, researcher, and clinical roles: how they deploy a range of interlacing multimodal resources – repetition, error correction, information packaging, prosody, register, one-upmanship, gesture, and other modal resources – to calibrate the doctor's inability to live up to role demands because of a lack of time, energy, and resources.

Academic Medicine

In the following data excerpts, the prosecuting attorney makes an initial contrast between academic physicians and private practitioners.

Excerpt 2

```
01 PA:   Would it be a fair statement, doctor, to say that
02       virtually all of your professional life (0.7) you have
```

03   been involved in (.) *academic medicine* (.) where
       you are employed or do work at some type of

04   university *setting* (.) ah: perhaps administrative

05   duties, lecturing, teaching (.) ah::: (.) >things
       like that<

06   (1.0)

07 RG: No that would not be fair

08   (.)

09 PA: That would not be fair

10   (.)

11 RG: No mam

12   (4.1)

13 PA: Isn't it a fact doctor the only *professional*

14   experience you've had in the private practice

15   of psychiatry (.) is for the last two years?

16 RG: No that's not true

17   (1.7)

18 PA: Well when were you:: (1.0) *licensed* as a psychiatrist?

19   (0.5)

20 RG: You don't *get licensed* as a psychiatrist

21   (.)

22 PA: **Well tell me what you do doctor** ((*very sarcastic tone*))

                             .
                             .
                             .
                             .

23 RG: In 1971, after actively practicing obstetrics

24   and gynecology in private practice in addition

25   to being on the faculty of the medical school ...
        ((continues for over a minute)) Somewhere

26   between twenty-five and thirty percent at least

27   of our time as full time faculty members were
        in seeing private patients ... in order to

```
28      [ get income for salaries  (.) we had to support
29      [((air quotes))
30      ourselves through private practice
```

Excerpt 3

```
01  PA:  Okay and you have been involved in academic medicine
         since
02           (.) nineteen fifty-seven.
03                         (.)
04  RG:  In one-way or another
```

In Excerpt 2, the prosecutor indicates that Dr. Good has been engaged exclusively in *academic medicine* and indexes the significance of that status first by the noticeably marked stress on the degree adverb (*virtually*), quantifier (*all*), partitive *of*-phrase, and prepositional phrase (*in academic medicine*), and second, by the preposed truth clause (*Would it be a fair statement*). By "academic medicine" she refers explicitly to work in a university setting and then proceeds to list the role obligations characteristic of that identity in lines 04 and 05 (*administrative duties, lecturing, teaching*) followed by the set-marking tag (*things like that*). Several noticeable aspects of the list are relevant to the fragmentation of identity. First, the list is important not only for what it includes but what it excludes: no mention of patients. Moreover, the set-marking tag instructs listeners to perceive his role as consisting largely of those items mentioned and foregrounds the significance of these over those left unsaid. Second, the prolongation on and slight pause following "*ah:::* " appear to signal that the prosecutor exhausts the relevant roles to assign to Dr. Good's status, still with no mention of tending patients. And, finally, the length of the list may function as an indexical icon of the length of time the doctor spends in academic rather than clinical roles.

In line 07, Dr. Good disagrees not only with the prosecutor's claim about his exclusive involvement in academic medicine but also with the suggestion that it would be a *fair statement*, and he does so through a partial repeat of her question (*No that would not be fair*). After a slight pause, the prosecutor responds with a third turn assessment of Dr. Good's disagreement by repeating his answer, a display that the response was not only unexpected but problematic as well. Her ensuing question in line 13 indicates that while Dr. Good has been in the private practice of psychiatry, this has been for the *last two years*, a question once more inheriting an immediate and emphatic rejection: *No that's not true.* Thus from lines 01 to 16, a finely synchronized pattern of repetition emerges, with the prosecutor's questions furnishing resources for the expert's rejections, and those rejections providing, in turn, resources for the prosecutor's response, setting the stage for an escalation of conflict in the ensuing sequence.

In line 18, she appears surprised by this second disagreement, a disconcerted stance marked through the 1.7-second inter-turn silence, turn-initial delay via the discourse marker *Well*, and one-second intra-turn pause prior to *licensed*. The conflict intensifies in the ensuing turn through a *one-upping* disagreement format, as Dr. Good challenges the presupposition that psychiatrists get licensed in (*You don't get licensed as a psychiatrist*). Notice too, that his non-referential *you* is not the same as the prosecutor's deictic *you*; it represents "institutional" *you* (similar to indefinite *one*). Dr. Good not only implements a shift from deictic to generic pronoun, but contemporaneously, recalibrates a shift in participation structure to animate and align with the institutional voice of medical authority: from lawyer/witness to expert/novice in an almost mocking lamination. He thus demonstrates that the prosecutor lacks even rudimentary knowledge of basic terms in the medical register. Put in more dynamic terms, Dr. Good activates technical terms in the medical register to accomplish the strategic interactional work of indexing professional identity and authority.

Just as interesting, Dr. Good's response never corrects the prosecutor's *faux pas*; it only offers a minimal negation without elaboration or account, and this alters the participation structure of the exchange a second time as the attorney opens up the questioning in the next turn (line 22). Instead of responding to the interrogative, Dr. Good is posed to respond to the looming *wh*-question at the behest of the attorney. This opens a discursive space for him to embark on a lengthy narrative that includes the amount of time he spends in private practice (lines 26–27) – an item that displays his orientation to the relevance of the projected conflict between private practitioner and academic physician. Notice an interesting aspect of this orientation occurs in lines 28–29. Dr. Good produces a conventional gesture or emblem, an air quote, that co-occurs with the *In order to get income* clause (see Figures 2.1 and 2.2). Although such a gesture – with both hands moving up to face level (palms facing outwards) and the middle and index fingers flexing several times – typically co-occurs with a quote or sarcastic remark (and euphemism), it appears to do something much different in this context. That is, it functions to emphasize and foreground the reason for engaging in private practice: that physicians had to support themselves by seeing patients.

Figure 2.1: (lines 28–29 upstroke of air quotes *to get income*).

Figure 2.2: (lines 28–29 downstroke of air quotes *for salaries*).

Two theoretical points of significance are worth noting here. First, answerers are not powerless relative to questioners or to some putative asymmetry imposed by the speech exchange of the courtroom. As we have seen, witnesses have a number of interactional resources at their disposal to steer the questioning in a more favorable direction, and in the aforementioned case the expert does so by escalating the discursive conflict in the unelaborated one-upmanship format. Indeed, the prosecutor's question in line 22 is heavily stressed to generate a sarcastic comment about the expert's adversarial error correction disagreement; it indexes an affective stance of frustration after two contiguous disagreements. Second, just as the expertise of the witness is being judged, so too is the competence of the attorney. Legal and professional identities – including the level of competence embedded in them – merge in the midst of these sociocultural discursive practices, at precisely this level of improvisational and contingent detail.

In sum, Excerpts 2 and 3 reveal an ambivalent opposition of norm and counternorm that contextualizes a role set hierarchy, a form of discursive power in the generation of epistemological dichotomies, and authorial boundaries of medical expertise. Dr. Good is an academic doctor with no hands-on experience in general and no hands-on experience with the victim in particular. He is not a compassionate "people" doctor, but a detached practitioner of academic medicine in a dynamic cultural opposition between physicians who examine patients versus academics who are scientists, teachers, administrators, and researchers.

To the detached academic physician who specializes in hypothetical opinions rather than compassionate concern, the victim is not really a patient but an object of abstract medical speculation. As a result, he is unqualified to know what happened. Once the prosecuting attorney creates the difference, she proceeds to show how the academic role is overburdened with role conflicts and overloads, and an inability to live up to role demands because of a lack of time, energy, or resources (Goode 1960).

The problem confronting Dr. Good, as we will see, is to challenge this underlying presupposition and articulate the conflict without appearing too detached from patients on the one hand, and any less an expert scientist on the other. How do attorney and witness negotiate the relevant interpretive frames for gauging expertise? How do they manage the opposition between "real" and "academic" worlds, a cultural distinction of no inherent value but salient as the underlying theme? Due to the ambivalent norms and counter norms between compassionate practitioner and detached scientist, if one is the former, it rules out the latter; and if one is the latter, it rules out the former. Following one medical norm makes it impossible to fulfill the other at the same time.

Teacher

In Excerpt 4, Dr. Good discusses his role in relation to residents, but as he does so, notice how he links his teaching to his practitioner role.

Excerpt 4 (continued from excerpt 2)

```
01 RG:    I planned the rotation of the residents (1.3)
          I- I pla::nned their educational activities

02        (.) and I wo[uld estima::te (1.5) that I

03                    [(((thinking face ...))) spent
```

```
04        (0.5) in that sort of [ planning (.) for the
05                               [ ((thumb and index
                                    finger gesture))
06        wo-work of the service [ (5.5)
07                               [ ((lip-point and head
                                    tilt thinking face))
08        [ maybe an hour a day? (1.0) For the rest of
09        [ ((Returns gaze to PA))
10        the time as the director of that service I was off
11        on the medical and surgical wards (.) seeing
          patients the residents had seen and we would
12        see them for follow-ups to be sure that they
13        were ah:::: their diagnoses and treatments
14        was consistent with our uh- uh training criteria
15 PA:    You were supervising your students then (.) er
          your interns
16                          (3.3)
17 RG:    Residents
18                          (.)
19 PA:    Residents
```

In line 01, Dr. Good launches into a lengthy narrative about his physician role relative to both students and patients. A beat prior to the verb of cognition (*estimate*) controlling the complement, he tilts his head upward, raises the eyebrows, and shifts into a "middle distance" gaze or "thinking face" display (Goodwin 1987), which aligns perfectly with the 1.5-second pause: an iconic mapping of verbal and embodied conduct (see Figure 2.3).[3]

When the utterance-in-progress resumes, he superimposes a marked yet quite delicate and precise gesture movement on the cognitive NP *planning* (see Figures 2.4. and 2.5), a gesture organized as follows (see Kendon 2004: 245). First, the tips of the index finger and thumb on each hand are pursed together (as if producing two half-circles or rings); second, each hand touches the other hand at the tips of the fingers on a symmetrical,

[3] Unlike Goodwin's (1987) discussion of the middle-distance gaze, the thinking face display here co-occurs not in the midst of a word search, but in the process of calculation.

Figure 2.3: (lines 02–03 thinking face *would estimate*).

Figure 2.4: (lines 04–05 *planning*).

Figure 2.5: (lines 04–05 *planning*).

horizontal plane in front of the body; and last, these are pulled apart in an in-out (horizontal) motion (as if *planning* moves "outward"), a metaphor organized as follows.

Lakoff and Johnson (1999) argue that abstract concepts like time are nested in concrete concepts like space, which can be experienced and understood directly (visually). Cassanto and Jasmin (2012) note that almost all aspects of time can be expressed in spatial words, with time appearing along the sagittal axis (front/back), especially when direction and orientation are noted. However, when speakers spontaneously produce co-speech gestures they often use the lateral axis (left/right), despite the fact that there are no expressions in English that specify time on the lateral axis.

Here, *planning* encodes direction to the extent that progress is implied in the NP (*of planning*). But the recapitulation of past events presents Dr. Good with a tempo-gestural dilemma, in particular, synchronizing past and present. As a solution, he bunches the fingers to create a precise point during his careful recollection of past events, demonstrating how experts are precise, delicately oriented to the details of their craft.[4] This "point" then locates deictically a present point in time and space, specifically the inception of *plan*. When his hands move outward on a horizontal or lateral plane, both left and right simultaneously – they depict, metaphorically, the linear passage of time, and the fruition of *planning*. Note, however, that the hands move right and left on the lateral axis, despite planning implying future progression. If rightward movement signifies future (as forward does sagittally), then left visualizes the past (as back does). The bidirectional spread of the hands reflects in space and motion the rhetorical infrastructure of the present narrative; this *planning* has already occurred (leftward, earlier), but must reflect the current use (rightward, later).

As the utterance continues, Dr. Good produces a much longer – 5.5-second – pause after *service* (line 06–07), that co-occurs with yet another noticeable embodied display. First, he looks upward (and to the side in a state of non-gaze with the prosecutor) in another thinking-face display, with a maximal widening of the eyes, eyebrow flash, upward head tilt, and chin jut. Second, he purses or compresses the lips to produce,

---

[4] According to Morris (1977: 58), such gestures are used when the speaker wants "to express himself delicately and with great exactness." Along similar lines, Kendon mentions (2004: 245) that precision gestures are employed when "a speaker is making a specific point, giving a specific piece of information on which he is insistent and which is … explicitly or implicitly in contrast to some other opinion or position." Of course, here the "other opinion" is from the prosecuting attorney. See also, Lempert (2011 and forthcoming).

Figure 2.6: (line 06–07 lip protrusion).

simultaneously, a non-deictic lip point or dual lip protrusion (see Figure 2.6).[5] Finally, he swings his head in a lateral to-and-fro movement, returns gaze alignment to the prosecuting attorney (relaxing the lip point), and completes the utterance with a markedly upward shift in pitch register (*maybe an hour a day?*).

After the 1.0-second pause, Dr. Good turns to the issue of seeing patients (line 11) and displays his orientation to being a hands-on patient doctor as well as teacher through the *rest of the time* phrasal quantifier, which grammatically marks the limited duration spent in the latter. Still, and with much greater precision, he might even be considered a "super" doctor, who examines both patients and residents to make sure that the latter have examined the former according to plan. However, although he spends only an *hour a day* supervising residents and the rest of the time *seeing patients*, the prosecuting attorney in line 15 refers solely to the teaching component of his prior answer. While it could be argued that the practitioner role here functions in relation to the teaching role, the prosecutor's follow-up question reformulates his answer in terms of its relevance to teaching rather than practitioner: as *supervising your students then (.) or your interns*.

Rather than dispute explicitly the prosecutor's reformulation, Dr. Good intensifies the conflict through an other-initiated other repair in line 17 after the prosecutor's self-initiated self-repair in line 15. In this one-upping format, he demonstrates his expertise by showing that *resident* is the appropriate term in the medical register, thereby legitimating his institutional identity as a physician and his legal status as an expert,

---

[5] That is, the *lip point* does not switch on what Enfield (2001) calls the "deictic vector of gaze," but activates something quite different as we will see.

in an interdiscursive drive for epistemological control and authority. As we saw in Excerpt 2, he synchronizes the one-upping correction with the enregistered voice of expert authority to accomplish strategic identity work in the escalating dispute. In the process, both prosecutor and expert negotiate claims to specialized knowledge and interactional competence through discursive form – mapping "what is said" onto "what is done" through the emphatic other and unelaborated corrections in the one-upmanship format (Silverstein 1998: 266), imparting an aura of certainty and authority to the unfolding dialogue (especially foregrounded in the wake of the self-correction attempt in the prior sequence). The expert is not just referring to supervision of students. Much more prominently, Dr. Good is "supervising" the interaction between himself and the prosecuting attorney, creating an asymmetrical context of instruction in the here and now as it is simultaneously represented in the talk: organizing the current interaction as he represents the past through the register repair.[6] As he challenges the presuppositions in the prior questions, Dr. Good demonstrates that he is more competent as an expert than Ellen Roberts is as a prosecutor through the repair sequence. Moreover, while the prosecuting attorney attempts to establish the role conflict between private practitioner and academic physician referentially, Dr. Good steers the relevant interpretive frame in the direction of expert by foregrounding identity through multimodal form and epistemic stance, perhaps a more optimal strategy than merely rejecting or agreeing with the prosecutor's position.

There are several observations to pursue about the multimodal and sociocultural emergence of professional identity. (1) While cognition might be considered a putative mental phenomenon, we should not lose sight of the fact that, in the aforementioned cases, it also functions as an interactive and embodied resource in the dynamic generation of meaning. In each of the body movements discussed earlier, Dr. Good foregrounds the process of mental deliberation and contextualizes the significance of not only temporal outcome but also epistemological stance toward the information imparted: a finely crafted stance of honest and thoughtful contemplation about the temporal span of occupational activities. Of specific interest here is the precision finger-touch gesture, which, as Kendon (2004) has noted, highlights and contextualizes a precise stance toward the forthcoming information. It does so through a spatio-temporal metaphor that uses motion in space as a metaphor for motion in time to demonstrate planning inception to completion. Such multimodal imagery could not be displayed

---

[6] According to Silverstein (1998: 266), this would be a mapping of denotation text to interactional practice or "what we are saying is what we are doing."

as vividly through language alone. (2) Although denotational text functions to provide a given representation of planning, estimation, and memory, an iconic, interactive performance of such putative mental abilities, with the complex inferences indexed through it, emerges only through the integration and juxtaposition of verbal and other modal resources, drawing the information so marked into a state of heightened prominence (Silverstein 1998). That Dr. Good's performance fosters an impression of thoughtful deliberation – that it contextualizes a heightened state of engagement or involvement with cognitive process – could not be conveyed, at least in the sense provided, through verbal resources alone.[7] What yields the interactional impact of his utterance is not the lone modal resource or verbal in isolation, but the temporal coordination among the array of multimodal resources – especially the sequential ordering of multimodal conduct and delay of turn progressivity – as they mutually elaborate one another via marked departures from the normal rhythm and flow of speech. (3) As the finger touching gesture and gaze movements merge into meticulous alignment with verbal and prosodic features – including turn-medial pauses – Dr. Good, first contextualizes and foregrounds the limited amount of time spent on teaching and, second, indexes his expert medical authority through performance laced features of epistemological stance. For instance, the final middle-distance gaze in concert with the lengthy pause, co-contextualize the punch line marked shift in pitch register at the onset of the epistemic stance adverb – *maybe an hour a day?* – to indicate that an hour a day is not a "big deal." In fact, although the epistemic stance adverb marks the level of doubt or certainty here, it may do quite more in conjunction with the head movement in line 7. It appears to lower the maximal threshold of doubt to one of little or no significance, as if to signal that the only thing that is certain is that it represents an insignificant doubt for an insignificant amount of time. In more oblique terms, this embodied process of estimation may constitute an inter-gestural and inter-visual ideology in which the "thinking face" movement projects a mental space in which to calculate temporal parameters and, in so doing, fosters the impression of involving a cognition state over contextualized performance (perhaps the lip pointing movement further contextualizes the deictic activation of gaze toward that projected mental space (see Enfield 2001). More accurately, however, such multimodal resources contextualize the position that the amount of time is not only

---

[7] Needless to say, we use "involvement" in the Goffman sense (1963: 43; see also, page 36): "Involvement refers to the capacity of the individual to give, or withhold from giving, his concerted attention to some activity at hand – a solitary task, a conversation, a collaborate work effort … a certain overt engrossment on the part of the one who is involved."

worth calculating but also worth showing the process of so doing in the finely synchronized coordination between verbal and other modal resources. In the case here, they project a virtual interactional space of deep involvement or engagement with the process of deliberation. As Kendon (2004) notes in considerable detail, multimodal conduct does not merely supplement semantic or pragmatic content; it also creates its own distinct strands of interactional relevance in the production of meaning, identity, and context.

To sum up the points thus far: Multimodal estimation displays the truthfulness and careful consideration of the expert's role or planning stage. The finger touching gesture draws attention to and contextualizes, the object of that estimation; the lip pointing gaze movement in concert with the shift in pitch register foregrounds the temporal contours and comparative relevance of that object. Together, each multimodal increment in the sequential movement interweaves a richly emergent, inferential lamination of identity relations and ambivalent voices in the dialogic pattern. Still more germane to the earlier point, the participants themselves bequeath a pristine sense of ambivalence to the ongoing exchange – ambivalence not as a static given of social life but as contingently emergent in the interactive particulars of sociocultural practice.

Researcher

According to the prosecuting attorney, Dr. Good's role as an academic physician is overloaded not only by teaching but by research as well.

Excerpt 5

01 PA: Didn't you also prepare applications for money grants

02   (1.4)

03 RG: Yes

04   (.)

05 PA: A:::nd you:: did all the paperwork required by

06   the University of Miami or the University of
        Texas justifying where the money went or

07   where the money was needed

08   (.)

09 RG: (hhh) I had a staff (1.2) that di- did much of

10   that paperwork, yes

Excerpt 6

```
01 PA:    Did you try to keep current with all the latest
02        things in medicine and psychiatry by reading
          the publications?
03 RG:    I not only read those publications I read the
          standard medical journals
```

In Excerpt 5, the prosecutor questions Dr. Good about writing grants and emphasizes the amount of *paperwork* required for this aspect of academic medicine. While he agrees superficially with preparing applications, he disputes the quantitative framing of the activity (*you did all the paperwork*) required for the applications, once again demonstrating his orientation to the putative role conflict by modifying the inclusive quantifier: *I had a staff that did much of that paperwork, yes.* More accurately, Dr. Good's turn-final agreement agrees with his own reformulation of her question, and in the process of negotiating the grant-writing conflict, he invites the inference that, since his staff does most of the mundane paperwork, he has time for more important matters, such as tending to patients.

In Excerpt 6, rather than contest the prosecutor's question, Dr. Good responds in a manner similar to what we saw in Excerpts 2 and 4. In this case, however, instead of challenging the prosecutor's assessment, he upgrades it through a contrastive structure to reframe the conflict. If he had just responded with agreement, he would have aligned with the prosecutor's overload claim. By upgrading the amount of reading – that he reads even more than the amount posed by the question – he may attempt to steer the relevant frame for calibrating competence into alignment with the expert rather than the academic physician. While it may be difficult for Dr. Good to contest the prosecutor's conflict frame and the presupposition embedded in the question, he may frame his own presuppositions in and through upgraded answers. Of strategic import: His upgrade might go against expectations that one would try to deny or justify or excuse the negative implications of the question, and in the process he may also appear more forthright than were he to engage in some type of evasive maneuver.

By the same token, the prosecutor's projection carries an identical sting in the tail. By highlighting Dr. Good's academic role activities, she also risks displaying his professional expertise, perhaps absorbing the distinction between them in a dynamic interaction between represented and discursive ambivalence.

Administrator

The attorney next supplements the teaching and research roles with that of administrator, increasing the strain in articulating role obligations.

Excerpt 7

```
01 PA:  Were you involved in curriculum changes and
        things like that?
02                              (.)
03 RG:  I had numerous committee responsibilities as
04      all faculty members did
```

Excerpt 8

```
01 PA:  And as part of you::r (.) work in academic
02      medicine you've had a (.) lot of administrative
        duties too haven't you, as part of that
03                              (.)
04 RG:  (hhh) It it- depended on what ah- my exact
05      position was on the faculty
                        (1.8)
07 PA:  But you would admit that you've had a lot of
08      administrative duties[(0.5) as part of that
09                           [(((extends palm of the right
                               hand as if beckoning the
                               desired answer))
11                      (1.7)
12 RG:  What would you define as a lot please
13                      (2.1)
14 PA:  Well tell us doctor exactly what you have
15      done then
```

In Excerpt 7, the prosecuting attorney questions Dr. Good about *curriculum changes* and *things like that*, items that involve the doctor's administrative obligations on the medical school faculty. As we saw previously, the set marking tag instructs the listener to include only

Figure 2.7: (lines 08–09 gesture *as part of that*).

similar administrative duties. Of course, private practitioners would have no such role obligations. In line 03, we see that, like other faculty members, Dr. Good had *numerous committee responsibilities.*

In Excerpt 8, the prosecutor refers to Dr. Good as an academic physician (*And as part of your work in academic medicine*), and then mentions how this role involves *a lot of administrative duties.* Instead of agreeing or disagreeing, Dr. Good mentions that the amount of administrative work would be contingent on *what my position was on the faculty.* After the qualified response, she repeats the question with the contrastive *but*-preface, which, in concert with the preposed factive (*you would admit*), is highly conducive of an affirmative answer (that is, *you would admit* is a highly biased question, strongly suggestive of an affirmative response). But there is more to conductivity here than language. As she begins her contrastive question in line 07, the prosecutor writes on and gazes at a notepad positioned on the podium in front of her. After the short pause she shifts her gaze and mobilizes an open hand supine gesture toward the witness that co-occurs with *as part of that* (see Figure 2.7). According to Kendon (2004: 272–273) such a gesture (not a full arm extension but bent at the elbow), indicates that the speaker desires to "obtain something from the interlocutor," in this case an agreement from the expert on her role conflict proposition about *a lot of administrative duties.* In so doing, the gesture escalates the coercive power of the question, something that would be missed by focusing on speech alone.

Instead of answering the question, however, Dr. Good responds with a question of his own. He requests a definition of the phrasal quantifier *a lot of* and, in so doing, sets the epistemological criteria for calibrating the legitimacy of her question, in particular, setting the felicity conditions for use of the quantifier. This also signals his expert identity by requesting a precise figure instead of the indeterminate quantifier, *a lot of*, which constitutes an imprecise and infrequent term in the formal medical register – a term characteristic of casual speech and informal registers (Biber et al. 1999: 276). Just as important, his remedial action alters, once again, the form of participation in the ongoing exchange from answerer to questioner, and, in particular, from answering *yes/no* questions to posing *wh*-questions (and with all the perquisites of being in that position). As it turns out, his question to the prosecutor inherits a *wh*-question from her in response. In a pair of powerful defensive movements, Dr. Good first produces a highly contingent response – that the answer would be relative – and, second, when the prosecutor repeats the question using a highly coercive combination of verbal and other modal resources, he poses a coercive question of his own, an epistemological hurdle on the felicity condition. Just as the prosecuting attorney upgrades the coercive form of her question, so too does Dr. Good one-up the level of resistance by questioning the transparent meaning of the phrasal quantifier, by challenging the presupposition. That is to say, these are not simply contiguous displays of one-upmanship but increasingly resistant one-upmanship formats.

Although the prosecuting attorney could have simply listed the administrative duties through a series of detailed *yes/no* questions and had Dr. Good agree with them, she is now put in the position (if she wants the answer that is), of allowing him to embark on another lengthy narrative (or put more prosaically, she attempts to take a shortcut and pays the price). After a noticeably marked pause in line 13, which fosters the impression of being caught off guard, she proceeds to do precisely that: *Well tell us doctor exactly what you have done then.* Quite transparently, the turn initial contrastive discourse marker *Well* and stressed components in line 14, constitute highly affective displays of frustration (simultaneously marking another display of incompetence), as his riposte confounds her expectations and compromises the integrity of her questioning strategy.

Professional Service

In the last excerpts to consider, the attorney escalates the role conflict representation, spinning a final web of significance, as she adds Dr. Good's professional service obligations to the growing list: attending meetings, teaching at conferences, and reviewing articles for scholarly journals.

Excerpt 9

```
01 PA:   And you have been an editorial reviewer for
02       about seven journals or magazines haven't you?
03                       (1.2)
04 RG:   Yes
05                         (.)
06 PA:   And doctor you would admit now that takes
07       u[h lot- (.)=
08 RG:   [((start and quick stop of headshake))
09 PA:   =uh lot[ of time to read those articles and review=
10 RG:          [((second more intense head shake))
11 PA:   =th[em and-
12 RG:      [((third and noticeably marked head shake
              with out-breath, alveolar click, closed eyes
              and downward gaze))
13                   (1.7) ((returns gaze to PA))
14 RG:   It doesn't take me a lot of time
15                         (.)
16 PA:   It doesn't take you a lot of time
17 RG:   Would you like to know how I do it?
18                         (.)
19 PA:   No I don't care how you do it doctor. I just
20       want to know how much of your time it took
21                        (8.5)
22 PA:   And then (0.9) you review for approximately
23       seven journals or magazines?
24                        (1.8)
25 FG:   I feel obligated to explain that
26                         (.)
27 PA:   JUST (.) please answer the question sir,
```

28   *do you review* for seven journals or magazines?

29   (.)

30 RG: Yes

Excerpt 10

01 PA: And you belong to::: (1.0) numerous scientific
        societies and you have over the:::

02   [(1.0) professional career?

03 RG: [Yes mam

04   (3.3)

05 PA: And in all of these societies that you have

06   joined doctor (.) they have meetings don't
        they that ya'll have to attend?

07   (2.4)

08 RG: You don't have to attend it's voluntary

09   (1.0)

10 PA: So you're saying that you joined these

11   societies but you don't attend the meetings?

12   (.)

13 RG: No I didn't say that

14   (.)

15 PA: Do you attend the meetings doctor?

16   (0.7)

17 RG: Some of th- them yes mam

18 PA: And have you tried to be a good (0.7)

19   member of these societies and attend (.)
        as many as you could attend?

20   (0.8)

21 RG: I'm well enough thought of to be the president

22   of a number of those societies, yes mam

23   (1.9)

24 PA: And when it comes to the conventions for

```
25      physicians you try to go to those (.) and
26      learn new things [ isn' t that correct?
27 RG:                  [ No- freq-
28 RG:  No, frequently, it is I who teach the others
29      the new things
```

Excerpt 11

```
01  PA:  And if you attend all those meetings (1.5) and go to
02       some of those conventions or even teach at them (0.8)
03       ah:: it keeps you pretty busy doesn' t it (.) with
         everything else
04                    (4.0)
05  RG:  ((turns to the left and back with raised eyebrows as if
         confused))
06  RG:  I' m not sure how pretty busy means
07                    (.)
08  PA:  BUSY DOCTOR.
09                    (.)
10  RG:  I'M A[ BUSY DOCTOR, yes
             [ ((hands thrust outwards smile))
11       ((outbreath burst of air + head shake))
```

The prosecuting attorney initiates this line in the ongoing conflict by questioning Dr. Good about his role as an editorial reviewer and the time it takes to read and review scholarly articles (Excerpt 9). In line 06 she deploys the rather imprecise phrasal quantifier (though aborting the projected final preposition "of" and NP "time"), along with the highly conducive pre-posed "confession" framing clause, *you would admit now*, to foreground the lengthy time involved in this role activity: that it takes Dr. Good *uh lot-* (line 07). That the phrasal quantifier designates a significant aspect of identity work inheres in the use of *now* (*And doctor you would admit now* in line 06), which is much more than a temporal (proximal) deictic – signaling the relationship between the proposition and time – at least in the case here. More accurately, while *now* is indeed

Figure 2.8: (line 08 lateral head shake).

polysemous, it functions as an affective stance marker to shift the form of participation into a more coercive frame, inviting Dr. Good to confirm the proposition in next turn while simultaneously imparting a strong sense of facticity to the impending phrasal quantifier (Schiffrin 1987; Aijmer 2002). That is to say, *now* contextualizes the significance of the phrasal quantifier and attempts to shape Dr. Good's response in next turn (linking epistemic and affective stance with discourse and ambivalent identities), especially given his prior resistance and disagreements (see Schiffrin 1987).

In the middle of the quantifier, on *uh* in line 6, Dr. Good launches a quick start into, then abrupt stop midway through, a lateral headshake: a forty-five degree, half-turn horizontal rotation of the head and return to original or home position (see Figure 2.8).

This, in turn, elicits a cutoff of the projected quantifier in the prosecutor's turn (line 07, just prior to the quantity noun *lot*) and restart in her turn-in-progress (line 09), as she recycles the projected yet aborted phrasal quantifier from line 07: *uh lot of time to read those articles and review them and-*. As she initiates the recycle, Dr. Good restarts his lateral headshake in line 10, a full forty-five degree, left to right rotation and back, to signal a more intense state of disagreement, without eliciting the same perturbation outcome from the prosecutor this time around.

However, at her completion of the second nonfinite complement en route to completion of a third in repetitive format, Dr. Good produces a noticeably marked – close to (but not quite) ninety degree horizontal rotation – third lateral headshake that co-occurs with an exaggerated alveolar click, closed eyes, and lowered head in line 12 – intruding on the prosecutor's turn in line 11 (see Figure 2.9).

Although the prosecuting attorney projects a third component post *to read those articles and review them and-*, she cuts off the conjunction and

Figure 2.9: (line 12 lowered head, eyes closed).

aborts possible turn completion at the precise moment Dr. Good initiates the third lateral head shake.

Let us unpack this densely interactive sequence of verbal and embodied turn competition between the participants. First, the prosecutor projects a phrasal quantifier that evokes a quick yet partial headshake from Dr. Good, which, in turn, disrupts her turn-in-progress in phrase medial position (line 07). Second, as she restarts and recycles the quantifier (line 09), Dr. Good resumes with a complete, horizontal forty-five degree rotation in line 10. Third, as she projects a third repetitive complement in a poetic format (*to read, review, and-* in lines 09–11), with embedded alliteration on *read/review* and *those/them*, Dr. Good produces a third, hyper-extended headshake (line 12), co-contextualized with shifts in gaze, paralinguistic features, and head movement that results in her ultimate turn withdrawal in line 11.

The competitive overlaps between participant's verbal and other modalities function as a type poetic collaborative coordination, each progressively and co-improvisationally threading an increment to the unfolding conflict, each escalating the struggle over ambivalent identity while simultaneously preserving – at least on a verbal dimension – the institutional order of the court. The prosecutor's turn-in-progress becomes progressively more salient to yield a richly emergent parallel structure, including repetition of and alliteration in the nonfinite complements, while Dr. Good's repetitive head nods occur in progressively intense increments, the finale incorporating a quite extraordinary multimodal display, as if to convey a resigned sense of frustration toward her persistent inaccuracies. Each repetitive movement contingently co-coordinates and co-contextualizes verbal and other modal resources not only between the prosecutor and Dr. Good, but also within each speaker and listener's

52   Co-Constructing Expert Identity

contribution as it simultaneously anchors a densely interactive sequence of alignment and misalignment in the resolution of overlapping body movements. When she starts, he starts; when she abruptly stops, he abruptly stops; when she restarts and recycles, he restarts and recycles; and when she projects an elaborate parallel structure, he responds with an affective bodily display. That is, the exchange incorporates not just a parallelism from a single participant but a multidimensional, interactive parallelism from both participants, with each increment moving along horizontal and vertical planes of multimodal space to reciprocally shape each self/other – each within and between turn – contribution in a mutually elaborative process. Each increment to the parallel structure on the one hand, and each increment to the headshake trilogy on the other, function interactively within and between each participant's activities to create a densely emergent clash of interpretive, epistemological, and emotive frames. In an analogy from Schegloff (2000), bodily conduct of the listener overlaps with talk of the speaker, activating the overlap resolution device – attempts to resolve discursive conflict laminated within identity conflict – creating perturbations in her turn-in-progress. In this instance, embodied overlap relates to turn organization and the overlap resolution device: an interactively managed device even in institutional settings such as trial cross-examination.

This reveals a more complex issue than mere turn encroachment or interruption of the turn-in-progress. Kendon (2002) notes that although headshakes generally (though not invariably) represent a negative assessment of a proposition, they may also add affective, evidentiary, and metapragmatic force to an utterance (and we can see a transparent instance in the doctor's third headshake). We would add, however, that such multilayering requires an analysis of (1) where the headshake is interactively positioned, (2) what other verbal and embodied resources co-occur with it, and (3) how a given headshake relates to preceding ones in sequential order. In the listener activity considered here, each headshake is positioned first, interactively relative to crucial information from the speaker and, second, sequentially relative to each prior shake – providing a mutually elaborative stance toward the speaker's position and the listener's own prior actions. A case in point: Dr. Good's final headshake registers an affective stance of frustration and disbelief concerning the prosecutor's proposition.

If we consider the headshake at this level of fine-grained detail, we can witness an intricate clustering of indexical features, from both speaker and listener activities, converging on the phrasal quantifier: headshake overlaps, cutoffs and recycles, affective stance marker, repetition of and alliteration in the nonfinite complements, and the co-occurrence of paralinguistic and gaze features. Why do these indexical features merge into alignment at precisely this sequential juncture – why this multilayered organization here and now? The prosecuting attorney marks ambivalent identity through grammatical structure (*a lot of time* line 09) and parallelism. In terms of the latter, she signals that it does not just take time to review scholarly articles. The parallel structure foregrounds the length of time iconically by dissecting the review process into distinct stages and thus expanding the strain: to read, review, and perhaps write up the reviews. In the midst of her production, Dr. Good attempts to fragment and displace institutional and discursive identities through embodied display. He disrupts the prosecutor's turn in progress at precise placement of the phrasal quantifier: the projected locus of ambivalent identity work. That the phrasal quantifier transacts crucial identity work inheres, first in the prosecutor's restart and recycle in the midst of Dr. Good's repetitive headshakes and, second, in the renewal of his bodily overlap over her attempts at resolution. Through repetitive head gestures, he gears shifting frames of epistemological authority into interpretive prominence and realigns forms of participation to shape ambivalent identity in the represented world through multimodal practice. Illustratively, the immediacy and progressive intensity of the doctor's multimodal disagreements, while displaying an affective stance that challenges and evaluates the presupposition about the time, also signals differential access to professional and expert knowledge because the prosecuting attorney is not in a position to possess such information.

In this sequence, we see an affective and multimodal disagreement unfold in a dense clash of multimodal resources that participants bring to bear on their interactive lives and legal realities. Dr. Good not only one-ups the prosecutor's authority through correction and register, but also one-ups and indeed preempts her verbal repetition through a multimodal one-upping poetic performance: a dynamic interaction between verbal and embodied conduct in the collaborative co-construction of ambivalent identity. As a theoretical and methodological aside, though certainly not an unimportant one, analyses of legal discourse that concentrate solely on the verbal dimension would miss how identity negotiations emerge interactively in such subtle dynamics of multimodal conduct.

After the prosecutor aborts her turn, Dr. Good's multimodal interruption evolves into its verbal modality outcome in line 14: *It doesn't take me a lot of time.* Her next turn repeats his assertion, which he then offers to explain in line 17, but that offer is rejected as she requests that he answer how much time it took. Whereas in line 6 she had used the indeterminate quantifier, she reformulates this in lines 19–20 as a more precise request for how much of his time it took. While Dr. Good attempts to explain the process of doing the reviews, the prosecutor underscores a sole interest in the temporal outcome of that process, and this negotiation reveals how both orient to the relevance of the role conflict impeachment strategy. Dr. Good asserts that the process of managing reviews occurs without a severe imposition of his time, while the prosecutor simply requests the time it takes. She recycles the question in line 22, but to no avail. Instead of providing the answer, Dr. Good recycles his request to explain the review process, which the prosecutor once again rejects.

Moving to Excerpt 10, the prosecuting attorney turns from Dr. Good's role as a scholarly reviewer to his involvement in professional associations, creating additional sources of intra-role strain in meeting role obligations and further developing the ambivalence between academic medicine and private practitioner. She broaches the issue of the number of scientific societies he belongs to and his attendance at professional meetings. After establishing membership in a number of professional associations and attendance at meetings, she asks if he has been a good member of those societies in lines 18 and 19. In the next turn, he one-ups the prosecutor's question (lines 21–22) to indicate that he is not merely a *good member* but *president of a number of those societies*. The prosecuting attorney in the ensuing turn asks if he *attends the conventions to learn new things* (as in ongoing professional development). Dr. Good's disagreement (in line 28) is framed in a sequentially contiguous, one-upmanship format. He produces turn-initial *No* to mark his disagreement, followed by the temporal adverb *frequently* and *it*-cleft contrast (with contrastive stress on *I*), which foregrounds his identity as teacher, not learner, as the relative clause backgrounds the presupposed information. Looking at these sequential one-upping movements, we can observe how both expert witness and attorney steer interpretive frames and legal identities in divergent directions through an interaction among grammatical structure, information packaging, and prosody.

Ironically, as she develops the conflict, she also highlights his expertise, and as he one-ups her assessments he aligns with the projected ambivalence: that he is primarily an academic who teaches students, colleagues and, of course, the prosecution in the here and now. By constructing expert identity in this fashion, Dr. Good upgrades the prosecutor's role conflict scenario, revealing his identity as a teacher embedded within the professional service role. Alternatively, this may be his optimal strategy in the discursive conflict: that is, to move into an expert identity by one-upping the prosecutor's ascription of role conflict. That Dr. Good teaches fellow physicians at medical conferences bestows a special degree of distinction upon his achievements, magnifying his expert identity (and perhaps moving beyond the threshold of mere teaching to expertise). Another way to think about the relationship between represented and discursive conflict is that her projected strands of ambivalence and his negotiation of these branch out into further – unintended – ambivalences in a never-ending cycle.

The final instance of conflict we examine occurs in Excerpt 11. In line 01, the prosecuting attorney mentions that going to and teaching at meetings keeps Dr. Good *pretty busy*, and by using the degree adverb she emphasizes the role overload that erodes time left for patients. Once again, Dr. Good challenges the presupposed transparency of the modifier both verbally and visually (visually he looks to the left and back, as if confused while simultaneously rolling the eyes in lines 05 and 06 and saying *I'm not sure how pretty busy means*). By activating a remedial exchange to request a more precise formulation, he derails the question and marks his expert identity in the process; *pretty* occurs infrequently in scientific and technical prose but more commonly in the conversational register (Biber et al. 1999). Instead of defining it, the prosecuting attorney simply repeats *Busy*, followed by the vocative *doctor* in an imperative construction with significant shift in stress and volume to generate a stern reproach. *Busy* means "busy" and this much should be intuitively obvious except to an academic, who would require such commonsense clarification. Here we can see how both attorney and expert negotiate the delicate contours of ambivalence, each striving to articulate divergent norms and counternorms in the conflict, and how multimodal conflict is superimposed on role conflict, shaping it as it is simultaneously shaped by that conflict. For the prosecuting attorney, only an academic physician possessing detached knowledge would seek clarification of such a commonsensical term. For Dr. Good, an expert requires terms in the scientific lexicon, and the conversational register lacks such precision. For the attorney, Dr. Good is a detached academic who lacks hands-on practice with patients in general and the victim in particular. For Dr. Good, the primary issue is not between academic and private practitioners and what that sociocultural opposition might yield, but rather his legal identity and competence as an expert. Indeed, his insertion query, *I'm not sure how pretty busy means*, represents a rather unconventional phrasing to manage the ambivalent struggle. He knows what "pretty busy" means but not *how* the PA intends it on this occasion, perhaps displaying that he is not "academically" isolated and withdrawn after all.

If we look at Dr. Good's response in line 10, *I'm a busy doctor yes*, notice another parallel over the repetition of *busy*. The attorney takes the meaning of *busy* as transparent; only an academic would fail to understand the meaning. Dr. Good's response occurs with heavily marked stress, an "exasperated" sigh, hand gesture, and headshake to signal, once again, his state of confusion with the prosecutor's question; only an incompetent attorney would broach his status as a "busy doctor," knowledge that should be obvious.

There is something else going on here that is not quite so obvious. If we look closely at the sequence, we can see a delicate negotiation over the nature of "busy," and this has significant bearing on legal-medical identity and role conflict. In line 03, the aspectual verb, degree adverb, and modifier (*keeps you pretty busy*) refer to Dr. Good's active involvement in and preoccupation with, academic obligations such as attending meetings, teaching at those meetings, and so on. Dr. Good's repetition of *pretty busy* requests clarification of the term in line 06, while the prosecuting attorney's repetition of *Busy* (line 08) employs it as a (definitional) subject preface to the vocative, such that it becomes a highly affective response: "Busy means busy, doctor." While Dr. Good's final turn in line 10 appears to accept the prosecuting attorney's "clarification," it does something much less transparent. *Busy* is transformed from the subject predicative of the copular verb, modifying Dr. Good's professional obligations, into an adjective modifying *doctor*, and doctor, in turn, is transformed from vocative to professional identity reference that precedes turn final agreement *yes*. Rather than accept the prosecutor's negative connotation, he mobilizes the connotation as a discursive resource to reference his identity as a busy doctor, marshalling the more generic and engaging identity as a private practitioner in the process. While turn-final *yes* fosters a tacit impression that his response refers to the meaning of the prosecutor's original role conflict representation from lines 03 and 08, he has significantly shifted the referential plane – transforming reference from the professional service role to that of private practitioner (and out of the discursive conflict, at least for the moment). That is to say, his turn-final *yes* agrees with an assessment the prosecuting attorney never makes: that he is a "busy doctor" (not a "busy" academic researcher). He reformulates her question and then answers his own reformulation in a strikingly nimble multimodal maneuver with the two-handed gesture, open-mouth smile, and headshake, reuniting the once ambivalent representation, balancing the conflict in a more generic format, and reconfiguring his response to the question.

Let us develop a more focused view of the reference shift as a process of shifting professional identity, for Dr. Good not only shifts the referential plane but just as important, the form of participation and structure of voicing in the dialogue. As mentioned previously, participation refers to

Figure 2.10: (line 10 *I'm a busy doctor*).

the interactive process of positioning speaker and recipient roles in conversation, dialogue or text, either real or imagined, and the epistemic forms of involvement social actors project onto their own and each other's words (Goodwin and Goodwin 2004). In a quite similar vein, Bakhtin (1981) noted that speakers take a moral and evaluative stance toward the voices portrayed in the dialogue, a stance reflecting their strategic interests in shaping the production and reception of utterances. We use the concept of participation to refer to the intertextual organization of voicing in which participants position, evaluate, and manipulate identity in multimodal practice. The attorney's first question in line 01 implements the canonical form of participation roles in courtroom questioning: attorneys pose questions, while witnesses answer them (Ehrlich 2001). With these points in mind, Dr. Good's response in line 06 activates an insertion sequence, embedding one canonical form of participation in the other as he requests more clarification on which to base his answer, which the prosecutor provides through her reproach in line 08. While his answer in line 10 appears to respond to the original question post the contingent insertion sequence, and thus resurrects canonical participation, it more accurately mobilizes a subterranean or transgressing participation structure with a distinct identity formation. Although Dr. Good appears to answer her question in exit from the insertion sequence, he actually reformulates the question and then answers his own reformulation, recalibrating participation, and realigning professional identity. Just as the insertion sequence embeds one sequence within another, so too does one overt participation frame embed a more covert one in a subterranean format. Dr. Good's *busy*, in concert with the perfectly aligned bilabial burst, hand gesture, smile, and headshake, repositions alignment from role conflict to role continuity by voicing the impression that it is commonsense knowledge that doctors are "busy" (see Figure 2.10).

In this intertextual shift, her "you are too busy to tend to patients" becomes *I'm a busy doctor*, inheriting our commonsense understanding in a down to earth display of incredulity, or even disbelief, that she would even pose such a question (the increased volume, stress, and embodied stance almost seem to say, "I'm too busy to deal with this question"). Indeed, Dr. Good comes down to earth, but it is certainly not the earth the attorney had hoped for. He shifts dialogue from conflict and ambivalence in the sense that *going to meetings keeps you busy* into (projected) dialogic form: "Are you a busy doctor? 'Of course I am.'" In the process, he transforms her remonstration into a much different sociocultural artifact: a "busy doctor" represents a professional identity that people can relate to, and he animates and voices that identity through multimodal practice. He uses her imperative and vocative construction as a multimodal platform to shift forms of participation and identity and thus reformulate the question, while fostering the impression of still responding to her original question.

More analytically, considering only speech in this segment erases a crucial aspect of identity work. While *I'm a busy doctor yes* captures denotational text or predicates some state of affairs as true or false (Silverstein 2014), it does not reveal the metapragmatic force of Dr. Good's utterance; that is to say, the two-handed gesture, smile, and headshake gesture work in concert to signal the absurdity of the prosecutor's question. In a more metaphoric vein, the more space between the two open palms, the more absurd the question.

Conclusion

In this chapter we have seen how participants orient to ambivalent norms and counternorms as they simultaneously circulate professional representations in the interdiscursive order. Of special interest, we have seen how a sociocultural dimension of expert identity emerges in and through a densely interactive synchronization of multimodal practice, demonstrating the relevance of the body, verbal dueling, and register in the epistemological grounding of knowledge claims. Within this conflict, the expert witness confronts not only an ambivalently projected social structure but an ambivalently structured discursive order so that if he agrees with the prosecuting attorney's questions he tacitly agrees with the epistemological dichotomy posed in them: that an "academic" physician, suffering from role strain, overload, and conflict due to competing obligations, is not qualified or competent to provide an expert opinion that has significant bearing on the ultimate issue in the case. On the other hand, if he disagrees with those questions, he might be seen as "evasive" with all the damaging implications and inferences such an identity might inherit. He manages the dilemma by one-upping, upgrading, or otherwise repairing those representations – foregrounding his expertise and his hands-on experience with patients – to shape a competing interpretive frame: that the prosecutor has created a false dichotomy and that he is even more of a qualified expert than her questions indicate. By the same token, the prosecution's ambivalent strategies create further ambivalences, both representational and discursive. Unlike the resolution of turn competition and overlap, they fail to resolve the conflict by creating further ambivalence of both types recursively. Still, one thing is certain. Whatever the outcome of the struggle between law and science, it will always happen in the multimodal order, with all its improvisational and contingent twist and turns. In the next chapter, we turn to a crucial element of formal legal rationality, and investigate how that formality is organized in and through the improvisational interplay of multimodal conduct.

3   The Transformation of Evidence into Precedent

Introduction

When making a decision, courts in the United States and other common law countries draw upon precedent – upon previously established rules and principles that deal with similar issues, facts, and cases. In technical legal terms, a precedent is a "narrow holding in a prior case that controls the disposition of the case before the court."[1] Indeed, scholars consider precedent as the hallmark of common law reasoning, a system of formal rationality that allows legal actors to calculate, predict, and plan a subsequent case based on analogized continuity with historically authorized rules and principles (Weber 1978). But, even in a system of formal rationality, such continuity only emerges dynamically and interactively in the concrete details of situated legal practice: a creative process of extracting text from some historical setting and naturalizing and authorizing it as the same in the here-and-now speech event. In the process, precedential text both shapes and is shaped by the indexical particulars and interactional contingencies of the current case under consideration (Mertz 2007: 46). As Mertz (2007: 46) observes, "The invocation of precedent involves an inevitable transformation at some level."

This chapter analyzes precedent as a micro discursive form of identity transformation in which evidence is placed under auspices of a rule, thus forging a connection with prior texts and legal principles. We demonstrate how multimodal conduct figures prominently in the constitution of legal evidence, identity, and sociocultural relationships in an intertextual drive to shape a coherent, precedential narrative. We show how a legal actor (1) selectively extracts or decontextualizes prior segments of speech, (2) reconfigures indexical facts from historical speech events, and (3) recontextualizes these in the current speech event to mobilize an authoritative account of behavior fitting under auspices of the rule, to invoke precedent as a meaning-making strategy.

---

[1] Matthew Lippman personal communication. See also, *Black's Law Dictionary* 1991:814.

More specifically, we examine how a prosecuting attorney (PA) invokes precedent in a rape trial; how she decontextualizes and recontextualizes evidence from three other rape victims to prove that the defendant possesses a *modus operandi*, or pattern of criminal behavior. Under the "Williams Rule" (*Williams* v. *Florida* 1959), prior conduct of a criminal defendant can be introduced as evidence if it shows a pattern of criminality (or *modus operandi*) rather than mere propensity to engage in such behavior. In more technical legal terms, the prosecution may prove the victim's state of mind pertaining to consent or lack of consent by proving the states of mind of the three other women and whether they had consented to sex with the defendant on prior occasions. If the PA succeeds in establishing such a pattern and the precedential link – the putative stability across multiple laminations of context – then the testimony of the three other victims would be introduced in the current case. This would have the effect of moving from the evidence of a single witness (in the he-said-she-said style typical of acquaintance or date rape trials) to evidence from four witnesses against the defendant, a favorable advantage for the prosecution even before the trial begins. But to do so, the prosecution must extract (that is, decontextualize and recontextualize), the relevant particulars of evidence from each woman's testimony, link these with evidence from the current victim, and then show how all four cases fall under auspices of the rule. How does the PA assemble a coherent narrative that displays a pattern of criminality? How does she transform the indexical particulars of each woman's discourse to establish a unique signature to the offense? How does an instance (or *token*) of "this" evidence from all four victims translate into a *type*-level pattern of "that" behavior on the part of the defendant?

Intertextuality and Participation

Words and speech from historical settings constitute the evidential infrastructure of the adversarial system. Thus, written documents, verbal statements, and electronic recordings from prior depositions, affidavits, interviews, and testimony form the evidential basis of legal order. We mentioned previously that researchers refer to this felt continuity between historical text and its recontextualization in a current text as *intertextuality* (that is, how structural features of a text come to resemble prior or historical discourse). In a closely related sense, *intratextual* continuities may also emerge within a segment of text and between segments in a single text, along with multiplex inter(intra)textual hybrids. Prototypic forms of intertextuality would include direct and indirect quotes; repetition; formulaic words as in greeting, closing, or oath-taking sequences; forms of address (like *Your Honor* or *Ladies and Gentlemen of the Jury*); and stylistic manipulations of represented speech, to mention but a few. In each case, the current use of language relies on and connects with some prior text for its full meaning (in the case of repetition, for example, the connection made might be within the same sentence).

Such continuities are always designed and negotiated with an eye toward the strategic interactional tasks at hand; that is to say, legal participants not only build textual linkages but contest and transform them as well, forging discontinuities and continuities across speech events as they frame, position, and evaluate their own speech and the speech of others to foster a particular impression on the jury. In this sense, extracting and recontextualizing elements of speech as either the same or different affects how forms of participation (or the social organization of discursive roles), real and/or imaginary, are projected in the interactive constitution of evidence and in the organization of dialogue. In his seminal work on participation, Goffman (1981) demonstrated how traditional conceptions of speaker and hearer were too simple to account for the complexity of speech. With his concept of footing, he permitted analysts to make distinctions within the constellation of discursive roles and figures in concrete instances of speech. Thus, using concepts such as animator (the one who physically produces the words), author (the one who composes the words), and principal (the one who authorizes those words as the responsible party), he was able to specify how speakers strategically position themselves and others relative to one another and to their utterances, embedding multiple laminations of participation even within a single utterance.

In what follows, we examine several segments of the prosecution's precedential narrative that flow in a linear ordering. Excerpt 1 focuses on the contrastive rhetoric in the PA's narrative and how this powerfully conveys an *iconic* (or mirroring) form of temporal opposition in the defendant's "bipolar" personality: a "one moment he was x, then next minute he was y" format. In Excerpt 2, we analyze how the PA rhetorically activates a sexual predator identity in which the defendant "entices" or lures victims into his "territory," an identity constructed through a rapist speech register or style. Excerpt 3 focuses on the multimodal integration of speech, gesture, physical objects, and forms of participation as the PA argues that the defendant fosters trust in the victims before the attacks, consolidating the sexual predator pattern. In the final section of the chapter, we consider how sociocultural patterns figure prominently in the production of gender and sexual identity during the PA's summary of the *modus operandi* she needed to establish. More specifically, we demonstrate how she positions herself into double-bind configurations indexed by stance adverbs, in a counter-hegemonic bid to denaturalize and pathologize patriarchal structures of sexual rationality. While the grammatical-lexical and text-metrical encoding of *stance* (the speaker's attitude or degree of commitment toward a proposition) has preoccupied linguistic analysis, we demonstrate how stance also embodies and reproduces sociocultural context.

Most importantly, we reveal how speech within and across the ensuing excerpts is not autonomous but synchronizes with the others in a rhythmically integrated form of type-token reflexivity. Each excerpt begins with a metapragmatic utterance type that categorizes (or classifies) the defendant and victim's words, which, in turn, contextualizes a reflexive interpretive frame for connecting each subsequent token with the type within a segment (Silverstein 2005). Each completed type-token segment then contextualizes the discursive frame for the ensuing type-token segment across the series, which, in turn, reflexively recalibrates the prior type-token segment as continuous with the ongoing litany (and so on recursively), as an instance in a progressively interwoven horizontal-vertical (*syntagmatic-paradigmatic*) linguistic pattern. Together, each vertical and horizontal increment in the inter(intra)textual pattern bears an iconic correspondence to the defendant's escalating pattern of sexually violent behavior. As these patterns collide and fuse, they synchronize a subtle yet iconic naturalization between social structure – patterns of interaction across space and time – and discursive patterning. In other words, the linguistic pattern makes the social patterning seem more natural through very subtle signaling devices.

A final note before proceeding. Our objective is not to assess the correctness or incorrectness of the legal judgment allowing or disallowing the testimony of the three other women. That is, we do not analyze the outcome of the precedential argument in a prescriptive sense – what the judge should have done – and the various pro and con claims. Instead, we address the linguistic, ideological, and multimodal resources that the PA brings to bear on the legal translation of evidence as an instance of following a rule. We illuminate how this process integrates crisscrossing, polyrhythmic currents of intertexual relations in the naturalization of precedential reality.

The Discursive Organization of Temporal Contrast

The PA's argument for introducing the testimony of the three other women begins with a type classification, summarizing prior deposition questioning of the defendant's change in behavior.

Excerpt 1

```
01  A::ll four of these girls stre:::ssed (.) the change in
    personality.
02                         (0.6)
03  Lisa (.) "he was charming. I danced with him. I felt
04  completely comfortable with him (.) Once at his home
05  (.) one moment he was standing in front of me talking
06  with me, saying goodnight to me (.) the next minute he
07  would- (.) tackled me onto the bed." Apologized.
    Seemed OK. Repeated the act.
08                         (1.0)
09  Lynn (.) "he seemed quiet, attractive, a well dressed, very
10  gentlemanly young man (.) Later I saw a complete change in
11  character (.) We were on the back side of the couch. At that
12  point without any warning (.) he grabbed my- (.) grabbed
13  me by the wrist (.) threw me over the couch" (.)
    Composed afterwards (.) unlocked the door n' let her out.
14                         (0.8)
15  Michele (.) "He said 'NO:: (.) you can stay upstairs' (.)
16  I just thought he was goin to be a gentleman and let me sleep
17  in his bed (.) Once upstairs he was such a ferocious (1.0)
18  almost animal like look to him." Composed the next day,
    very indifferent toward her.
19                         (1.0)
20  Patricia (.) "talked and danced with him. Very interesting
21  to talk to, very nice (.) had a nice demeanor." The defendant
22  went skinny dipping, invited her in. She declined, he
23  grabbed her ankle, tackled her onto the lawn (.) Described
24  him as ferocious composed afterwards (.) very indifferent.
```

In line 01, the PA mobilizes the quantifier (*all four of*) + specific determiner (*these*) + collective noun (*girls*) type-level classification to show how each victim *stre:::sed* the defendant's change in behavior. Here she moves beyond a focus on individual instances to unify the arguably different occasions and people as part of a single type. Notice how she delivers the main verb with marked stress and vowel lengthening (*stre:::ssed*) to emphasize the proposition and, in so doing, instructs listeners that each woman did not merely notice or mention the behavioral change but accentuated it to create a distinct intertextual continuity. Still more specifically, we see in vivid detail how the PA authorizes an interpretive template for the ensuing tokens not only through denotational text, but also in the iconic correspondence between the proposition and noticeably marked stress in the reporting verb. She offers a poignant demonstration of intertexuality in motion as she *enacts* the represented word in the current narrative, a symbolic interaction in which what was said becomes what we are doing.

After a short pause in line 02, the PA unpacks the type classification with an incremental and progressive listing of tokens from each victim (also drawn from prior deposition interviews taken some months previously), a repetitive litany occurring as a temporal contrast. The litany begins in lines 03–07 with a proper name, a short pause, and then a quote drawn from Lisa's speech: an intratextual pattern repeated for each subsequent victim statement. Put another way, the PA omits the reporting verb and instead deploys the simple first name and short pause to contextualize the direct report. Notice how the quote consists of a parallel structure that assembles a contrast between the defendant's initial mild demeanor and subsequent rough assault. More explicitly, the quote lists the defendant's positive attributes along with Lisa's actions and feelings: *He was charming. I danced with him. I felt completely comfortable with him.* Just as important, her sense of certainty about those attributes – indexed through the degree adverb (*completely*) – contextualizes and intensifies the contrast via the temporal locator noun phrases or NPs (*one moment* and *the next minute*). In this iconic correspondence between linguistic form and behavioral pattern, the PA instructs listeners that such dramatic mood swings constitute an abnormality – a unique criminal signature – in the defendant's personality, perhaps a bipolar disorder or split personality indexed by the poetic (or intratextual, rhythmic) construction. To complete Lisa's testimony, the PA moves out of the direct quote and produces two additional behavioral anomalies in elliptical format, a format repeated in each ensuing victim account: first he *apologized* for his behavior and second, after the apology, *repeated the act*. Although the defendant apologized for his untoward behavior, he repeated it nevertheless, displaying total disregard for his victim(s) and a complete lack of self-control – another increment to the emerging *modus operandi*.

In the next token of the unfolding litany, after a one-second pause, the PA moves from Lisa to Lynn, once again, repeating the *turn-shape format* (proper name + micro pause + direct quote). She then repeats and recalibrates the epistemic verb from line 07 (*seemed*) followed by a poetic listing of positive attributes through the predicative adjectives – including the degree adverb on the last adverbial – that intensifies the forthcoming contrast: (*he seemed quiet, attractive, a well-dressed, very gentlemanly young man*). However, while Lisa's contrast above consists of juxtaposing the temporal locator NPs, Lynn's statement involves something different. After the temporal adverb, the PA uses the evidential verb *saw* (in line 10) to generate an appearance/uncertainty versus reality/certainty contrast

(*Later I saw a complete change in character*), grammatically marked through the temporal deictic (*later*), variation in perception verbs (*seems, saw*) and, most important, absolute quantifier (*complete*). On the one hand, the epistemic stance verb (*seems*) marks the degree of certainty in the proposition: Lynn's inference about the defendant's character based on appearance. The evidential verb (*saw*), on the other, marks the source of information: Her sensory evidence about those attributes that becomes the reality. As the oppositional structure develops, we see that what Lynn initially presumed turns out to be inaccurate and later "corrected" via sensory experience. After elaborating the details of the attack, the PA withdraws from the direct quote format to produce, once again, two post-attack descriptions that delete the subject and *be*-verb in an elliptical construction (*Composed afterwards (.) unlocked the door n'let her out*).

In line 15, the PA turns from Lynn to Michele with the same repetitive representation. However, rather than use a direct quote referring to the victim's initial impressions, she introduces a direct quote from the defendant ('*NO::* (.) *you can stay upstairs*') embedded in Michele's direct quote from the historical deposition. Here we see multiple laminations of participation and multiple forms of embedded social organization across an intertextual medley of speech events, each designed for strategic interactional effect. The defendant's speech in the rape event is embedded in Michele's deposition testimony which is, in turn, embedded within the PA's current precedential argument. Increased loudness, vowel lengthening, and stress in the defendant's *NO::* indexes a conversation with Michele in the rape incident where the defendant appears emotionally concerned about her leaving his apartment (as we will see in Excerpt 2, he does so because she is in an intoxicated state and he invites her to stay in his bedroom as a matter of "safety").

As it turns out, however, affective marking in rejecting her reported request (to leave) reveals something other than the defendant's altruistic motives. While multifunctional, *just* (*I just thought he was going to be a gentleman*), may operate as a modal discourse particle, locative or temporal construction (among other functions), it possesses, in this context, an intensifying function designed to "tone up" an argumentative strategy (Aijmer 2002: 158–173). The epistemic mental verb *thought* prefaced by the *just*-adverb contextualizes and intensifies the impending opposition, repeating the discursive patterning from both Lisa and Lynn. That contrast escalates full force in marked degree modification (***such***) of the stressed extreme adjectives (***ferocious*** and ***animal like***) to evoke an image of the defendant as a dangerous, violent predator – not only to characterize him as a psychopath with uncontrollable sexual impulses, but also to pathologize the unfolding pattern (*Once upstairs he was **such** a **ferocious***

(1.0) *almost **animal** like look to him*). As in the prior two statements, the post-rape depiction of the defendant departs from the direct quote with clause-final *ellipsis* (or omission of part of the quote), though this time repeating the degree modifier (*very indifferent*) – just as we would expect an *animal* to display no emotion after an attack.

In line 20, the PA describes the defendant with the same contrastive rhetoric, starting the sentence with initial first name, micro-pause, and extracts of Patricia's prior police statement. Those extracts consist of first, ellipted direct quotes with repetition of the degree adverbs, and modifiers of the defendant's attributes (*very interesting, very nice*) and second, movement of the second adjective to modify the clause-final noun (*nice demeanor*) for a third repetitive structure. Following this, the PA moves from the direct quote into a description of the sexual assault by repeating the stressed evaluative lexical item (***ferocious***) from Michele's statement followed by the ellipted post-rape recitation (*composed afterward/indifferent*).

To sum up the points made thus far: The type utterance frames an intertextual continuity for the ensuing token, which, in turn, foregrounds the next token as another instance of "that" type as they mutually elaborate one another and the framing type in a recursively interwoven intratextual structure. Inter(intra) textual continuity in linguistic form and content naturalizes an iconic continuity of sexual violence and, as this microcosmic gestalt unfolds, type-token calibrations and recalibrations yield a recursive ensemble of inter(intra)textual coherence to "pathologize" the defendant's behavior, building up a polyrhythmic temporal pattern of charm, violence, and indifference to bestow a unique criminal signature to his actions. One way that is done is through an iconic connection organized around changing certain words through stress and lengthening (***ferocious***, ***animal like, stre::sed***) to emphasize the startling change in the defendant's personality. As we are beginning to see, inter(intra)textual repetition not only or even primarily functions as a referential link with the past – building up a coherent pattern – but provides a dynamic sense of persuasive involvement and evaluation in current text as well. As we will next discover, type-token repetition within Excerpt 1 furnishes the reflexive frame for interpreting Excerpt 2 (and so on recursively and reflexively) in the progressively linked linear pattern.

Enticing the Victim into His Territory

In Excerpt 2, the PA presents another type classification – this time characterizing the defendant as a sexual predator not by virtue of his reported behavioral pattern, but in terms of a pattern in his speech. Instead of simply re-presenting the victim's statements, she translates the defendant's verbal action using direct and indirect quote formats: what he told each victim to lure them into his territory for the attacks. As in Excerpt 1, she deploys heavily marked stress, increased volume, and vowel lengthening in the main verb (*enti:::ced*) and then proceeds to list what he told each victim in chronological order.

Excerpt 2

```
01   The defendant enti:::ced the victims into his
02   territory with false pretenses judge.
03                               (0.9)
04   He offered Lisa a place to stay? in- in the guest
05   room of his family's home (.) after the people she
     was supposed to stay with had left.
06                               (1.1)
07   He told Lynn there was a party at his house (.) when
08   in reality there was no party (.) But he invited her there.
09                               (0.7)
10   Michele (.) he told her (0.5) "I'll give ya a place to stay
11   for the night" ya' know "You're too drunk to go home."
12                               (1.3)
13   And with Patricia (.) he told her he needed a ride
14   home (.) and once there he invited her in to see the
15   Kennedy estate and then to walk onto the beach.
16                               (0.6)
17   Every single one of these people he got to his house
18   by false pretenses.
```

While the PA uses one type frame in Excerpt 1, she employs two framing types for Excerpt 2, enclosing the tokens with variant repetition of the initial type to mark beginning and closing of the excerpt (lines 01 and 17–18) (*enticed ... by false pretenses; got to his house by false pretenses*). That is, she bounds the tokens by type-framing clauses in an inter(intra)textual repetitive structure that foregrounds the defendant's planning for the attacks, so that each example within the frame is set up as a token of the larger type (predator's speech). Moreover, type-to-token translation functions not only through repetition of the type-frame enclosure but through repetition of the reporting verb (*told*) in triplet. Much like the extreme adjectives from Excerpt 1 (*ferocious* and *animal- like*), the marked verb *enticed* and locative phrase *into his territory* suggest that the defendant "lured" the victims to his "lair" for the attacks, as a predator would, recalibrating and repeating the intertextual imagery from Excerpt 1, but adding the theme of intentional and premeditated false statements.

In a very transparent sense, such specialized lexical items percolate through her narrative to build a type-level conception that there is a sexual predator speech style or register that can be traced through many different instances of the defendant's speech.

We can make several observations about the intertextual litany. First, type-token reflexivity produces a cumulative effect, building up the predator identity and criminal pattern vertically (or intratextually) within each segment through stressed verbs, linear ordering of each victim, pausing, and reported speech. Second, each type-token segment reflexively generates a horizontal cumulative effect as it frames the next segment, recalibrates, and stabilizes our interpretation of the prior one, and builds up the pattern intertexually across segments. Such patterning organizes reflexive continuities between the segments, a prior segment shaping the next as the next shapes the prior, as both shape one another through repetition and variation of linguistic features. Lastly, in this dense constellation of sense-making resources, inter(intra)textual continuities – in both form and content – combine with type-token reflexivity to synchronize the developing criminal pattern.

Fostering Trust in Multimodal Detail

To entice the victims into his territory the defendant must first gain their trust, and in this excerpt we illuminate how multimodality, identity, and participation figure in the PA's logic as it makes connections with legal precedent.

Excerpt 3

```
01  [The defendant        [fostered trust in his victims.
    [((gazes at board))  [((closed hand point at the board))
02                                 (.)
03  [Lisa trusted him- (.) [he was a cousin of her boyfriend
    [((gaze to judge))     [((gaze to board))
04  [No reason not to trust him
    [((gaze at judge))
05                                 (1.5)
06  Lynn (.) he was a[ fellow medical student (.)
                     [((left arm bent at elbow/waist
                       level extended outward
                       open palm facing
                       judge/fingers spread.))
07  [ No reason not to trust [him =
    [((fully extends arm))] [((points at blackboard
                              with closed palm facing
                              downward+gaze at judge))
```

```
08  = as comp[ared to some stranger on the street=
           [((left arm thrust backward in "flip"))
09  =[that would come up and ask you out
       [((hands return to home position in front of body))
10                        (0.8)
11  Michelle (.) she attended Georgetown with him (.)
12  He was acting like a bi- big brother (.) No reason
    not to trust him ((gaze to judge))
13                        (0.6)
14  Patricia (.5) she discussed the medical condition of
15  her child. That's the first thing she discussed with Mr.
16  Smith (.) that she had a child and that the child had a
17  problem at birth (.) and that the child was very ill (.)
18  She completely trusted him as a physician and as a
19  person (.) There was no reason not to.[((gaze to judge))
```

We have seen that multimodal conduct refers to the integration of gesture, gaze, materiality, and speech in the coordination of coherent courses of improvised action, creating a focus of joint attention and generating emergent forms of participation in the unfolding dialogue (Goodwin 1981). In the courtroom, attorneys may employ multimodal conduct to insert their own voice and evaluation into the evidence and thus circumvent legal constraints on their speech.

With these points in mind, note how the PA (in Excerpt 3) stands to the right of, and parallel to, an artist's "easel" that consists of a large sketch-pad with an inscription of each victim's first name, while simultaneously facing the judge with arms held down and hands folded in front of her body – the "home" or base position (Sacks and Schegloff 2002). To gaze at the easel, she must torque her upper body and tilt her head upward to the left. In line 01, her type utterance (*The defendant fostered trust in his victims*), telling us what overarching type of behavior each subsequent example fits into, coincides with gaze and closed hand pointed at the easel in perfect alignment with production of the verb. See the figures to follow.

After a short pause, she begins the token listing with Lisa (line 03) – but rather than mention how the defendant fostered trust, the PA produces an explanation based on a triangulation of kinship reference (*he was a cousin of her boyfriend*), followed by utterance-initial ellipsis (ellipting *there*-existential and *be*-verb – in other words, leaving out *there was*) and post-token frame (the negative adverb + infinitive clause *No reason not to trust him*) – directing gaze shift from easel toward judge at the infinitive. This post-token frame (based on the "no reason" theme) represents a final expansion and a variation on the single type frame we witnessed in Excerpt 1, and the type boundary-repetition we saw in Excerpt 2. At a

Figure 3.1: (line 01 *The defendant*).

Figure 3.2: (line 01 *fostered trust in his victims*).

finer level of granularity, a series of unmarked lateral head nods accompanies gaze toward the judge to reinforce and stabilize the co-equivalence relation between type ("fostering trust") and post-token frames ("no reason not to"), on the one hand, and corresponding tokens on the other.

As the incantation unfolds, the PA includes Lynn and the defendant (line 06) as co-incumbents in the student identity (*fellow medical student*), followed by repetition and expansion of the post-token type with the comparative (*as compared to some stranger on the street*), and relative clause (*that would come up and ask you out*). By virtue of their shared student status, the victim inherits legitimate grounds for the trusting the defendant, as if mere co-student identity naturally "extends" their relationship to a higher level of trust.

Similarly, if we consider lines 06–10 in more detail, notice that speech-gesture synchronization expresses not only an affective layering of emphasis but a laminated form of participation unavailable from just the spoken word, demonstrating how forms of gesture integrate with speech to

Figure 3.3: (line 06 *fellow*).

Figure 3.4: (line 06 *medical student*).

produce an additional dimension of meaning in courtroom interaction: a densely organized choreography of gesture that animates Lynn's mental state. At the modifier *fellow* (Figure 3.3), the PA produces a pleading, open-palm gesture (arm down with wrist bent, parallel to her waist, and directed to the judge) as if to indicate the "reasonableness" of Lynn trusting the defendant and then extends her left arm (with palm still open and fingers spread vertically at waist level and still directed toward the judge) on *medical student* (Figure 3.4), suspending the gesture for a moment in a post-stroke hold, as if extending the initial pleading gesture to invite or implore the judge to agree with the reasonableness of *her* position (see Figures 3.3 and 3.4). Much more speculatively but not so remotely, arm extension may constitute a metaphoric gesture of how co-identity would extend or expand into a trusting relationship (as it simultaneously synchronizes with phrase expansion).

As her arm gesture decays, the PA first shifts the open palm into a closed and downward palm pointed toward the easel, extending her arm in its

Figure 3.5: (line 07 *no reason not to trust him*).

Figure 3.6: (line 08 *some stranger*).

direction on the post-token frame *no reason not to trust him* (see Figure 3.5), and, second, shifts gaze from the judge to the material artifact. On the phrase (*to some stranger*) she redeploys the pointing gesture to execute a backward hand toss, a *brush-off* gesture that takes the outstretched arm pointing toward the easel, bends it at the elbow, and then flings it past the head with the palm facing upward and fingers spread. In the process she projects – better yet *enacts* – an imaginary participation structure to demonstrate in vivid detail how Lynn would have summarily *brushed off* such an advance or "come-on" by a stranger on the street (see Figure 3.6). In an intricate display of multimodal dexterity, the PA expands the *trust* proposition with the comparative plus relative (as compared to some stranger out on the street that would come up and ask you out), as she simultaneously expands the brush-off gesture in perfect synchronization with utterance-final clause, integrating verbal and gestural expansion by putting participation and epistemic stance in motion in the very details of their multimodal realization. *In a dynamic gestural movement, she adds an intricate lamination of participation and embodied stance that would be unavailable from the spoken word to show not just "what" Lynn would have done with the imaginary stranger but performs "how" she would do it in the here and now, performing epistemic and affective stance in the deictic immediacy of multimodal action.*[2] In more symbolic terms, the brush-off gesture appears as a metaphor representing how Lynn would have brushed off such an advance for casual sex (before the PA's hands return to "home" position in front of her).[3]

But the PA's verbal representation and gestural reenactment of Lynn involve much more than the integration of language and gesture, for any discussion of embodied activity would be incomplete without understanding the role of material artifacts and how they penetrate the stream of multimodal conduct – what Heath and Hindmarsh (2002: 117) refer to as the "local ecology of material artifacts." As mentioned in Chapter 1, while material artifacts appear to possess a physical facticity based on mere presence in context, they function, much more dynamically, as discursive resources only at specific moments within unfolding courses of action. That is to say, participants utilize them as dynamic resources to enliven distinct interactional tasks. In this sense, the easel functions as a disembodied semiotic resource that directs gaze to it, creating a joint focus of attention that channels evidential orientation. Just as important, when the PA gazes at the easel she executes another crucial form of interactional work. She projects and naturalizes a "passive" animator footing toward the evidence, that she is merely animating Lynn's figure in the narrative (Lynn's brush-off reaction to the stranger), rather than inserting her own voice – her own position and evaluation as author and/or principal – in the imaginary multimodal dialogue, circumventing legal constraints on attorney speech in the process.

---

[2] This example provides a poignant illustration of Volosinov's (1973:119) comments on reported speech. "Earlier investigators of the forms of reported speech committed the fundamental error of virtually divorcing the reported speech from the reporting context." We see here how that "dynamic relationship" between both contexts is thoroughly infused with not just speech but multimodal conduct as well: the prosecutor's gestural representation of Lynn's hypothetical performance (or an embodiment of a hypothetical embodiment).

[3] This is a variation on Tebendorf's (2014: 1549) notion of the metaphoric "brushing-aside" gesture. "The source domain as the action of brushing small, annoying objects aside in order to get them away from one's immediate surrounding is mapped onto the target domain: the chasing away of real people, which is part of the proposition of the utterance."

She recruits the easel as an evidential and instructional tool that erases and leaves no residue of its assembly process, a tool containing only the objective and authoritative voices of the four women. Notice too how she shifts from third person (*he was a cousin of her* boyfriend) to free indirect speech (without the reporting clause: *no reason not to trust him*), that appropriates the voice of the represented speaker under the guise of and laminated in the third person. Thus the artifact's meaning comes into play as the PA animates its relevance and punctuates its significance in a dynamic multimodal configuration, gearing distinct spheres of institutional relevance into discursive prominence, setting into motion the circulation of discourse across time, space, and speech events – in essence, anchoring her entire precedential narrative around the easel. In this instance, easel, speech, and gesture mutually elaborate one another in the embodied materialization of meaning to perform behavior that fits within the governing precedent.

More theoretically, the PA extracts, lists, and positions relations in the ongoing dialogue not just through language but in the contextually situated and multimodally emergent construction of precedential evidence, creating a joint interplay of polyrhythmic voices and intertextual continuity. More symbolically, she orchestrates what we might think of as an improvisational, melodic, and staccato "gestural phrase" (see Kendon 2004) – a four-part multimodal excursion that flows in tight, crisp phrases – in which the criminal pattern percolates through variant forms of inter (intra)textual repetition. More practically, but no less interestingly, the intertextual link to the victim's statement superimposes an allusive participation structure that instructs the judge on the role of trust in understanding acquaintance or date rape (in stark contrast to stranger rape), and how that figures prominently in the application of precedent – the precedent applicable in this case.

Turning to Michelle and Patricia, notice the same identity translation regarding the "foster trust" frame. After the pause in line 10, the PA repeats the co-student identity structure (she attended Georgetown with him), adds kinship analogy (He was acting like a big brother), and ends with the ellipted reason-clause and gaze redirection toward the judge.

The PA employs a more complex construction in discussing Patricia. First, she brings up the medical problems associated with her premature child, packaged in a parallel repetition of *that*-complements (*that she had a child, that the child had a problem at birth, and that the child was very ill*): a mother worried about a sick child. While the PA initially refers to the defendant with formal address (*Mr. Smith*) in line 15, she switches reference first to occupational identity (*physician*), and second to the prepositional complement person, inserting occupational identity and person reference prior to the post-token type as an "internal" expansion. The victim trusted neither Mr. Smith nor even, for the most part, the defendant as a person but trusted him, most critically, as a physician, someone who helps patients. Second, the PA foregrounds maternal identity with the degree adverb (*completely trusted him*), parallel repetition of the adverbials (*as a physician, as a person*), and flip-flop repetition of the reason clause from clause initial to clause final ellipsis (*There was no reason not to*), ellipting the infinitive. In so doing she constructs a participation structure that portrays a mother consulting her sick child's physician, and this makes the defendant's behavior even more deplorable, more despicable: that he is violating doctor-patient trust and exploiting a distraught mother for criminal purposes. Lastly, this displays how person reference functions to construct legal identity and to craft persuasive work in contextualizing precedent – more specifically, how maternal identity translates in the process of fostering trust through doctor-patient identities and multimodal performance.

Sociocultural Forms of Domination

We have seen how intertextual circuits repeat form, content, and imagery and how that process is stabilized, calibrated, and recalibrated in type-token reflexivities not only across historical texts but within and across current text segments. In the process, the PA produces an iconic correspondence between discursive patterning on the one hand and legal identity under auspices of the Williams Rule on the other. Still, the translation is ever problematic as she must maneuver an ambivalent gauntlet of norm and counternorm, and steer an interpretive route through this discursive maze. Consider her concluding comments.

Excerpt 4

```
01   Judge there was absolutely no sexual innuendos exchanged
02   between any of these victims and the defendant at any
03   ti::me. And I submit to the court this is the defendant's
04   pla:::n, to meet unescorted young women at some kind of
05   social gathering, to lure them to his house under false
06   pretenses and once there to make a violent, swift, sudden
07   attack with absolutely no sexual innuendo beforehand
```

In this concluding meta-intertextual frame, the PA delivers a densely metricalized pattern consisting of parallel repetition of the *to*-infinitives (*to meet, to lure, to make*), including alliteration in the first and last lines (*meet, make*), repetition of the *any*-modifiers (*any of these victims/at any time*), and a parallel listing of the modifiers in line 06 (*violent, swift, and sudden*), with alliteration in the final adjectives (*swift, sudden*), to summarize and foreground the predator image.[4] Just as impressively, she repeats the intratextual imagery from the main verbs in Excerpts 1 and 2 but this time in the stressed *pla:::n* in line 03, producing an iconic alignment in vowel lengthening in the NP on the one hand, and a lengthy amount of planning for the violent attacks on the other. The most interesting repetition lies with the epistemic stance adverb in lines 01 and 06–07 (*absolutely*) and what the PA indexes about her utterance – perhaps even what she indexes about her entire precedential narrative – with this grammatical choice. As mentioned previously, stance refers to positioning of speaker's utterance and to the degree of certainty regarding the proposition: how speaker grounds the authority of knowledge. We argue here that it also encodes broader forms of sociocultural context and it is this latter dimension that will occupy our final analytic concerns for understanding legal identity and the performance of precedent, for while the PA's interlaced lyricism and lush impressionism are doubtlessly sophisticated, several socially structured issues require consideration.

First, while the jury in the adversary system understands that parties will only select evidence that best supports their case, they also expect attorneys to present a persuasive argument of the facts brought before them. In Goffmanian terms, attorneys must manage the impressions of the judge or jury by projecting an appearance of objective neutrality rather than presenting an argument that appears too explicitly biased. Komter (2000: 420) captures this ambivalence as follows, "The task of both prosecution and defense is to present the jury with the more convincing story. The problem is that too conspicuous orientation to 'winning the case' might undermine the persuasiveness of their story. Thus establishment of the facts is managed by implicit persuasion and persuasion is disguised as 'establishing the facts.'" In other words, if persuasion appears too persuasive – too oriented to winning at the expense of truth – it undermines the facticity of the legal narrative and "spoils" the impression management performance. The PA has to find the seam between coherence and fracture to cultivate the threshold of objective neutrality for the jury.

Second, superimposed on this aspect of the adversary system lies a system of power and domination, infused with the adversary system in such a way to conceal itself. The *patriarchal logic of sexual rationality*

---

[4] Text-metricalized speech (poetics) like repetition, rhythm, and rhyme creates not only a sense of cohesion but a sense of involvement in the message as well. For Silverstein (1985), speakers use them to signal how participants should interpret what is said and done.

constitutes a linguistic ideology – an interpretive template – for assessing the victim's and offender's actions during the rape event, a representational logic of power based on male standards of sexual preference contingently enacted in the courtroom to accomplish distinct interactional tasks (Matoesian 2001). Most important, patriarchal logic conceals itself within the adversary system – as it simultaneously misrepresents itself – as the adversary system. That is to say, at key moments patriarchal logic appropriates the adversary system as the adversary system arrogates patriarchal logic in a way that something novel emerges, something as concealed and naturalized as the adversary system, and gender neutrality in the process. This linguistic ideology conceals and naturalizes male standards as commonsense reasoning that appear as legal inconsistency. Any form of "sexual innuendo" or "interest" or innocent flirtation (and so on) is interpreted, according to male logic, as granting sexual access and is misrepresented and concealed as an inconsistency – as a logical incongruity among aspects of evidence – when claimed otherwise.

Third, given the dominational logic of this system, the PA must stabilize translations among type and tokens (and between these types and precedent) within and across each segment of her narrative to avoid intertextual "ruptures" or "fractures" that would expose even minute forms of sexual "innuendo." Her narrative must bleach the account of any hint of sexual interest between the victims and defendant – any conspicuous orientation to or relevance of sexual identity. The women must appear as completely devoid of sexual interest or identity. More sharply put, the PA must bleach out all sexual references, pathologize male heterosexual desires, and sanitize sexual content from each woman's narrative. Any exposed sexual residue (of even the most innocent form of flirtation) will be governed by calibrations and recalibrations emanating from patriarchal logic and colonized as a legal inconsistency.

And, in each excerpt, we can see this process at work in dynamic detail. The PA attempts to give date or acquaintance rape the characteristics and moral status of stranger rape and blur the artificial distinction between the two, as the lexical items *ferocious* and *animal-like* suggest. Through her invocation of the type-level rapist register or speech style, the PA recalibrates characteristics of stranger rape, superimposes these on the date rape scenario, and thereby displaces normative male sexual preferences as to how flirtatious cues should be interpreted. More pointedly, her narrative must pathologize not only the defendant's actions but also his male-hegemonic form of sexual desire. The problem is this: her counter-hegemonic tactics (attempting to undercut a more male view of consent) still yield intertextual ruptures that reinforce and naturalize hegemonic sexual rationality. That the victims, in Excerpt 1, were in the bedroom or near the bed or sitting on the couch could lead to some degree of sexual interpretation, though not necessarily sexual consent. Of course, an intoxicated woman sleeping in a young man's bed could lead to more direct sexual interpretations, and the fact that he was indifferent afterwards could lead to the motivational issue of fabricating the charges. Her claim of no sexual innuendo is inconsistent according to the ideological order of male standards of sexual access, under which information such as the fact that the women went with the defendant into more intimate settings would be interpreted as the giving of consent.

When the PA switches reference from the victim to defendant in Excerpts 2 and 3, more problematic representations arise with the "enticed into his territory" and "fostered trust" frames. Given that it would be inappropriate for a man engaged in a "normal encounter" to expose sexual interests blatantly (or at least be inadvisable), then he would have to be more or less indirect and "entice" a woman with an offer of a drink or cup of coffee or an invitation to walk on the beach (and so on), as an avenue for obtaining sexual access later.

Notice in particular how the PA uses the verb "entice" instead of the more generic "seduce." Even so, according to the Oxford English Dictionary, the verb "entice" carries connotations of "allure" or "seduce" and "to attract physically" (not to mention the connotation of "tempt" and the connotation of "getting someone to do something that is morally questionable").

The "fostering trust" frame, for example, could represent a "pick-up line" that men use (as a ruse) to attract women, once again with an eye to sexual conquest. Moreover, since *foster* is an active verb one would expect a degree of defendant agency; yet the sole impetus behind the frame is identity co-membership with the victims: a passive relational attribute. Indeed, the PA must "stretch" considerably to stabilize asexual translations when "normal" male heterosexual behavior involves using a "line" (or foster trust) to "pick up" a woman at a bar or elsewhere (entice), getting them over to his place (or territory) and trying to have sex with them (see Matoesian 2001).

Fourth and with the earlier points in mind, why would the PA deploy such extreme or absolute representations, permitting no gradations on the ordered scale, leaving all other degrees ripe for the DA to exploit? Why not simply state that the women were interested in the defendant for any number of reasons but not sexually interested? Why not admit that there was, perhaps, some sexual innuendo but nothing in the way of sexual consent? The patriarchal logic of sexual rationality erases the female perspective in the gendered order, displaces it with male standards of sexual access, and governs any type of interest as sexual interest, the way men are interested in women (see Ehrlich 2001; Matoesian 2001). In this ideological process, the woman is interested in the man the same way that he is interested in her: sexually. The patriarchal logic of sexual rationality is not just a system of logic but logic of power that shapes discourse as discourse shapes it, even as it submerses itself under auspices of the adversary system. In the legal-linguistic ideology of inconsistency, no moderate position is possible; the PA must commit to the most extreme end of the ideological spectrum, leaving her mired in the sexual abyss she so studiously sought to avoid, leaving her with no interpretive latitude. This is how the stance adverb *absolutely* encodes quite more than a grammatical or text-metrical or interactive way to signal the degree of commitment to, or level of certainty about, the proposition. In this context *absolutely* incorporates broader forms of sociocultural domination, indexes the patriarchal logic of sexual rationality, and drives the ambivalence in the PA's discursive representation.

Last, this ambivalence imperils the PA's extreme representations and precedent-framed narrative, leaving her in a dominational double-bind and dangerously exposed to the defense attorney's more "modest," objective, and thus "neutral" counterclaims, with all remaining gradational points to exploit. That is to say, if we consider this as an ordered scale, the defense attorney can exploit everything after the extreme representation (*absolutely no sexual innuendo*) and thus maneuver in a much wider field of opportunity. The PA's melodic attempts to bleach sexualized identity, pathologize the defendant's actions via type-token reflexivity, and mobilize stance/degree adverbs demonstrate how the patriarchal logic of sexual rationality is normatively oriented to and relevant to discursive practice even in absence. That is, it is not just absent but, to adapt a line from Sacks (1992), noticeably and powerfully absent. Indeed, we can see how type-token reflexivity functions to not only create a predator identity but, just as importantly, to bleach sexualized identity from representation organized around precedent – a representation that turns out to be problematic because type-token relations will recalibrate, under auspices of patriarchal logic, as type-token mismatches. Indeed, the PA not only attempts to pathologize the defendant but to denaturalize normative male sexual preferences – a system of domination.

She loses either way, and that's why the judge denied the motion to introduce the testimony of the three other women. On the one hand, her claim of absolutely no sexual innuendo is incredible; on the other hand, if she admits innocent flirting or some sexual innuendo, the patriarchal logic of sexual rationality recalibrates such action as sexual interest and thus sexual access – yet hidden under the auspices of the linguistic ideology of inconsistency. These reciprocally infused ambivalent systems – the adversary system and the patriarchal logic of sexual rationality – pressure the PA into extreme versions of the events using characterizations like *absolutely*, making her precedential narrative appear too persuasive, too conspicuously oriented to winning the case. In the process, it shapes and co-opts resistance and re-channels it into male-hegemonic forms, concealed as legal inconsistency. Because of the dynamic interpenetration of social structure and linguistic structure, there is no way to build precedential narrative by taking a more moderate stance. Despite the intricate and artful type-token coordination, articulated at times in dense multimodal form, the PA could not overcome the intertwined sociocultural and linguistic barriers encountered in this courtroom.

4   Negotiating Intertextuality

In the last chapter we saw how multimodal conduct anchored the inter-textual infrastructure of the legal order in the narrative of a single speaker. In this chapter, we turn our attention to the intertextual interplay of multi-modal conduct between an attorney and witness in cross-examination: how participants mobilize multimodal resources to orchestrate an ensemble of metapragmatic realignments for organizing epistemological stance, recon-figuring turn organization, and recalibrating the putative asymmetry in forms of participation (Philips 1972; Goffman 1981; Goodwin and Good-win 2004). In so doing, we illuminate the emergent and shifting dialogic relations as the witness attempts to take control of the turn-taking system to recontextualize a glaring inconsistency in her prior speech, an inconsistency crucial to the legal interpretation of evidence in the case. We examine the strategic opportunities and multimodal resources that participants bring to bear on the interactional and epistemological contingencies confronting their legal identities and relationships in the courtroom.

Language, Power, and Participation

An important focus in legal discourse involves the role of power and how it affects trial outcome. Rather than merely assert or presume that witnesses, especially victims of sexual violence, are dominated in the courtroom, researchers have documented the legal–linguistic and institutional constraints imposed on witnesses attempting to tell their side of the story during hostile questioning by defense attorneys (Matoesian 1993, 2001; Taslitz 1999; Ehrlich 2001; Luchjenbroers and Aldridge 2007). Attorneys dominate witnesses through leading questions that attack credibility and generate inconsistencies, while witnesses passively provide answers, foreclosing opportunity to clarify inconsistencies or actively steer questioning in a more favorable direction.

Numerous analysts have made observations about asymmetries of participation in the courtroom (Conley and O'Barr 1998: 21; Ehrlich 2001: 67–69; Archer 2005: 76–77). According to Cotterill (2003: 105), "Witnesses are poorly placed in the interactional hierarchy of courtroom talk; they have no control over the talk of other participants in the trial process and only a very limited control over their own contributions." Raymond (2006: 126) notes, "In courtroom cross-examinations, participants operate within a specialized turn-taking system where the order of speakers and the types of actions they can produce are pre-allocated; lawyers ask questions and witnesses respond to them."[1] Pascal (2006: 383–84) claims, "In the adversarial legal system, talk-in-interaction is extremely fixed and regulated ... a set of pre-established and highly regulated communicative structures." Pascal goes on to state that "conversational roles are strictly allocated and turns are extremely constrained."

However, analytic focus on questions and the power of questioners to control testimony, important as it is, requires a more balanced consideration of how witnesses may subvert power and recalibrate differential access to the mechanisms of discourse. That questioners control witnesses rests not only on the assumption that turn departures can be legally sanctioned by both attorneys and judges, but also, more methodologically, on a near-exclusive analysis of attorneys and their questions, a structural bias built into the notion of the courtroom speech exchange system (speaking roles in court are pre-allocated and predetermined in contrast to the locally managed system of natural conversation) – a bias that reifies institutional variation in participation roles, obviates extralinguistic legal strategies that may influence discursive action, and conceals the power of witnesses to resist and displace institutional constraints that sanction turn departures.

Such a narrow focus on discourse in the courtroom envisions meaning as the product of a sole speaker rather than a collaborative, multimodal, and interactive co-construction between speaker and listener, with each shaping one another's contributions on a moment-by-moment basis (see Goodwin 1981). As we saw in Chapter 2, speech in court, like other forms of co-present discourse, is not the province of an autonomous speaker isolated from the contributions or influence of other participants, but is a thoroughly interactive communicative activity (Goodwin 2000). Here we question the assumption that the questioner – by virtue of questioning – controls the topic, trajectory, and ideological presuppositions of ongoing dialogue, with witnesses occupying a passive answering space rather than actively shaping and reshaping questions, or creating strategic opportunities that challenge restricted modes of participation.[2] We consider a

---

[1] Of course, this characterization is quite inaccurate as it ignores the role of objection sequences and the objection option space inserted between questions and answers (see Matoesian 1993).

[2] In a formal sense, this bias reflects the legal–linguistic ideology that only answers from witnesses, not questions from attorneys, represent evidence in a case.

radical departure – a deviant case – from this turn-taking system and the types of extralinguistic and multimodal leverage the witness exploits to realign participation roles and reconfigure identity.[3] If identity represents a performance of participants in interaction, as Mendoza-Denton (2002) correctly argues, then approaches to legal discourse must focus not just on the static linguistic practices of attorneys but also on the dynamic multimodal interplay between attorney and witness.

In a police statement given just after the alleged event and during examination statements to the prosecutor and defense attorney the prior day in the trial, the witness, Ann Mercer, mentioned that Bowman told her that Senator Kennedy, the defendant's uncle, who was present at the estate when the alleged assault occurred, had "watched" the rape incident. As it turned out, however, the alleged victim never stated – at least explicitly – that Senator Kennedy was watching (and there was no evidence that he did), but Mercer "inferred" this from a conversation she had with the victim afterward, even though the basis for such an inference was never revealed. According to defense attorney Roy Black, this "outrageous" statement provided firm evidence that the rape charge was designed – to some extent – to embarrass the Kennedy family in general and smear the senator's reputation in particular. In the ensuing segment, Mercer attempts to "rehabilitate" her prior testimony, resurrect the prosecution's case, and reaffirm the victim's credibility by revealing the basis for her inference.

Cross-Examination of Ann Mercer by Defense Attorney Roy Black

```
01 DA:   You knew that you were going to be asked
02       questions only twelve hours ago. It was only
         twelve hours isn' t that right?
03                              (1.1)
04 AM:   Yes
05                              (7.3)
06 AM:   ((slight head tilt forward and back at 7.0))
07 AM:   ((lip smack/alveolar click and head movement forward
            toward microphone with thinking face display at 7.3))
08 AM:   I would like to complete my answer on uh:: the question
09       (.) about (.) saying that Senat[or Kennedy was watching
                                        [((gaze moves to DA))
10                              (0.9)
```

---

[3] An issue that requires ethnographic access to trials and participants.

```
11 AM:    ((raised and sustained eyebrow flash with open mouth
          co-occurring with three micro vertical head nods))
12                            (3.3)
13 DA:    Uh::: (.) which question are you answering now:: miss::
                                                        [
14 AM:                                            You
15        had asked me uh::: (.) yesterday (0.5) n' you also asked
16        me this morning (0.5) about my statement to the police =
                              [                 ]
17 DA:              You want to-
18 AM:    = saying that she told me that Senator Kennedy was
19        watching. I would like to complete that answer for the jury
          please.
20                            (0.9)
21 DA:    You mean this is an answer that I asked you yesterday you
22        now after thinking about it overnight want to complete the
23        ah::: answer
          [
24 AM:     Ah::: No. I didn' t have the opportunity to answer your
25        question yesterday ((staccato delivery)) I
26        [ believe=
          [ ((slight gaze movement from DA to Judge and back))
27        =we had stopped[ at that point
                         [ (((45 degree turn to Judge and back to DA))
28                            (1.2)
29 DA:    I' m sorry I thought you had uh:: completed your answer
30        If you want to say something to the jury that you' ve had
31        time to think about (.) [ please go ahead ((low volume
          29-31))
                                  [
32 AM:                         No- it- >I haven't had time to
33        think about it. I would have said the same thing
34        yesterday when you asked me.< ((Sped up))
```

In what follows, we first describe the multimodal contextualization of Mercer's radical turn departure and the extralinguistic leverage she exploits to take control of participation structure, and the dilemma imposed on the defense attorney as a result. As mentioned previously, participation designates how speaker-hearers build micro forms of social organization through multimodal activities in the ongoing course of co-present interaction: the dynamic and emergent fragmentation of discursive roles. According to Goodwin and Goodwin (2004: 222), it refers to how participants "display to one another what we are doing and how we expect them to align themselves toward the activity of the moment." As we will see, however, participation may include more than the current social organization of discursive identities, and may impose historical configurations onto the pragmatic present (Irvine 1996).

In the second section, we investigate metapragmatic, intertextual, and interdiscursive negotiations between defense attorney and witness as both strive to shape the prior realignment in an ideological drive to establish epistemological hegemony over a projected course of speech. We consider these forms of textuality as dynamic multimodal resources in the joint negotiation of legal–linguistic ideologies, epistemological stance, and speaker–recipient alignment.

In the final section, we display how the micro-historical circulation of utterances functions to fragment participation roles in the current speech situation, how the interaction between current and historical speech implicates novel forms of institutional dialogue and projects an intricate ensemble of laminated voices in the legal co-construction of sexual violence.[4] In the process, we see how linguistic ideology or folk beliefs about language use aligns with multimodal conduct to manage a particular impression of reported speech – even before that speech occurs – endowing it with epistemological relevance and interpretive significance. We analyze the multimodal strategies that witness and attorney bring to bear on the interactional contingencies confronting their legal realities: how they rotate alignment in multiple laminations of participation. We hope to show, more modestly, that witnesses in court, even in cross-examination, are not as powerless as researchers often claim.

A Deviant Case Embodied

Discourse in the courtroom possesses a formal institutional signature or fingerprint, a distinct speech exchange system: pre-allocation of turns and turn types. Attorneys control the turn-taking system, asking questions, while witnesses respond to them. Departures that invert either turn type or turn order may be sanctioned by formal, metalinguistic reprove. On the other hand, they may be interactionally marked in some fashion to display an orientation to the legal order while simultaneously violating it – or

---

[4] Lamination (Goffman 1981) refers to the embedding or layering of voices, footings, and forms of participation present in a speaker's utterance. As we hope to show, such laminations represent not only the speaker's contribution but also an interactive co-production/ projection among both co-present and non-present participants.

both.[5] We can witness discursive marking in the earlier segment. Defense attorney Roy Black came to a break in questioning, and his lengthy silence in line 05 appears to project the genesis of a new topical frame. However, before he launches a new line of inquiry, Mercer initiates a request to "complete" her prior testimony about "Senator Kennedy watching" (line 08).

In terms of marking the violation, notice that Mercer's utterance consists of neither an answer nor testimony she wishes to contribute. Moreover, her departure from the provisions of the turn-taking system occurs not only in request format, seeking the attorney's permission before continuing, but also in the midst of a lengthy silence – Black's silence (since attorneys control the turn-taking system, once the witness completes the answer turn, order reverts back to the attorney) – that appears to signal the end of a topical sequence. In a delicate balancing act, her verbal request maintains alignment with the participation structure of the court while contextualizing a realignment of institutional arrangements and identities, violating the normative order of the court while simultaneously displaying an orientation to its relevance.

But there is much more than a verbal request here. In fact, to focus solely on Mercer's verbal component would neglect not only the multimodal constitution of emergent forms of turn distribution and participation, but the distinctively assertive stance she undertakes to index specialized speaking rights – that is, to warrant her departure from the institutional order.

With these points in mind, at seven seconds into Black's silence (line 06) Mercer produces a fleeting, "hesitating" head movement forward to the microphone and back, as if contemplating a course of activity while still maintaining an indecisive stance about going forward with it. In a duo of visually and verbally marked pre-violations, she tilts her head forward, aborts that movement, and retracts forward progression.[6] Then, at 7.3 seconds (in line 07) she first activates an alveolar click that projects a forthcoming utterance, then executes a forward head movement to initiate the request.

Just as interesting, although Mercer gazes at Black during the silence, she diverts her gaze in a middle distance look or "thinking face" display during production of the request, then redirects it back to Black after completion. In a more speculative vein, given the contemplative dynamic,

---

[5] Of course, this applies to both attorneys and witnesses.
[6] The to-and-fro movement toward the microphone (which here may function as a semiotic artifact) could well provide a focus of joint attention by contextualizing a pre-activity, in this case, moving into speaking position.

Figure 4.1: (line 11 eyebrow flash with micro head nods).

we might wonder whether Mercer would have made the request in the absence of Black's lengthy silence.

Although Mercer's request definitely projects an operative transition-relevant place, Black does not respond, and after close to a second after the request, she activates a progression of embodied increments organized at discretely layered micro intervals to simultaneously elicit and scan for his withheld response, recycling the request multimodally.[7] First, moving into a state of gaze with Black, she produces a raised and sustained eyebrow flash, with widening of the eyes and an open mouth display (see Figure 4.1).

Second, after a split-second delay in turn transition – another recipient delay some two seconds into the silence – she initiates a compressed yet accelerated sequence of three vertical head nods synchronized with the suspended flash (as if seeking an "OK" response). Third, even as the last head nod increment decays, she "holds" the eyebrow flash until, after 3.3 seconds, Black finally responds (line 13). Thus, Mercer is not just eliciting a response from Black but first, contextualizing a specific type of response preference – granting of the request – and, second, escalating the velocity of turn-transfer attempts as she modulates her turn-in-progress by adding post-verbal embodied increments.

This shows, however, more than the interactive dynamics between speaker and listener, and how multimodal practices engineer and shape the organization of deviant turn activity. It also shows more than how Mercer's turn-in-progress unfolds as an interactive co-construction in

---

[7] A transition-relevant place is a projected environment where other speakers may begin to speak or gear into a speaking role, at least in natural conversation. Of course, it is not clear if the same applies to the courtroom.

which Black's delayed response triggers her multimodal turn extension. Rather, it displays the contingent and improvisational multimodal practices that rotate institutional arrangements and identities. This dynamic interplay of multimodal resources indexes a linguistic ideology of speakership rights based on the historical circulation of utterances: she fashions an intertextual link with her prior text as something left unsaid or incomplete. Her post-verbal embodied increments index a discursive right to complete the prior text and, even more importantly, signal an assertive stance toward those rights, even appearing to "normalize" the realignment of participant roles. The accelerating head nods shape a conducive format that normalizes her verbal production, and finesses Black to grant the request. Her post-verbal embodied increments represent not just an "adding" on of the nonverbal to verbal, a further turn-transfer device, but a conducive attempt to shape the attorney's next turn (grant the request) and recalibrate institutional order. This is not to say that deviant case marking is equivalent to witness resistance; rather, it is to stress that her resistance, in this instance, emerges contingently, incrementally, and multimodally in the dense clustering of deviant case features to reframe participation structure.

We have seen thus far, in just a brief snippet of this exchange, how our institutional identities and arrangements function in the interactive moments of multimodal practice – how the witness takes the interactional initiative in cross-examination. Often neglected in the study of institutional discourse, these multimodal resources constitute the interactional architecture of the courtroom: they shape intertextual and ideological relations, reconfigure participation roles, and recalibrate the historical circulation of utterances and epistemic stance. Mercer's multimodal conduct is responsive to and interacts with, the delay in Black's response; her multimodal extension increments are triggered by his lack of recipiency; her turn is not an autonomous utterance that belongs to an isolated speaker but is, much more dynamically, a multimodal co-construction emerging contingently and improvisationally in the performance of the turn-in-progress. A detailed analysis and appreciation of these situated and embodied turn practices – conducive head nods, post-verbal turn extension increments such as gaze, facial expression, projecting, and recycling transition relevant places – is a basic, not tangential, requirement for specifying how witness resistance emerges as an interactive and multimodal accomplishment in the courtroom.

On line 13, Black finally responds to Mercer's request, although with several perturbations at turn onset to go along with his withheld response: the elongated delay marker and slight pause to indicate its coming "out of the blue" status. Just as Mercer marks her departure from the canonical pattern, Black marks her turn as well with inter- and intra-turn delay components and, in so doing, shows an orientation to the courtroom order. Along similar lines, just as Black co-marks Mercer's violation, he also builds that marking out of resources from her request. His response transforms her predicate noun phrase (*my answer*) into the progressive verb (*answering*), while repeating her *question* as the turn-initial selective interrogative (*which question*) – but with an odd twist.

Rather than grant or reject Mercer's request, he produces an unorthodox metapragmatic formulation – a query that treats her utterance not as a request but as an answer to some unknown question: *Which question are you answering now?* Although Mercer's request indicates a desire to complete a prior answer, the deictic adverb *now* marks her utterance neither as a request nor a precursor to some unfinished utterance, but as an answer, though a referentially ambiguous one. Black's speaker–recipient realignment – a realignment of the realignment – first reaffirms or maintains the integrity of institutional boundary and the canonical form of participation within it by treating her request as an answer, and second places Mercer in the canonical sequential location of providing an answer to his question, although now housed in the insertion sequence format. Her request has to work its way through this format, a format that delays, expands, and highlights her depart-ure while simultaneously "normalizing" institutional turn protocol.[8]

Moreover, while it might be tempting to attribute the realignment to asymmetrical participation rights or institutional power, we should con-sider that it is also and contemporaneously, an artifact of the insertion sequence: Black's question deals with problems in Mercer's request, a request coming "out of the blue" as it were, rather than (solely) realigning institutional boundary. Thus, what we see emerging in all its multiplex deviant case manifestations resembles a contrapuntal dialogue conjured with transparent institutional crosscurrents, a dialogue incorporating dif-ferent elements but still maintaining a delicate harmonic balance.

You Might Win the Battle but Lose the War: Strategic versus Tactical Maneuvers

Why does Mercer even attempt to direct the course of talk? If the discur-sive division of labor in the courtroom represents such a rigid structure as the earlier commentators have noted, how could she even contemplate altering institutional arrangements? Just as important, why doesn't Black suppress the attempt, and quash it immediately, instead of letting her continue? Why risk the possibility that Mercer might say something

---

[8] By *normalizing* here we refer to Black's treatment of her request as an answer.

injurious or damaging to the defense? In a lengthy interview the first author conducted with him after the case (see Matoesian 2001), we discussed Mercer's turn departure (along with several from the victim) in terms of strategic versus tactical objectives in a trial. When asked why he failed to suppress Mercer's speech, he stated, "You might win the battle but lose the war." He went on to explain that witnesses "might strangle themselves with their own words." In the first case, jurors might draw the conclusion that he was trying to withhold vital evidence about the issue at hand, especially since she wants to complete the answer *for the jury*; in the second, the witness might say something that harms his or her own case. Although certainly within Black's legal rights to limit the victim's discursive role, his legal-linguistic rationalizations about suppressing or permitting role departures, and the effects this might yield, mediated his handling of Mercer's request. Otherwise, even though perhaps surprised, he could have delivered a quick and emphatic "just respond to the questions," or "don't talk unless questioned," and so on. While a decision to constrain or limit the witness's attempt to expand his or her discursive role might, on the face of it, seem like good tactical logic, it could also pose a hazard to the strategic objective of prevailing in the case: winning the war. Put in more Goffmanian terms, attorneys seek to foster a particular impression on the jury, and that gives witnesses limited leverage to exploit strategic versus tactical dilemmas in the trial, in Mercer's case to recontextualize a matter relevant to the legal constitution of sexual assault. Although she is not in control of the inferences (by drawing attention to the inconsistency), she still constructs a discursive dilemma for the defense attorney, a dilemma that influences the realignment of attorney–witness participation.

This is not to say that witnesses can alter institutional arrangements at any time or any place. Nor is it to claim that attorneys will always allow witnesses a discursive space as a strategic maneuver. Rather, it is to document the interactional dilemmas and contingencies confronting courtroom participants, and how these may be managed to shape the organization of discursive opportunity, strategies often ignored by focusing on concepts like pre-allocation or asymmetrical speech system. It also illustrates, more theoretically, the difference between law as a system of formal rationality – and by analogy a formal pre-allocation system – versus the law in action, the discourse of law as a strategically emergent co-construction, and the tension between these.

We can recognize that the courtroom represents – to some extent – a distinct speech system with differential participation rights while simultaneously taking account of legal and extralinguistic factors that mediate such constraints and provide a more flexible movement of discursive practice, practices that shape the opportunity for witness resistance. While the discursive division of labor in the courtroom may bear some variable relationship to institutional identity, this is not a direct relationship as Heritage (2004: 237) claims, but one mediated by the emergent interplay of extralegal strategies and contingent multimodal resources. Discursive practices always possess a dynamic status that can never be "read off" of institutional structure, even in the rigid moments of cross-examination. In more critical terms, while Mercer's request components may bear the institutional signature of the legal institution, they also bear the local imprint of ordinary conversation; to echo a position from Hester and Francis (2001), there is little about the request components – silence, pauses, head nods, and so on – in terms of representing some distinct institutional signature.

The Art of Impression Management: Intertextual and Interdiscursive Epistemologies

The preceding sections examined the dynamic interplay of multimodal resources and legal strategy in shaping a discursive space for witness resistance, how the attorney oriented to the practical objective of winning the case, and how this mediated institutional constraint. In this section, we turn to a metapragmatic negotiation between intertextual and interdiscursive relations and the epistemological oppositions circulating through these.

As we saw in Chapter 3, intertextuality refers to the decontextualization of historical text and its recontextualization in current context; interdiscursivity refers to the use of one form of discourse or genre (or hybrid of genres) in another genre (Fairclough 2003; Johnstone 2008). The former relates words, utterances, and text from one context to another; the latter relates one genre or speech event to another. Together and in terms of the present analysis, they organize the historical circulation of voices, identities, and contexts in multimodal laminations of strategic activity.

Viewed from this perspective, Mercer intends to recontextualize her incomplete speech and insert it into the current speech situation. But that depends on Black granting the request, and in the ensuing sequence we see an intertextual and interdiscursive opposition take shape and come into focus as Mercer elaborates its content.

First, in line 14 she overlaps Black's utterance-final tag in line 13 (preempting its completion), referring to the temporal coordinates of her prior speech in the conjoined clause (*You had asked me uh::: (.) yesterday (0.9) n'you also asked me this morning*). Second, she produces a complex embedding of *that*-complements to refer to her previous cross-examination, police statement, and post-rape conversation with the victim (*about my statement to the police saying that she told me that Senator Kennedy was watching*), synchronizing a multiplex lamination of participation roles within a complex grammatical construction – even embedding an indirect quote from the victim within her own indirect quote (line 18). Third, in this iconic embedding of grammar and participation, she generates an intertextual continuity between historical and current text by representing her prior speech as incomplete and currently in the process of being finished, with noticeably marked stress on the final clause (*I would like to complete that answer for the jury please*).

In this instance, notice that her answer is *for the jury*, so the jury would be the projected recipients of the information now developing in significance. If Black curtailed her request, he would deprive the jury of crucial evidence, and that might spark their interest in his reasons for doing so.

When Black detects the significance of her request and attempts to respond (*You want to*), Mercer – perhaps gaining a glimpse of the looming opposition – increases her pace and volume to engineer his withdrawal from the overlap, illustrated in the cutoff at the beginning of the *about*-phrase. In more detail, Black interprets the end of Mercer's conjoined clause in line 16 (in the environment of her pause) as a complete utterance, but that projection turns out to be inaccurate as Mercer expands her turn – now a multiunit turn-in-progress – with the post-modifying prepositional phrases followed by the embedded *that*-complements. Moreover, focusing on the multimodal interaction we can ask how (or if) Mercer contextualizes turn continuation instead of turn withdrawal. While we can offer only a provisional account here, as Mercer begins construction of the multiunit turn, she lowers her head and gazes at Black. At the end of the first clause she pauses for 0.5 seconds, and, even through Black's overlap, the pause after the second clause is of identical duration (0.5 seconds), a perfectly balanced case of temporal clause synchronization, perhaps designed to display turn continuation rather than withdrawal.

Of course, we can contemplate why Black would not wish to intrude on Mercer's turn extension, an issue that may have less to do with witness resistance or turn competition than legal strategy. Mercer organizes the request as a completion of unfinished prior speech, and although she never states explicitly *why* that speech was left incomplete (at least up to the present point), we can speculate that Black interrupted her or constrained her speech in some fashion – at least, that is the impression she is attempting to foster. If Black interrupts Mercer's current turn extension or turn-in-progress, it would be an instance of what we are "saying" becoming what we are "doing." A potential interruption of her current utterance would be an indexical icon of what Mercer's request is, to some extent, attempting to redress.

Although Black withdraws from the competitive overlap, his aborted turn incursion escalates the looming intertextual-interdiscursive opposition and its epistemological significance. That opposition materializes full force to ignite the textual clash beginning in line 21. First, Black produces the turn-initial and heavily stressed *You mean* discourse particle that functions not as an explicit repair initiation, or an attempt to clear up an ambiguity or seek clarification. Instead, it operates as a stance marker of disbelief, a contrastive marker that registers surprise as it simultaneously evaluates the request. Second, he mobilizes three temporal deictics and a mental state verb to indicate the content of that evaluation: that the projected recontextualization from *yesterday* was something Mercer had been *thinking* about overnight. Of special significance is the temporal adverb *overnight*: that she had been thinking about her recontextualization and planning it for an unduly long period of time. Third, it is not only the case that Mercer thought about her testimony overnight but also that this *thinking* included rehearsal or coaching with her attorneys the prior evening, adding another lamination of participation onto the intertextual request. As previously mentioned, participation refers to the current division of discursive labor, but it may also designate the historical circulation of voices that can be imposed on the pragmatic present, what Irvine (1996) refers to as "shadow conversations." In this case, we can see a micro-social organization assembling a complex combination of voices in historical and current dialogue, unleashing a flood of damaging inferences in the process. In Goffman's (1959: 175) terms, Black constructs Mercer's request as a type of "staging talk" or team collusion, a scripted or contrived impression management scheme rather than authentic (and, of course, truthful) speech in the legal order.[9]

---

[9] Consider further evidence of this interpretation from the following *edited* excerpts, the first two from Black and Mercer shortly after she completes her request (which we see shortly), and the third from the Court TV news commentator who "breaks in" after Mercer's utterance in example 2.

(1) BLACK:	Did you discuss this with your lawyer Mister Felder last night.	
MERCER:	*No I did not!* ((increased loudness and stress))	
(2) BLACK:	You have two attorneys representing you in this case do you not?	
MERCER:	Yes I have.	
BLACK:	I'm sure they've gone over this statement with you haven't they?	
MERCER:	*No they have not!* ((increased loudness and stress))	
(3) COMMENTATOR:	Our guest commentator Mickey Sherman and I suspect that Ann Mercer has a different attitude and responsive demeanor today in this second day of cross-examination. She may have spent the evening talking with her attorney, Raul Felder, to try and figure out a way to better respond to the questions.	

If we bear these considerations in mind, Black discloses discrediting information about backstage rehearsal with attorneys the night before, doubtlessly encouraging her discursive assertiveness, and projects a disembodied yet implicated form of dialogic voicing consisting of her legal coaches in the pragmatic present. Her current request, as it turns out, bears the dialogic imprint of these historical voices, and that cabalistic or Machiavellian form of collusive participation lies outside the parameters of legal propriety – outside legal truth.

While Mercer projects an intertextual continuity between historical and forthcoming speech by portraying her prior speech as incomplete, Black recalibrates that speech as an interdiscursive discontinuity: a speech event originating from a different genre to constitute an epistemologically contaminated hybridization of speech styles. In this crisscrossing circulation of polyphonic voices, epistemological value is mapped onto textual relations and institutional identity. He shapes the epistemological criteria for gauging the authenticity and truth of evidential knowledge; utterances that are planned or thought out beforehand, that are not in a state of deictic immediacy to canonical question–answer format, and that are rehearsed with professionals constitute an epistemologically invalid method of discovering legal truth.

Thus, Black not only realigns Mercer's realignment roles in his inserted query but also produces a more powerful epistemological re-realignment consisting of a hierarchically organized opposition of temporal truth values, a linguistic ideology of spontaneity that establishes the epistemological criteria for calibrating the legitimacy of legal utterances.

In line 24, notice the increasing intensity of disagreement. Following Black's lead, Mercer's response tacitly naturalizes the epistemological division that Black proposes (by responding to it and responding to it first). She interrupts Black's (projected) turn final component "answer to," triggering his withdrawal, to produce an emphatic *Ah::: no* followed by *I didn't have the opportunity to answer your question yesterday,* with the clause-final component stressed in staccato for emphasis. To illustrate the delicacy of Mercer's resistance and its interactive relevance, notice how she appropriates and repeats Black's vowel lengthening (from his turn preservation attempt in line 23), to rhythmically integrate her turn incursion as syntactically continuous with the prolonged component, retooling it for turn-entry position, and to enhance the significance of her rejection.[10]

---

[10] Perhaps we could refer to this type of repeating resource as a "turn-fluid interruption," in which Black's delayed completion furnishes the opportunity space for her to preempt his turn.

Figure 4.2: (line 27 *gaze to judge*).

In an ironic twist, as Black is questioning Mercer's desire to complete her historically interrupted speech, she takes the opportunity to interrupt and preempt his utterance in progress – power indeed! And, in line 27, Mercer claims that *we had stopped at that point*, thus explaining the basis for making the request in the first place.

If we consider her utterance in more detail, we see again the importance of including embodied along with verbal activity, for Mercer creates a multimodal realignment of participation in her response. As she delivers the epistemic verb *believe* (line 26) – expressing doubt and evaluation (Precht 2003: 242) – she gazes toward the judge in a slight movement and back. After the judge fails to respond, she recycles her gaze and torques her upper torso toward the judge in a second confirmation try at turn final deictic (*at that point*), in the form of a subordinate alignment (Goffman 1963; see Figure 4.2).

As this happens, she first conveys an uncertain stance toward the information imparted, and second realigns participation structure to secure the judge's confirmation of the time, a delicately laced integration of verbal and embodied conduct (i.e., the brief gaze toward the judge is perfectly synchronized with the epistemic verb *believe*; the second longer gaze and body torque is synchronized at onset of the deictic phrase *at that point*). The cognitive verb marks a lack of certainty; her embodied conduct orchestrates realignment and expansion of participation; and both coordinate a multimodal form of "evidential participation" in which the witness *attempts* to augment epistemological authority. In a slightly different reading, however, Mercer's action may represent less an uncertain epistemic stance or an attempt to find an evidential "ally" than an interactive resource to shape a visible focus of attention for interpreting her intertextual claim. Whether or not the judge responds may be of little relevance in the truth status of temporal coordinates.[11] That is to say, when Mercer gazes at the judge, holds it for a moment, and then realigns to Black, this constitutes an epistemological *display* of grounding a *certain uncertain stance*. This important aspect of witness resistance would be omitted by considering only the verbal dimension of discursive practice.

In a stunning maneuver out of the dilemma, Black formally "grants" her request in line 29, concluding the lengthy insertion sequence through the metapragmatic conditional (using the *if*-conditional to present the directive in a polite form), which provides an alternative interpretive frame for her forthcoming speech – an explicit (supra) metapragmatic calibration of its textual status. Although Black formally "grants" the request, he more accurately reconfigures it, and this is hardly the same intertextual object preoccupying Mercer's interactional efforts. Now, the optimal strategy is to let Mercer continue, but with the epistemological provision in the reconfigured participation structure: a projection of team collusion or staging talk (not Mercer and Black in current testimony but Mercer plus coaches in a prior rehearsal genre, another laminated form of participation that will hover over the rest of Mercer's multimodal actions). Black's counterstrategy thus fosters the impression of not concealing evidence, with the added bonus of pre-framing and reframing Mercer's historical speech. Moreover, he preempts the possibility that the prosecution might bring up the issue on redirect, leaving him little recourse to shape the "collusive teamwork" interpretation.

Even after granting the request (prefaced with the apology and mistake acknowledgement), Black puts Mercer on the defensive. In line 32, rather than unpack the (now "granted") request, she rejects the conditional and reasserts the intertextual continuity with emphatic stress, increased tempo, and loudness prior to addressing the content of her forthcoming speech, signaling a heightened state of aggravated opposition: *No- it- >I haven't had time to think about it I would have said the same thing yesterday when you asked me<*. Still more accurately, Mercer opens her mouth well before she starts to speak, indicating her pre-rejection of Black's claim (in line 31). For those keeping count, this is the fourth time that Mercer interrupts or overlaps Black's speech, and in each case Black withdraws from the

---

[11] Unfortunately, because of the camera angle we cannot see if or how the judge responds.

simultaneous talk – a marked difference from the discursive passivity often
attributed to witnesses. As Mercer's response demonstrates, this is no mere
apology and granting of the request. Much more accurately, his conditional functions as a thoroughly unveiled accusation, realigning Mercer in
the canonical participation format of responding to the attorney's blame-
implicative utterance.

Reported Speech as an Interactive and Embodied Activity

In this final section, we consider the epistemological implications of
the aforementioned textual negotiation for Mercer's reported speech.
What follows is the discursive culmination of Mercer's recontextualization efforts.

```
32 AM:   No- it- >I haven't had time to
33       think about it. I would have said the same thing
34       yesterday when you asked me.< ((Sped up))
         ((gazing at Black from 32-34))
35                          (1.4)
         [((torques upper body, tilts head/shoulders, and
         shifts gaze to thinking face/middle distance
         display in 35-41))
36       When Patty:: (1.6) came over to my house (.) when
37       she was at my house (0.4) she was sitting on my
38       couch (.) in a state of hysteria (1.6) a::::nd I had
39       asked her (.) uh few questions (1.7) Uh:: she repeated
40       (2.5) th- that he was watching, he was watching
41       (2.8) I (.) then in return asked her (.) who
42       was watching (0.8) [Was Senator Kennedy watching?
                            [((eyebrow flash))
43                          (2.0)
         [((realigns body and gaze to Black))
44       [ A::nd at that point (.) she became[more hysterical (.)=
                                             [((slight lateral head
                                                shake))
45       =[more shaky (.) and I assum::ed (1.2) that Senator=
         [((marked lateral head shake))
46       = Kennedy was watching. But she never (0.8) told
47       me he was watching. I made that assumption
48       by her affirmative (0.8) display of hysteria
49       ((Move to an upright position and juts chin))
```

Reported speech – direct, indirect, and free quotes – functions in a number of different respects. It dramatizes, demonstrates, evaluates, and enacts prior speech; it displays affective stance and constitutes a subtle persuasive device in which speakers insert their own voice into the speech reported. In legal settings, in particular, reported speech possesses an important evidential function in the representation of historical utterances. However, rather than being an accurate representation of some state of affairs, it constitutes, as Tannen (1989) notes, a form of constructed speech designed to accomplish some interactional task in context. How does Mercer's speech intersect with embodied activity in the joint production of epistemological authority?

We have seen that Black's metapragmatic conditional recalibrates the epistemological significance of Mercer's impending statement, and because of that we can also see how linguistic features of her narrative *retrospectively* and reflexively index a degree of planning or formality: long pauses, embedded parenthetical (*then in return*), repetition of direct quotes, and explicit metaindexical frames (*she repeated*), to mention but a few. But there is something else just as significant that may bestow such interpretive force.

After the noticeably marked rejection in lines 32 to 34, Mercer torques her upper torso from Black to the right, tilts her upper torso and head to one side, and shifts her gaze downward in a thinking face display, appearing deeply engaged or heavily involved in thinking while speaking. According to Goffman (1963: 36), "To be engaged in an occasioned activity means to sustain some kind of cognitive and affective engagement in it, some mobilization of one's psychobiological resources; in short, it means to be *involved* in it." We can see this clearly in the previous segment – although in neither the mobilization of "psychobiological resources" nor in her bodily conduct, but in the multimodal and interactive negotiation between her and Black (see Figures 4.3 and 4.4). Retrospectively, Black's pre-framing conditional imparts an iconic alignment and reflexive sense of epistemic coherence to Mercer's bodily action and reported speech – to her contemplative activity while speaking. Her body shift and gaze foreground a state of mental activity – thinking or remembering – and foster the impression that she is in the process of enacting the rehearsed object of the prior evening.[12]

---

[12] In another sense, the shift contextualizes her involvement with her narrative about the historical conversation and coordinates her departure from the disagreement sequence with Black.

Figure 4.3: (line 34 *pre-body torque*).

Figure 4.4: (line 36 *body torque*).

Even more germane to the just mentioned points, Mercer mobilizes a specific bodily activity during production of the direct quote in line 41. In her report of historical dialogue, Mercer first quotes Bowman's speech, then responds with a direct quote of her own. Although the reported speech of Bowman appears, given the *that*-complementizer, syntactically marked for an indirect quote trajectory, the sharp fluctuation in intonation and shift in pitch register recalibrate the reported speech as a direct quote, and this shift signals a key portion of Mercer's message. In her ensuing narration, Mercer first embeds represented speech, *I then in return asked her who was watching,* and second inserts her historical speech in the form of a direct quote, *Was Senator Kennedy watching?* While both appear, on the face of it, configured as reported speech, there is a crucial difference: the first represents a paraphrase (*who was watching* functioning as a quotative

Figure 4.5: (line 43 body returns to 'home' position).

frame), the second a direct quote. In a finely synchronized multimodal display, only the direct quote occurs with a shift in intonation and pitch register, and even more important, with marked alteration in facial expression: an animated eyebrow flash that decays after the quoted speech (as she realigns her body and gaze back to Black at the 2.0 pause in Figure 4.5).

By synchronizing facial expression and gaze with the direct quote, Mercer may not only signal a division between quoted and represented speech but also foreground the ambiguity in historical dialogue. In a delicate balancing act, she needs to extricate herself from the damaging implications of prior speech about Senator Kennedy, while maintaining her credibility and that of the victim. Mercer's dilemma appears linked to an issue of footing: she needs to suppress or at least "disperse" her involvement as the *principal* behind the statement about Senator Kennedy. As mentioned in Chapter 3, Goffman (1981) found that traditional depictions of speaker and hearer were inadequate to capture the complexities of our discursive activities. As a result, he decomposed the speaker into the well-known taxonomy of footing, or the relationship the individual takes to their utterance: the animator physically produces the words, the author composes them, and the principal authorizes those words and assumes the role of responsible party. Although Mercer attributes the statement in question to Bowman (originally), there is no evidence that Bowman ever made such a statement, leaving Mercer dangerously "exposed" as the animator, author, and principal.[13] She

[13] Given that Mercer received a large sum of money from popular tabloids for her story, one could speculate why she would wish to introduce the "story" about Senator Kennedy. Of course, defense attorney Black does a bit more than speculate later in his cross-examination (see Matoesian 2001).

needs to "distance" her involvement in, and relationship to, the production of the statement, especially since she provides no substantive hint of the questions, only the gloss (*I had asked her (.) uh few questions*) that elicited the *He was watching* response from Bowman.

To do so, Mercer creates an interpreter role and inserts her voice as a figure in the reconstituted dialogue, suppressing her involvement and maintaining the boundary dividing Bowman, the principal, and Mercer, the animator. The principal's position must always be interpreted, and if it can be interpreted, it can also be misinterpreted. As Mercer maps facial display onto direct quote (once again following the *who was watching*-quotative), she highlights an interpreter footing, displacing her role as a possible principal or co-principal in the production of the statement through a visually animated verbal production. Given her question and Bowman's "hysterical" response, the assumption that Senator Kennedy was watching represents a quite logical inference – a logic conveyed by instructing the jury to view that response as an *affirmative display of hysteria*. In more strategic detail, by disambiguating the *who*-relative (*asked her who was watching*) with the direct quote (*Was Senator Kennedy watching?*), Mercer instructs hearers to treat both utterances as referentially equivalent, the former being a formulation or representation of the latter. Given the direct quote of Bowman's exact repetitions (*He was watching. He was watching*), clearing up the referential ambiguity appears as a logical inference in the sequential progression of historical and current speech, especially since the exact repetition foregrounds the indefinite reference as a matter of special interest, even intrigue. The *who was watching* representation shapes the ensuing Senator Kennedy quote as a mere logical inference based on or triggered by the principal's – Bowman's – speech.

Moreover, if we look at the outset of Mercer's narrative beginning on line 36, consider a further item relevant to her performance. In addition to the body torque and middle distance look, she tilts her head and shoulders in noticeably marked fashion (see Figure 4.4). According to Calbris (2011: 96) such a tilt "represents a point of view" and "the slanted imbalanced position of an object." Such differentially positioned segments of the body impart rather interesting alignments to her different interactional activities. She signals first a new viewpoint, her "enacted" interaction with Patty and, second, the rather strange or "slanted" conversation about Senator Kennedy watching, marking this aspect of the narrative through multimodal conduct. On line 43, Mercer moves out of torque (see Figure 4.5), squaring her shoulders and head, to move into an analytic (or objective) interpretation of Bowman's speech and hysteria, igniting the possible inferences she made in lines 46–48: *I made that assumption.* As she completes her

Figure 4.6: (line 49 moves to an upright position to end the narrative).

narrative (Figure 4.6), she sits upright and juts her chin out in a display of aggressive confidence, as if emboldened by her assertive behavior. More theoretically, when looking at the lone linguistic individual we may see one viewpoint. However, when considered multimodally and inter- actively, multiple viewpoints may emerge: one from Black, another from Mercer, and still another from the reflexive recalibration between Black's metapragmatic frame and Mercer's defensive multimodal response, differentially ranked laminations of involvement in different types of activity.

Just as germane to the aforementioned points, notice how Mercer superimposes repetition of lateral head shakes onto repetition and stress of the intensifying adverbs (*more hysterical (.) more shaky* in lines 44 to 45) to create a multidimensional iconic imagery. Her lateral head shakes not only beat out the rhythm of the modifiers but also foreground Bow- man's *shaky* and *hysterical* traumatic state. Still more substantively, her multimodal parallelism indexes how Bowman's ambiguous comments and erratic behavior could relate to rape trauma syndrome and the acute disorganization phase associated with it, allowing Mercer to consolidate her interpreter-figure role in the unfolding drama – and the "shaky" role of trying to interpret the traumatized Bowman – as well as to downplay any collusive footing on their part.

Thus, Mercer manages the dilemma, the inconsistency, and her credibil- ity (and that of the victim) by molding an interpreter-figure footing in the historical dialogue and transmitting the import of that involvement in a dynamic multimodal form of impression management. Mercer creates not only an intertextual link but also an intertextual ambiguity – which she proceeds to set aright – as a strategic interactional resource for saving face.

Whatever the outcome of the case and Mercer's overall performance, this is a sophisticated form of witness resistance in cross-examination.

Even so, because of Black's framing conditional and the epistemic authority it imparts, the animator footing Mercer assembles is, to some extent, infused with the principal-author voices of her legal "coaches" and the truth values embedded in and constructed through this collusive footing – projected voices that infiltrate and contaminate her narrative production. That is, Mercer positions herself as an animator–interpreter relative to Bowman. Black projects her as an animator relative to her principal legal coaches, which recalibrates Mercer's animator–interpreter role and repositions the collusive conspiracy by her and Bowman. As Goffman (1981: 153) notes in his discussion of collusion, "We not only embed utterances, we embed interaction arrangements." Footing and other forms of participation, as Goodwin and Goodwin (2004: 225) have noted, are not products of the isolated speaker but interactive, multimodal co-productions between participants as they mutually shape footing alignments in the intricate rhythms of the unfolding dispute. Mercer does not merely "adapt" a particular footing in her reported speech, but, much more dynamically, a particular footing emerges as an interactive, multimodal coproduction between her and Black. At a finer level of granularity, footing emerges in the contrast between Black's perversely restrained – a tauntingly composed lower volume – *if*-conditional metapragmatic frame (*If you want to say something to the jury that you've had time to think about (.) please go ahead*), as it interacts with Mercer's body torque, middle-distance look, or thinking gaze (lines 35–43), and sonorous defensive stance in line 32 (the increased loudness, stress, cutoff, and sped up speech), drawing attention to itself and making it appear rehearsed (thus subtly invoking the negative inferences associated with rehearsed testimony).[14] Put another way, her "interruptive" and prosodically marked defensiveness interacts with Black's metapragmatic frame to draw disparaging attention to the authenticity of her forthcoming quotes in lines 40–42. This in turn confirms Black's interpretation that she is speaking from a prepared script. Just as crucial in the negotiation is how Black, while foregrounding Mercer's multiple forms of participation, manages to background his own voice and role in the implicated and current dialogues.

Along with the numerous forms and functions of reported speech, we can add that it is a thoroughly interactive and embodied communicative practice, a collaborative accomplishment of co-present and historically implicated forms of participation. Reported speech not only inheres in

---

[14] Of course, the rather formal parenthetical *in return* contributes to this rehearsed interpretation also.

the grammatical and paralinguistic properties of an isolated speaker's narrative or utterance (or in the immediate sequential environment), to project onto extralinguistic reality; it is contingently grounded in the broader constellation of multimodal activity and the epistemic circumstance in which it is interactively encrusted. In precisely this sense, reported speech and an epistemic conditional mutually elaborate one another in a multi-laminated ensemble of intertextual and interdiscursive voices, such that Mercer's direct quote (as well as her entire narrative) becomes – to some extent – retrospectively displaced and reconfigured even prior to being spoken. As isolated and autonomous activities, neither Black's epistemic conditional nor Mercer's embodied conduct foster an aura of rehearsed performance. Rather, it is the co-improvisational interplay in and through multimodal practice that contextualizes such a collusive impression, an impression that emerges *in the moment*.

Conclusion

If power refers to what it might ultimately yield in terms of practical outcome or effectiveness (as if we know how practices are linked to outcomes), we suspect Mercer fared quite poorly, for Black may have let her "strangle" herself in her own words, and let her "win the battle but lose the war" because she focused undue attention on the inconsistency and its significance. What started out as a prosecution theory of the case in terms of a Kennedy conspiracy to cover up evidence – with all the "intertextual" intrigue alluding to the assassinations of John and Robert Kennedy and Senator Kennedy's "incident" at Chappaquiddick became a conspiracy by Mercer and Bowman to implicate members of the Kennedy family in a heinous crime of sexual assault – for whatever reasons. That dialogue itself assembles a historical – perhaps even current – form of participation dealing with the reasons for discussing Senator Kennedy in the first place
  On the other hand, if power implicates the multimodal resources and extralinguistic strategies that witnesses bring to bear on the discursive contingencies confronting them, and how they co-coordinate and negotiate forms of participation in the historical circulation of textual forms, then we open up analytic possibilities for uncovering the interactive logic of role departures and witness resistance in the legal institution. In this regard, we have seen how ideological forms and linguistic rationalizations function not only through verbal form but also through the dynamic integration of verbal and embodied conduct; our *legal* interpretation of sexual assault is shaped, to some extent, in and through these microcosmic multimodal episodes. Although Mercer may not have fared well in this round, she was far from passive in the proceedings, far from just providing

answers in the witness role. While it is well known that attorneys constrain witness's choices, we have seen here how the witness limits the attorney's choices: his ability to openly quash her speech. The dynamic negotiation between Black and Mercer over the pre-framing of her reported speech and the emergent mapping of crisscrossing legal epistemologies onto textual oppositions, is just as crucial to an understanding of institutional power and witness resistance as the structural asymmetry of participant roles. We would miss this crucial feature of constructing legal reality without detailed consideration of interactive and multimodal forms, a research agenda necessary to re-specify and reinvigorate language and law studies.

Part II

Trial Practice in Multimodal Conduct

5   Motives and Accusations

In this part, we turn to several items in the prescriptive culture of trial advocacy such as motivation, control, and credibility, and how the incorporation of multimodality can enrich the study of these classic strategies. In Chapter 5, we demonstrate how gesture, gaze, and postural orientation are interwoven into the stream of verbal activity in a victim's motivational narrative during direct examination. Incorporating a sociocultural focus, we also display how multimodal resources function in the ascription of blame, constitution of identity, and the emergence of multiparty participation frameworks in a victim's narrative performance.

More specifically, we analyze an instance of multimodal activity from a victim in a rape trial as she addresses motivational issues during redirect examination. As Ehrlich (2001: 108–9) notes, direct examination permits the victim to construct a narrative in her own voice, making the narrative come "alive" and captivate the jury's attention, in contrast to cross-examination which involves deconstruction by the defense attorney. Redirect examination (also called re-examination), in particular, is of crucial significance because it allows the prosecution and victim to rebut the defense attorney's impeachment from the immediately prior cross-examination. Considered by some as the penultimate moment in the prosecution's case, the victim's narrative in this instance creates an emotionally charged moment of high drama as she discusses ulterior motives for going forward with charges against the defendant. However, her narrative consists of quite a lot more than just speech. She synchronizes talk, gesture, and gaze as co-expressive resources to shape a rhythmically integrated and affective form of persuasive discourse. In the process, she grounds victim resistance in a sophisticated multimodal constellation of multiple participation frames to forge identity, orchestrate epistemic stance, and distribute responsibility in the sociolegal organization of sexual assault. More generally, we will see how multimodal conduct is brought to bear on the local contingencies confronting the victim's motivational narrative, and the incremental alignments and realignments she deploys to shape a coherent accusation against the defendant, rebutting the defense attorney's impeachment attempt in the process.

The next section provides background information on this segment and the motivational issues surrounding the case. The ensuing analysis of motivational data demonstrates not only how multimodal conduct is relevant to the study of the victim's narrative in direct examination, but also how institutional forms of speech-synchronized gestures may reveal sociocultural directions for the study of gesture, gaze, and talk as situated forms of activity.

Data Extract 1

After a lengthy cross-examination, in which the defense attributed a host of unsavory ulterior motives to the victim (see Chapter 8), the prosecuting attorney (in re-direct) posed the following question, in Extract (1), to the victim.

Victim Re-Direct Examination

(PA = Prosecuting Attorney; DA = Defence Attorney; J = Judge; V = Victim; D = Defendant; p = point; b = beat; pb = pointing beat; IFT = index finger touching thumb.)

```
01    PA:   Do you have any ulterior motive for going
            through this Ms Bowman?
02                       (1.7)
03    V:    Yes.
04                         (.6)
05    PA:   What is that?
06                         (.4)
07    DA:   Objection yer honor (.6) motivation
                   [
08    V:                  ((gaze moves toward DA))
09                       (2.3)
10    J:    Overruled.
                [
11    V:                ((gaze returns to PA))
12                     (1.7)
13    V:    ((V moves from home position to gaze and
            point at D)) =
14    V:    = What he did to me was wro:::ng (1.3)
                 (p)    (pb)    (pb)      (pb+hold)
            [ ((gaze and left hand pointing toward D
              at turn-initial position))
```

```
       ((short beats on did and was))
       ((post stroke hold on wro:::ng into the 1.3
       pause with 3 micro beats embedded in the hold))
       ((on was gaze moves to PA))
15     I have a child
       [((gaze to PA))
       [((points to herself on I then downward bunched
       fingers point with index finger extended on child))
16                          (0.8)
       ((point and gaze moves toward D during pause))
17     ((in-breath)) What he did to me was wro:::ng
                          (b)        (b)        (b+hold)
       ((gaze to D on What he did to me))
       ((gaze shifts to PA on was,
         to jury on wrong+post-stroke hold))
       ((3 micro beats during post-stroke hold)
18                          (1.0)
       ((slight head shift to the right toward jury))
19     n' it's    not              right (.)
                  [(beat upstroke) [(beat downstroke)
       [((gesture shifts to PA))
       ((gaze to PA on n' it's, shifts to jury on not right))
       ((first head shift increment right towards jury))
20     n' I don't want to live the rest of my life
       (IFT)              (b)        (b)        (b)
       [((gesture shifts to PA n' I don't want to live))
       ((shifts to jury on the rest))
       ((second head shift increment to right))
21     ((arm and finger shifts moving toward D))
22     in fear of that        man ((staccato))
          (b)    (b)          (b+hold)
       [((gaze at PA in fear of that, then shifts to
         jury on man+post-stroke hold))
       ((third head shift increment to right))
023                         (0.5)
024    n' I don't wanna be responsible for him
       (b)                          (beat upstroke)
       [[[((gaze to PA))
025    doin it                  to somebody=
       [(beat downstroke)       [(beat upstroke)
       ((gaze to jury for him doin it, to PA on to somebody
        and then gaze to jury on utterance completion))
       =else
       [(beat downstroke)
026 DA: I object yer honor
```

```
027  V:     [((return to home position+gaze/head to DA))
             ((high elevation on the upstrokes and marked
             acceleration on downstrokes in 19, 24 and 25))
```

Multimodal Accusations

In rape trials – like other criminal assault trials – defense attorneys routinely raise questions about the victim's extralegal motives for making the accusation, and the case under scrutiny here represents a poignant instance. During cross-examination, the defense questioned the victim at length about ulterior motives for fabricating the charge against the defendant, some conscious, others unconscious: that she disliked men, that she was hurt because the defendant would not let her spend the night, that she was mentally disturbed, that she was looking for publicity, that she was upset about being "used" sexually and being "misled" by the defendant's true intentions. By ascribing ulterior motives, the defense assembles an interpretive template for framing and assessing the credibility of the victim's account, an account based not on legally relevant criteria but on malicious factors irrelevant to the ultimate issue in the case (as we will see in Chapter 8).

By the same token, the prosecution and victim must convince the jury otherwise: that the victim's accusation consists solely of legally relevant facts. In line 01, the prosecuting attorney begins her re-direct examination of the victim with a question about ulterior motives *for going through with this*, and after the victim's avowal (*Yes*), she poses the further question: *What is that?* That the victim admits possessing ulterior motives seems, on the face of it, a rather unorthodox response because the defense, rather than the prosecution, typically ascribes such motives to impeach the victim's credibility in rape trials. Given the defense attorney's vigorous imputation of ulterior motives in the prior stage of questioning, however, more than a simple denial appears warranted in response.

After the objection sequence, we see the victim steer the logic of motive ascription and avowal in a quite unanticipated yet favorable direction, elaborating her "ulterior" motive in line 14: *What he did to me was wro:::ng.* There is more than a verbal component to the answer, for if we consider the victim's actions in line 13, notice that she begins with an embodied response well before the start of the utterance. Following the judge's overrule on the objection, she turns from DA to PA, moves out of home or rest position (Sacks and Schegloff 2002), and raises her left

Figure 5.1: (line 14 *What he did to me was wrong*).

arm/wrist and finger to point at the defendant: an elevation and extension of the arm in a bent elbow position with the index finger extended and other fingers tightly curled under the thumb. As she switches on the deictic vector of the point, she also shifts postural alignment and projects her gaze toward the defendant, creating him as the focus of joint attention. As her utterance proceeds in line 14, the pointing gesture coincides with onset of the verbal component (*What he*) – a delicately laced synchronization of verbal and embodied modalities so that both arrive simultaneously in a semantically coherent course of action. Just as important, while the victim realigns gaze from the defendant to the prosecuting attorney on *did,* she maintains the pointing gesture at the defendant – a noticeably marked post-stroke hold on *wro:::ng* (where the gesture is suspended in position for a period of time after the gesture stroke) – not only over the entire verbal component, but also into the 1.3-second utterance final pause (in line 14, Figure 5.1).

However, the victim does more than orchestrate a semantically coherent and temporally synchronized course of gesture-speech action; her pointing with the index finger does more than locate the defendant's bearing from a deictic center. In fact, the gesture involves quite a lot more than just pointing as deictic reference – more than indicating the defendant's location in space.

According to Kendon (2004), McNeill (2005), and Kita (2003), index finger pointing refers to those actions whose primary or sole function is to indicate direction, or locate objects in space, and in lines 13–14 we indeed see how ostensive gestural deixis is directionally anchored, projecting a vector from the finger to the defendant. As she switches on the spatial vector, we see gesture, gaze, and speech align perfectly in the production of her utterance (each arriving simultaneously on the pronoun *he*), and that reflects our prior discussion of the joint interplay between speech and gesture: that speakers adjust and readjust gesture-speech ensembles to achieve intricately interwoven structures of discursive action.

When we dissect this in more microscopic detail, however, notice that her pointing gesture evolves into short beats on the stressed syllables *did* and *me*, and a series of unaccented "shaking" beats on *wro:::ng*.[1] As mentioned previously, beats refer to the rhythmic function of gestures – how gestures visualize or (perhaps more accurately) orchestrate aspects of discursive structure through horizontal and/or vertical movements. According to Streeck (2008), they enact the musical and informational flow of an utterance, highlighting points of emphasis, parsing significant segments into discretely organized units of relevance. In this case, the victim resets the pointing gesture as a multifunctional – double duty – narrative resource for not only switching on the deictic vector but also mapping out significant segments of her utterance, fusing the deictic on the one hand, with the pragmatic function on the other, to create a hybrid gesture of considerable complexity. When these two functions collide and fuse, they yield an accusatory moral stance that ascribes blame and allocates responsibility for the sexual assault. Put another way, gestural deixis mutates into accusatory beats. Indeed, upon closer inspection, the pointing beat recalibrates into an accusatory gesture during vowel lengthening (on *wro:::ng*) and further into the 1.3-second ensuing pause (in line 14), where it not only stands alone as a post-stroke hold but simultaneously displays an unmarked finger shake (three micro beats while pointing at the defendant) – intensifying blame by foregrounding the defendant as a joint focus of attention.

In a recent work, Goodwin (2003) demonstrated how the ostensibly simple deictic gesture of pointing derives its meaning from the broader stream of semiotic activities in which it is embedded, and in line 14 (Figure 5.1) we can witness such meaning construction in the victim's narrative-in-progress. First, she maintains index finger extension in a post-stroke hold toward the defendant while simultaneously withholding speech, and second, she shifts participation structure via gaze realignment toward the prosecuting attorney to map an accusatory moral stance onto the deictic vector of the point: a highly affective and emphatic stance toward the information imparted. That is, once the deictic vector rotates into directional alignment, she retools and redeploys it as a beat to hammer out points of emphasis. Just as germane, pointing and shaking

---

[1] As Kita (2003: 2) notes, "pointing does not merely indicate a vector, but it can serve to create further types of signs." As we are starting to see, it can serve multiple communicative functions and do so simultaneously.

an accusatory finger at the defendant while directing speech to a different recipient, packs an additional modal punch, transforming her "ulterior" motives into an accusatory account. That imagistic meaning would be lost without detailed consideration of the embodied component.[2]

Thus far we have seen how gestures and other bodily actions possess a type of emergent flexibility and multifunctionality that, in concert with speech, are specifically tailored and adapted to the contingencies of direct examination: assembling accusations and blame (and, as we will see, in a more or less "ulterior" strategy in legal terms). Moreover, although the victim's words convey very little stress, her utterance is still laden with affective evaluation – with intense modal meaning – in the temporal coordination of multimodal stance and speech, forms of meaning that would be lost to description and analysis by focusing only on the latter.[3] As we will see shortly, she is just getting warmed up.

Gesture and the Emergent Organization of Maternal Identity

In line 14, the victim realigns gaze from the defendant to the prosecuting attorney on the *do*-verb, and in line 15 (Figures 5.2 and 5.3), she continues this gaze pattern in the ensuing comment: *I have a child.* On the first person pronoun, Bowman points to herself with the left hand but then immediately, in a fluid improvisation, aborts the point and produces a downward gesture consisting of several bunched finger beats (with the fingers facing down and palm inwards), that reach the stroke phase on *child.* In this supple movement, she transforms personal reference deixis with the extended index finger to a bunched three- or four-finger display to make an emphatic point; her self-reflexive finger point transforms into the bunched gesture on the downward motion, a type of discontinuous gliding gesture that begins as a self-point, but one displaced and merged immediately into a different form that synchronizes with her production of the noun phrase *child.* Put another way, she accelerates tempo of the self-point

[2] Indeed, we might reflect on pointing gestures more generally at this juncture in the analysis. Does the witness's finger project a vector toward a particular direction, toward the defendant? Or does it direct us to the crime or an evaluation of the defendant's actions? Are these even isolable functions, at least empirically (rather than analytically), or do they exist simultaneously as possible functions of the deictic – well beyond the deictic? Needless to say, Wittgenstein (1953) pointed out this problem with ostensive definition and pointing in his classic example of the child and the apple.
[3] Stance possesses an array of meanings and as mentioned in Chapter 3, we use it quite generally as the multimodal marking of the speaker's degree of certainty of, or commitment to, their statement (epistemic stance), and to evaluation, attitude, and affect conveyed in propositional content (see Matoesian 2005).

Figure 5.2: (line 15 *I*).

Figure 5.3: (line 15 *child*).

and then implements a cutoff on that gesture to reconfigure a new gesture
that coordinates with the emphatic finger points on *child.*

Mobilizing an ingenious demonstration of displaced rhythm to preserve
the integrity of talk-gesture synchronicity, she produces a parenthetical
afterthought or aside – but not an unimportant one. While the defense
attributed an array of unseemly motives – that she was a woman scorned
or revengeful – the victim reframes ulterior motives as an issue of moral
authority, a discourse of maternal responsibility. She contextualizes
gender identity not as sexual relation (a woman picked up in a bar) but
as a family relation, where the downward gesture on child consists of an
up-down spatialization metaphor in the sense that the child is lower in age
and smaller than herself. The defendant did not merely sexually assault a
woman but a mother with a child, and the bunched finger beats, by
visualizing both pragmatic and propositional structure in an emphatic
display of bodily stance, intensify the immorality of such a crime. Thus

we see the role of gesture not only to coordinate interaction, adjusting and readjusting its form and trajectory to keep pace with the emergent contingencies of utterance construction, but also in concert with speech, to contextualize maternal identity, activate epistemic stance, and build creative accusatory accounts in sociolegal performance. We see how identity and stance are not only realized through grammatical resources but also contextually situated and multimodally emergent.

Repeating and Recycling the Accusation

Where is the victim's ulterior motive in all this? What is becoming transparent at this stage is that the victim's avowal of ulterior motive represents less a rebuttal of the defense attorney's impeachment strategy than a symbolic vehicle for assembling a litany of accusations against the defendant. Doubtless, the only thing "ulterior" is not the victim's motive but her deployment of motive as a sociocultural resource for attacking the defendant's moral character. Still, and with much greater precision, the victim and the prosecuting attorney mobilize ulterior motive as an explicit metapragmatic resource for shaping a sonorous recitation of moral condemnation against the defendant, steering the topic toward his unscrupulous behavior rather than the victim's state of mind. As we saw in Chapter 4, although legal research often notes that rape victims in particular, and witnesses in general, are powerless on the stand, less research has shown how witnesses compose a persuasive voice in court, and the victim's accusatory narrative here constitutes, mutatis mutandis, a mirror image of defense strategy: a powerful form of multimodal resistance.

In line 17 (Figure 5.4), the narrative develops further as the victim repeats and recycles her accusation (*What he did to me was wro::::ng*),

Figure 5.4: (line 17 *What he did to me was wro::::ng*).

repeating not only verbal but embodied conduct as well (demonstrating speech-gesture synchronization in the process), returning her pointing gesture to the defendant during the pause in line 16, and gazing in his direction on *was*. Although the victim repeats the accusation, she alters gestural configuration in terms of tempo and elevation: slower tempo and steep upward/downward motions for more pronounced emphasis. That is to say, the second recycled and repeated accusation is accompanied by marked pointing beats – heightened elevation on the upswing, and increased acceleration on the downswing – though still incorporating the autonomous post-stroke gestural hold toward the defendant during vowel lengthening (on *wro:::ng*), and after utterance completion. By withholding speech on the post-stroke hold, the victim bestows a powerful sense of modal intensity to her verbal conduct: a pronounced shift in the fused relative, now the first component in an emerging multimodal parallel structure.

Just as crucial, she not only shifts gaze to the prosecuting attorney after her initial gaze at the defendant, but also, while still maintaining a pointing gesture in his direction, realigns her gaze and postural orientation to the jury during the post-stroke hold (albeit briefly), adding an emergent dimension of subordinate participation into the unfolding narration. As mentioned in previous chapters, participation refers to the interactive and multimodal positioning of speaker and recipient roles in the micro social organization of discourse (Goodwin and Goodwin 2004; Goodwin 2007: 53). In a powerful display of multimodal dexterity, she intimates a high degree of contempt toward the defendant – perhaps inviting the jury to agree with that assessment – by pointing at him while simultaneously moving into a state of gaze with other participants, participants responsible for prosecuting and evaluating his actions. To "rearrange" Goffman (1959), she directs a form of "uncivil" inattention toward the defendant by discussing his blame relevant actions and immoral traits while directing her speech to other co-present recipients.

The sequence progresses through a multimodal parallel structure consisting of the contracted coordinating conjunction (explicitly marking the parallel structure in progress), general ascription concerning the defendant's actions built as a contrast off the prior blame component (*n' it's not right*), and elevated pointing beat to the prosecuting attorney: a steeply marked elevation on the contracted conjunction, and acceleration on the downswing stroke *right* in line 19 (Figure 5.5).

From the pointing beat's downswing position (at the bottom of the motion) in Figure 5.5, she retracts her hand shape to execute an index finger touching thumb or precision gesture (in which the tip of the thumb touches the tip of the index finger to form, as Kendon (2004: 225) notes, a

Figure 5.5: (line 19 *n' it's not right*).

Figure 5.6: (line 20 *n' I don't want to live the rest of my life*).

"ring" shape that "makes prominent some fact or idea"), directs this new gesture (still with the left hand) via a low vertical arc movement to the jurors, and aligns her gaze to the jury box in the middle of the utterance (on *rest* in line 20) to shape a new – and main – participation structure. Next, she redeploys the precision gesture to map beats onto stressed syllables and, in the process, mobilizes postural adjustments in the form of three distinct incremental shifts to the right (on lines 19, 20, and 22), a progression of short head shifts imposed on each intonation unit that culminates in perfect gaze alignment with the jury and that accentuate their institutional relevance. Finally, the third verbal component in the emerging parallel structure repeats the contracted coordinating conjunction to link the accusatory litany in Figure 5.6.

Thus far we have seen how the victim's embodied activity – her beat gestures – moves laterally/horizontally from defendant to prosecutor to jury (interturn participation), and up/down vertically on the first two pointing beat gestures (intraturn). Put another way, she employs multi-party (moving from the defendant to the prosecutor to the jury and back to the defendant, etc.), multidimensional (horizontal and vertical/up-down), and polyrhythmic (beating in a parallel sequence of arcs rotating along the inter clause axis) hand gestures to organize her narrative. In a finely orchestrated alignment of fused gestures, the arc motion ties episodic points and beat rhythms into a continuous narrative stream, maintaining continuity across each clause. Moreover, the micro-embedded gestures (up-down) during the post-stroke hold to the defendant add a further measure of poetic complexity to her narrative.

At the same time, her verbal activity consists of parallel blame imput-ations regarding the defendant's behavior coordinated through the con-tracted conjunctions. The first two parts of the litany refer to general blame attributes (*wrong* and *not right*). The third and fourth segments, however, shift to more specific, first-person mental attributes (*n'I don't want to live the rest of my life in fear of that man* and *n' I don't want to be responsible for him doin' it to somebody else*) that repeat the verb of cognition, contracted negative and infinitive (in lines 20–25).

Consider the relation between grammar, legal identity, and the body as this unfolds. The first general attribution is in the past tense (*was wro:::ng* in line 17), in which gaze and pointing beat are directed at the defendant, indicating past behavior. The second intonation unit (*it's* in line 19) is in the present tense and directed to the prosecuting attorney, who is institu-tionally responsible for prosecuting the case in the here and now. On the other hand, the jury, who would be responsible for evaluating the crime in the future deliberation, is the primary (not sole) recipient of the specific components in the parallel structure (*I don't want to live* and *I don't want to be responsible*), each referring to grammatically marked future projections. Specifically, the *want*-type (mental desire verb "want" to the infinitival complement) infinitives encode future projections, and it is the jury's institutionally endowed obligation to evaluate these; that is to say, the jury is institutionally responsible for the future outcome of the case. Just as crucial, the shift from general moral evaluations (*not right*, *wrong*), to specific cognitive verbs (*wanna* in line 24), corresponds metaphorically to gestural shape. The victim deploys pointing beats for the former, but shifts to the gesture of precision or specificity in the latter, and this alternation in gestural form activates not only a change in participant alignment, but also a new relation to her utterance (from past and present to future projection): an embodied shift in footing (Goffman 1981). In so doing, she contextualizes a delicate or vulnerable identity (perhaps a delicate gesture for a delicate woman) and that her fate (and the fate of other potential victims), will soon be in the jury's hands. As Morris (1977: 58) observes: the ring or precision gesture is used when the speaker wants to "express himself delicately and with great exactness. This hand emphasizes the fineness of the points he is stressing." Just as interesting, the ring gesture onset is prominently marked – almost as if she is "winding up" for a delivery in the arc motion – to convey precisely this point.

Here we can see in vivid detail how grammar, gesture, and participation merge into a multimodal constellation of institutional relevance. We see how stylistic features of multimodal conduct are not only rhythmically integrated – how verbal and gestural parallelism intersect in polyrhythmic modalities – but institutionally anchored as well. When her gesture moves from the prosecutor to the jury, she shifts from a steeply elevated, vertical pointing motion to a horizontal index finger tip touching thumb gesture movement with a very low arc trajectory en route. Once at its participation destination, the gesture is recalibrated and redeployed to beat out her main points of emphasis, still using the precision gesture shape. In an agile multimodal performance, both gestural form and trajectory are significantly altered to recontextualize the new participation structure and new activity being transacted: a different participation structure in play with a different texture of legal relevance. In more theoretical terms, gesture shapes the infrastructural context in which such poetic improvisation can take place.

Multimodal and Multiparty Forms of Participation

At the end of the intonation unit (*in fear of that man* in line 22 Figure 5.7), the victim reactivates the deictic vector – retracting the precision gesture and restoring the index finger extension – but not until gesture onset begins, early enough to co-occur with its verbal complement, the

Figure 5.7: (line 22 *in fear of that man*).

noticeably stressed demonstrative *that man*. As this occurs, she realigns her point back to the defendant while simultaneously adjusting her gaze and postural orientation to both jury and prosecuting attorney (indeed, the stressed demonstrative imparts a marked pragmatic sense in addition to reference). In so doing, she maps an emphatic moral stance onto the deictic vector of the point, while maintaining multimodal frames of participation encompassing multiple strands of relevance. That is, she not only switches to the deictic vector to coincide with the demonstrative but, once syn-chronized, resets it to beat out the rhythm of her accusation, engaging the defendant without disengaging from either the jury or the prosecuting attorney by maintaining gaze and postural orientation. Following this, she first adds the final element to the parallel structure by repeating the contracted coordinating conjunction, cognitive verb, and infinitive, and second, maintains the pointing beat into the indefinite pronoun (*n' I don't wanna be responsible for him doin' it to somebody else* in lines 24–25) to complete the dense rhythmic structure: a gestural hybrid of deixis, beat, and bodily stance.

More substantively, the victim reframes ulterior motives as an issue of moral order, of moral authority. By downplaying the sexual, and fore-grounding a protective mother identity, she demonstrates how she is responsible not only for protecting a child but for protecting others against future crimes by this sexual predator, engaging the jury's sense of responsibility for the well-being of other vulnerable women in the process (see Figure 5.8). It is her responsibility to keep him from doing *it* again. Still more symbolically, this demonstrates how the sociocultural voice of maternal authority emerges not only from denotational text, but in the intricate polyrhythmic texture of multimodal form itself; that is to say, the victim not only conveys her sentiments to the jury and PA but

Figure 5.8: (lines 24 & 25 gaze shift from PA to jury on *for him doin' it*)).

also, in and through the accusatory beats, fosters the impression of reprimanding an obstinate and impenitent child – the defendant. Just as germane to this point, by pointing at the defendant while directing her gaze and postural orientation to other participants, she projects her legal identity as a rape victim: a victim unable or too afraid to gaze at her assailant. In the process, we can see how, in Michael Silverstein's (1998: 226) words, "what was said maps onto what was done," or how "denotational text maps onto interacting text." The victim not only constructs forms of participation but also enacts culture in the iconic form of multimodal performance.

Back to Ulterior Motives

If we consider the re-direct narrative in technical legal terms, the victim's ulterior motives neither resurrect her credibility nor broach her motivational state after a sharp defense impeachment. In a furtive turn of events, she reinforces and repeats the criminal charges against the defendant through an emotionally riveting spate of accusatory accounts. Still more accurately, she goes beyond the charge of rape to portray the defendant as a dangerous individual, shifting from the criminal act per se, to criminal character (*in fear of that man*) and moral identity (*wrong, not right* as an entire course of conduct): an indirect attack on the defendant's moral character. That the defendant has not even taken the stand at this juncture in the case, bestows a further measure of distinction to her narrative; since he has not yet taken the stand it is legally improper to attack his character unless he opens himself up to impeachment (notice the defense attorney's objection in line 26). The points we wish to make are these. First, rather than consider rape victims in the courtroom as passive recipients for defense imputations of motive, for fabricating the assault charges (often with a psychoanalytic twist), we can see how Bowman not only resists defense impeachment of motive but also assembles rather ingenious – multimodal and social organizational – resources for directing her own character attacks against the defendant. This is not to say that ulterior motives are absent in her narrative. Rather, her multimodal stance, especially her deictic beats, bequeaths a strong accusatory sense to her speech – meaning that would be lost to analytic description without considering the role of the body in and as cultural-legal action. Second, rather than consider gestural conduct as some type of nonverbal leakage that reveals an objective inner truth (often with a psychoanalytic twist), we can see how it functions as a sociocultural resource in the constitution of legal realities and organization of direct examination.

Conclusion

In this chapter we have demonstrated – indeed the participant has demonstrated – how a dense constellation of multimodal resources – gaze, gesture, and speech – is brought to bear on the emergent and contingent social projects confronting the victim in direct examination, including accusations, identity, and stance. As her narrative unfolds, we have seen how accusatory accounts are differentially distributed to institutionally anchored recipients in temporally synchronized gesture-speech units – how verbal and embodied laminations of participation, legal identity, and epistemic stance are generated through multimodal patterns and off-kilter rhythms. *Such multimodal actions display how the law is not only talked but embodied into being as well.*

In the semiotic division of labor, each multimodal increment contextualizes distinct accusatory activities, and fragments legal recipiency into institutionally emergent forms of relevant participation. Speech specifies the moral grounds of the accusatory litany; pointing gestures pick out the defendant's location in the deictic field; rhythmic beats ground affective and epistemic stance by hammering out points of significance; and gaze movements draw multiple participants into the motivational account and keep shifting institutional alignments in play simultaneously. More theoretically, bringing multimodal analysis into the realm of language and law opens up a microcosmic direction for a more discriminating exploration of how the victim can dramatize her story – construct her own voice spontaneously – in a rhythmically intricate, highly interactive, and emotionally compelling narrative, a sociocultural performance that is fluidly improvised yet uncannily synchronized. That she manages to foster such a persuasive impression reveals the value of multimodal analysis not only for direct examination in rape trials but also for legal discourse more generally.

6   Nailing Down an Answer

In Chapter 4, we saw how the witness exercised a multimodal and extra-linguistic maneuver to coerce the defense attorney to honor her request to finish testimony from the previous day. In this chapter, we watch the defense attorney employ a coercive and multimodal maneuver to overcome the resistance of an evasive witness – the same witness who turned the tables on him previously. More theoretically, we investigate a questioning strategy in trial cross-examination that is designed to control an evasive witness, and how that control functions through multimodal conduct to index identity, construct multidimensional forms of participation, and circulate intertextual relationships in the legal order.

Control

The issue of control represents a central theme in the study of law: the power to shape the content, form, and flow of evidence (Harris 1984). Nowhere is the issue of control as significant as in trial discourse, where tangible outcomes such as guilt, innocence, and monetary award hinge on the ability of lawyers to influence the witness's testimony (Harris 1984; Philips 1987; Walker 1987; Ehrlich 2001).[1] In the context of adversarial trial cross-examination, especially, attorneys often discredit a witness's testimony and damage credibility through unflattering questions about moral character, while witnesses, on the other hand, may resist such imputations and deflect degrading inferences by offering qualified or evasive answers (Drew 1985, 1992; Conley and O'Barr 1998; Cotterill 2003). But to discredit testimony and make their version of reality count, attorneys must gain and maintain control of a usually hostile witness. By

---

[1] In the trial context, more specifically, control represents the attorney's ability to not only extract the desired answer from the witness but also impose the relevant legal and cultural frames on those answers through the form and substance of the question. Of course, the ultimate goal of such questioning is to "erase" the answer, as it were, and speak directly to the jury. See Hobbs (2003) for an excellent example of this.

the same token, the hostile witness must manage resistance – and the damaging moral inferences evasive techniques often inherit – in the face of ever escalating and finely discriminating strategies of control. At the intersection of this conflict, a continuous and oscillating to-and-fro struggle of control and resistance may emerge – especially in the midst of intensely oppositional and emotionally charged moments of questioning – where neither party prevails. Strategically, the issue is important enough that the prescriptive culture of trial advocacy advises attorneys to overcome such unyielding resistance by using a strategy of control referred to as *nailing down an answer*, as the authors of a recent textbook mention.

Witness weaseling is an age-old art and the examiner will miss the witness' equivocal responses or qualified answers unless he is listening to the answers. If the advocate catches the attempted evasion, he can nail the witness down. (Perrin et al. 2003: 309)

The authors go on to provide a pointed example of "nailing down," a nonresponsive witness (Perrin et al. 2003: 310):

LAWYER: As you approached the intersection, you were going
50 miles per hour, true?
WITNESS: I guess that's right?
LAWYER: I'm sorry Mr. Weasley, I don't want you to guess. You
were going 50 miles per hour, true?
WITNESS: I suppose so.
LAWYER: You were going 50?
WITNESS: Yes.

In a descriptive, linguistic study on the language and ideology of judges, Philips (1998) studied how Arizona judges nailed down unequivocal admissions of guilt from defendants in plea bargain sentences, overcoming their often evasive and ambiguous answers. In these instances, a clear admission of guilt is of considerable legal significance for appellate review, since the Arizona Statutes state that the defendant must know the consequences of pleading guilty. In taking guilty pleas from defendants, a judge "nails down" an answer when he/she overcomes the defendant's resistance by going "over the same ground until he elicits the admission he is seeking" (Philips 1998: 97) or "asks question after question in the critical areas of denial until he has enough admissions among the denials to satisfy himself" (Philips 1998: 95). The following is a striking example from her study (Philips 1998: 95–98, and edited here from the much longer transcript).

JUDGE: And what did you do on the ninth of January that makes you
think you're
guilty of this crime. Did you take
some property or money from him?

DEF: No, I received the money from him.
JUDGE: Okay. Then how was it that he gave it to you?
DEF: I asked him for it.
JUDGE: Did you ask him for it in such a way that there wasn't much
           choice on his part?
DEF: I asked him for it in a derogatory tone.
((several lines omitted))
JUDGE: Did you suggest to him that you had some weapon there?
DEF: How would you say "suggest"?
((several lines omitted))
JUDGE: At that time you said to him, "I want your money" or words
           to that effect?
DEF: I asked for his money.;
JUDGE: All right.
DEF: He asked me if he could help me and I says, "Yes, you can
           give me some money."
JUDGE: Okay. And at that time you thrust your finger forward in
           your pocket which suggested you might have a weapon?
DEF: Yes.
JUDGE: Lemme ask you this. Do you think he would have given you
           the money if you hadn't done that?
DEF: I don't know.

Thus both prescriptively and descriptively, nailing down an answer (here-after, ND) refers to the techniques in which attorneys attempt to control a witness's testimony, overcome their steadfast resistance to questioning, and obtain confirmation of a specific version of "the facts." In a quite transparent sense, ND is a form of conflict speech between adversaries in the micro politics of truth.

As interesting – and legally significant – as this verbal conflict appears from the work of both Perrin et al. and Philips, neither scholar analyzes the concrete discursive details in and through which control materializes, and resistance overcomes during the ND process (keeping in mind that neither set out to do so). While numerous researchers have identified how variation in question form exerts coercive control (succinctly summarized by Gibbons 2003), few have analyzed how coercive questioning practices are collaboratively and interactively negotiated over longer sequential exchanges and incorporate embodied resources, such as the body, gesture, and facial expression.

In this chapter we analyze the discursive process of ND and demonstrate how it is not only or even primarily a form of coercive syntax designed to control an evasive witness and overcome resistance. Indeed, as we hope to show, "doing" evasion might be a more complex issue than it *prima facie* appears. Much more significantly, we demonstrate how ND represents a multimodal struggle of identity, participation, and power, strategically forged in a constellation of legal linguistic ideologies, cultural practices unfolding incrementally, contingently, and interactively over a lengthy exchange between defense attorney and witness in cross-examination. We have seen how *linguistic ideologies* represent folk beliefs or rationalizations about language structure and use, and how these beliefs relate to the naturalization of power: the social conditions underpinning the production and reception of discursive action (Silverstein 1993; Woolard 1998). We have also seen how *participation* refers to the interactive process of positioning speaker and recipient roles in conversation, dialogue, or text, either real or imagined, and the epistemic forms of involvement social actors project onto their own and each other's words (Goodwin and Goodwin 2004). Together, they contextualize the relevant interpretive frames for signaling to one another, "what we are doing now?," providing the resources for coordinating ongoing communicative activities and channeling the indexical ground for the situated interpretation of meaning.

However, the "now" of the current conversation is not the only dimension to participation, as actors invoke broader forms of social organization for producing and interpreting their activities, as Irvine (1996: 157) notes:

There is no necessary limit to these contextualizations and discourse histories – to the sense in which a multitude of other dialogues are implicated in the one at hand. By the same token, I believe, there is no necessary limit to the participation frames that can be imposed on the pragmatic present, fragmenting its participation roles and recombining them, in a complex calculus of mapping roles onto persons present and absent ... The intricate laminations of participant roles, the many shadow conversations they reflect, and the discourses they inform belong to the same dialogue.

In a similar vein, Wortham (2001: 138) writes:

Voices and relationships that get *represented* by the narrator can come to organize the storytelling event itself, as narrator and interlocutors act out relationships partly analogous to those represented in the narrative.

The current chapter builds on this sense of participation by setting intertextuality and participation "into motion," by showing how the represented dialogue is enacted in the current speech event (Silverstein 1998). In such cases, we can witness the emergence of a symbolic interaction in which "what was said maps onto what is done" (Silverstein 1998: 266; or what Silverstein also refers to also as a "mapping of denotational text to interacting text"). We explicate the dynamic intertextual relations among participation, legal identity, and language ideology and demonstrate how these are epistemologically organized for strategic purposes. We show how the persuasive power of ND emerges not just from syntactic form but the broader range of intertextual and multimodal practices in which those forms participate. In the process, we demonstrate how an intertextually-fused field of participation that hovers over the current conflict imparts a tacit yet richly inferential and strategic sense of moral relevance to the ongoing exchange between attorney and witness.

The first section describes a commodification issue, how the witness sold her story about the case, an issue that stimulates the ND sequence. This legal linguistic ideology and the epistemological practices relevant to it place the witness in a normatively accountable double bind. As we will see, while the commodification ideology places the witness in a face threatening moment of blame, it is little more than a developmental stage for a much more important ideological agenda to unfold. The ensuing section shows how a prior conversation between the witness on the stand, and the victim of the crime interacts with the commodification of utterances to shape – in quite powerful and unanticipated ways – the intertextual criteria for determining the legitimacy of legal discourse, for grounding and calibrating belief about legal truth. In such instances, ND may function under the auspices of much more authoritative ideological and epistemological interests.

The remaining sections examine the discursive and multimodal dynamics of ND, and consider how recycling, repetition, and embodied conduct implicate multiple dialogues – position multiple voices – and their complex laminations of participation to impeach credibility. In this instance, ND is situated in an interactive, reciprocal, and co-constructed relationship between the immediate utterance event and historical episodes of discourse. This is more than a positioning of voices in a single speaker's narration; it represents an interactive and collaborative projection of multidimensional voices and contexts in an intricate lamination of participation and power. Specifically, we address the following. How does ND emerge interactively, incrementally, and contingently through multimodal conduct to shape our commonsense presuppositions of legal knowledge? How do processes of control and resistance contextualize identity, signal relationships, and ground the legitimacy of legally relevant modes of belief? How does the micro-naturalization of these beliefs function in and through intertextually-laminated *forms* of participation? We not only describe how ND is multi-modally and interactively realized in the concrete details of situated practice, but how it simultaneously synchronizes multiple planes of participation at the intersection of multiple participations of power. We examine not just the fragmentation of participation but also a parallel fragmentation of power that functions in and through impeachment strategy.

Data

The extract we analyze here is a segment of defense attorney Roy Black's cross-examination of Mercer, the witness from Chapter 4. Although the prosecution envisioned Mercer as a crucial witness because she could contrast Bowman's condition immediately before and after the alleged rape incident and thus testify directly about her being in a state of "hysteria" at the Kennedy estate, she turned out to be a disappointing liability. First, she sold her story to the tabloid television show, *A Current Affair*, for $40,000, even though she was initially offered $150,000 (along with similar rival offers from the *National Enquirer*, *Globe*, and *Star* tabloid newspapers). Second, she took $110,000 less than what she was initially offered, which became a central theme in Black's questioning.

Commodification of Utterances and Normative Accountability of Profit Maximization

((camera focus on Mercer from lines 1–74))

```
01   RB:   Now you found ou::t (.) did you not that (.)
02         as time went o:::n the price started dwindling
           (.) isn't that correct.
03                        (3.1)
04   AM:   After I- (.) after the uh::: (.) statement was
           public yes.
                        (0.9)
06   RB:   The price for your statement started going
07         down in value isn't that right Miss Mercer?
08                        (.)
09   AM:   Yes that's correct sir
10                        (.)
11   RB:   You began ge- you began getting worried
12         that you weren't going to get enough money
           for your statement (.) isn't that right?
13                        (2.4)
14   AM:   No not exactly
15                        (.)
16   RB:   Well you wanted to maximize your profits
           didn't you?
```

```
17                          (1.6)
18  AM:  No:: I did not.
20  RB:  You wanted to make as much money as
         you could?
21                          (0.9)
22  AM:  If I wanted to make more money- if I wanted
23       to make the most money that I could of I would
24       have taken the hundred and fifty thousand
24       dollars. I did not take ((staccato)) the hundred
25       and fifty thousand dollars. (.)
```

Why would selling a story about an alleged crime constitute an issue in court? Even more important, why would the defense attorney raise the issue of Mercer taking less money than what was initially offered? Does this evidence have any bearing on the ultimate issue in the case?

In line 01, Black notes that after a period of time, marked with an iconic vowel stretching (*o::n*), the price for Mercer's statement dropped in value. The highly animated verb *dwindling* fosters the impression that the value of her statement was gradually yet noticeably shrinking – perhaps even to the extent that she became concerned. After a 3.1-second pause, Mercer agrees with Black's assessment that the monetary value of her statement declined. In response, Black (line 06) does a partial repeat – omitting the *you found out* frame (main clause) – of the *price started going down in value* (replacing *dwindling* with *going down in value*). And on line 09, Mercer once again agrees with the question: her profit margin was evaporating slowly.

After focusing on factual matters, Black begins a series of questions in line 11 about Mercer's mental state relative to the shrinking profit margin: that she became concerned about her profit making potential (*worried about getting enough money*). Instead of being concerned about her friend, she exhibited a callous preoccupation with profiting from her friend's misfortune. In line 14, Mercer first rejects (*No*) and then qualifies Black's assessment with the sentence final adverbial *not exactly*.

In lines 16 and 20, Black presses the unseemly case that Mercer began to worry about her evaporating profits. He mobilizes the turn-initial discourse marker *Well* to index a forthcoming disagreement (with Mercer's *not exactly* in line 14) in the form of a parallel structure with repetition of the desire verb and infinitive across lines 16 and 20 (*you wanted to maximize your profits* and *you wanted to make as much money as you could*), once again exposing Mercer's unscrupulous pursuit of self-interest by profiting from the sexual assault of her friend.[2] Notice too, the heavily marked parallel stress (and alliteration in the verbs) across Black's turns on *maximize* and *make*, on the one hand, and *profits* and *money*, on the other, that function to animate the significance of Mercer's calculating rationality through a highly affective and engaging poetic form.

Although Mercer was certainly mindful of the price slipping, her corresponding mental state turns out to be quite another matter. Despite the form of Black's questions, Mercer delivers an emphatic rejection about wishing to maximize profits in line 18: *No:: I did not.* Especially revealing about the questions and answers thus far is the absence of any reason for the putative contradiction in the price "dwindling," on the one hand, and Mercer's disinterest in maximizing profit on the other. Mercer merely disavows without account the face-threatening questions posed in lines 11 and 16, a noticeable absence given the legal presuppositions embedded in these. That Mercer failed to capitalize on her linguistic opportunity is normatively accountable in the micro legal order. What is at issue here is not just the commodification of utterances but the rational maximization of profit and departures from this cultural construction.

Seen in this light, Black's questions and Mercer's answers highlight the forthcoming climax to the contradictory matters of Mercer's declining profits and imputed desire to maximize profits. In lines 11, 16, and 20, one gains the impression that he is almost taunting her on the matter, indeed that he wants more than a mere rejection or agreement. If we look at these sequences closely, it becomes clear that Black is after more of an answer than his questions indicate. Otherwise he could stop at *maximize your profits* or even his prior question in line 11. Doubtless, he wants her to provide the rationale for doing otherwise. The interaction between Black's questions and Mercer's answers not only produce but even more importantly, foreground absence of maximization as a relevant legal linguistic ideology in the courtroom.

Of crucial importance here is this. While Mercer is initially portrayed as an unscrupulous opportunist, cashing in on the misfortunes of her friend (and the defendant), her callous indifference appears seriously compromised by accepting a less-than-favorable outcome for her statement. By making much less than she could have, Mercer's identity as a risk-minimizing, profit-maximizing strategist – her rational pursuit of

---

[2] Discourse markers like *Well* in this context (and line 26 in the next extract) are polysemic discursive objects, and may work to not only signal a forthcoming disagreement, but also to reject the answer or signal it as inadequate in some way (Schiffrin 1987; Hale 1999; Innes 2010). Or it may function in all these ways simultaneously.

economic self-interest – appears questionable to say the least. In a quite unanticipated turn of events, Black now positions Mercer as the inept capitalist. If she does possess a capitalist mentality, it is certainly not one that will lead to other worldly salvation.

After Black's third question (line 20) on the issue, Mercer produces a more elaborate denial in line 22 and takes the bait, as it were, to provide a partial defense for failing to maximize. Yet still, she only provides a minimally responsive answer without the rationale, and thus leaves it as a puzzle, one building up suspense as the sequence progresses.

In more detail, Mercer (in line 22) uses a counterfactual conditional + emphatic assertion as an evidential, with superlative repair in the counterfactual. This is accompanied by heavily marked stress, staccato-like delivery, and uncontracted negative in *I did not take the* ... By not contracting she adds prominence to the negation and thus foregrounds an assertive, oppositional stance.

Unfortunately for Mercer, she also foregrounds the absent rationale in a double bind configuration. On the one hand, if she accepts money for her statements, then in the legal epistemological order the truth-value of those statements decline. On the other hand, if she fails to capitalize on her linguistic opportunities, an account is normatively warranted. And if that were not enough, another legal-linguistic ideology looms on the discursive horizon.

Legal Epistemology in the Collaboration between Witnesses

```
26  RB:  Well you didn't take the hundred and fifty
27       thousand dollars because you had a deal
28       with Patricia Bowman[that you wouldn't=
29  AM:                      [((shakes head twice
                                w/mouth open))
30  RB:  =do it isn't that right?
31  AM:  THAT IS NOT CORRECT SIR NO=
         [((head shake))
```

Black knows that Mercer took much less than what she was initially offered and that, while she may have wanted to maximize her profits, she failed to do so – but not because she was an inept capitalist. In fact, she hired a nationally prominent attorney to negotiate the contract with *A Current Affair*. Much more importantly, Black does not want to highlight Mercer's calculating rationality but demonstrate that her monetary transactions were guided more by irrational considerations such as friendship. While Mercer may not be much of a businesswoman, she is a very good friend.

Black begins to demonstrate precisely that by providing the reason in the most face-threatening form possible (in line 26). In a powerful linguistic bind ideology, Black first produces another disagreement marker *Well* to preface his question in line 26 and then activates the bind in an oppositional contrast format. As it turns out, Mercer failed to capitalize fully on her linguistic opportunity because she made an agreement with the victim. In this discursive economy of utterances, we find Mercer and the victim engaged in a cabalistic interaction concerning issues in the criminal case. Black's question depicts Mercer as actively engaged in the legal conspiracy. *You had a deal with Patricia Bowman* indexes Mercer as perhaps even initiating the impression management scheme to avoid charges of sensationalism and thus make the prosecution's case more "convictable." Just as epistemologically significant, Black's strategy may connote a legally questionable plot against the defendant.

In response to the damaging and face-threatening implications of the question, Mercer displays a strongly aggravated oppositional stance, displaying the affective intensity of opposition multimodally, during and after Black's question. First, she produces a head shake with open mouth component as a preliminary to the disagreement (at recognition point of Black's accusation), one that displays a strong multimodal pre-disagreement with Black's proposition, and keen recognition of the blame implicatures as she gears into the turn. Her multimodal pre-entry to vocal turn activity signals a heightened state of affective involvement toward Black's proposition, and thus manages a spontaneous rejection of blame while simultaneously maintaining the integrity of his turn. Her multimodal conduct coordinates precisely with Black's face-threatening blame component and heightens the sense of opposition to his assessment (see Figure 6.1). More specifically, Mercer (line 29) dips her head to the left at a slight angle on *that* and does a marked lateral recoil head movement or head shake on *you wouldn't*: an iconic recoil as if recoiling from Black's assessment.[3] Second and simultaneously, she moves from staring at Black to rolling her eyes. Third, as she returns to original position, she gazes at Black with her mouth in an open, gearing-to-speak, position. Finally and additionally, during the verbal component of her answer in line 30, she displays heightened commitment to the proposition through emphatic stress, uncontracted negative, and increased loudness in conjunction with

---

[3] As Kendon (2002: 148) notes, head shakes may not only function as a negative assessment but also mark the "evidentiary status" of an utterance.

Figure 6.1: (line 29 pre-turn entry embodied disagreement).

a further head shake movement (as well as the double negative *That is not correct sir, no*).

Even before her answer, Mercer engages pre-turn entry bodily conduct to comment on Black's question in progress and contextualize her forthcoming yet not currently realized (verbal) oppositional stance. This shows in vivid detail the interaction between verbal and embodied conduct between participants as Mercer withholds (verbal) turn entry while still displaying a highly embodied rejection and assessment of Black's proposition. When we reach her answer in line 30, we can see that her verbal component is perfectly aligned with its embodied counterpart to generate a highly aggravated state of opposition.

In just this sense, multimodal conduct pre-figures and intensifies semantic content, providing a preview of forthcoming speech (Streeck and Hartege 1992). Moreover, Mercer's embodied actions occur not at the transition space between turns but at recognition point of the disagreeable lexical token: an epistemological stance that equates gesture spontaneity with the calibration of legal truth. That is to say, multimodal conduct adds more than emotive meaning to propositional content; it also incorporates both onset and intensity of that affect in the calibration of truth – a type of *multimodal epistemology*. As we can see, there is more to ND and resistance than just speech. Speakers and witnesses negotiate strategies of control, blame, and resistance through the multimodal coordination of self and other's utterances. This perfect synchronization between legal participants would be unavailable for analysis without attention to the fine-grained details of multimodal conduct.

To summarize the points thus far: By producing a highly face-threatening question without any incremental question/answer building up of the facts sequence, Black has opened the door for Mercer to vigorously deny the collaboration charges and paved the way for a ND sequence of considerable duration.[4] Indeed, *prima facie* he is now forced to backtrack and retool his questions in more factual terms to produce a more thorough recasting of blame. He now has to recycle the exchange to establish the basic facts of evidence and restart the blame sequence. Perhaps this is a strategy he has foreseen, even orchestrated for special effect.

Nailing Down the Facts

```
31  RB:  =Didn't you and Miss Bowman have
32        a conversation about whether or not
          you ought to do an interview.
33                                  (2.0)
34  AM:  I don't recall that sir no=
35  RB:  =You do not recall having a
36        conversation with Patricia Bowman is
          that correct, is that your testimony here.
37                                  (1.6)
38  AM:  Concerning what sir?
39  RB:  About whether or not you ought to give
          give an interview.
40                                  (1.9)
41  AM:  I believe I talked to her about that at
          one point yes.
42  RB:  So you did talk with her?
43                                  (0.5)
```

Mercer's strong opposition in line 30 prompts Black to recycle and reformulate his ensuing questions in a more factual direction by having her confirm the existence of the conversation with Bowman (line 31). After a two-second pause, Mercer offers a qualified response that reveals lack of knowledge about the conversation in line 34: *I don't recall that sir no.*[5] In line 35, Black latches a repeat – repeating Mercer's *recall* – question with heavily marked stress on the final utterance component *testimony here* that signals his state of disbelief in Mercer's answer.[6] Interestingly, just as

---

[4] That is to say, at the very outset Black exaggerates Mercer's role in the collusive scheme without setting up that blame with a series of factual questions.

[5] Tsu (1991) mentions that modal adjuncts like *I don't know* or *recall* often function to tacitly disagree with a prior question, especially when the adjunct occupies entire turn.

[6] Goodwin and Goodwin (1987) and Goodwin (1990) note that partial repetition with expansion is one method to signal a state of aggravated opposition. Of course, this operates here in concert with the quality of latching (that also indicates something of import).

Mercer attaches prominence to her denial by not contracting the negative in line 22, so too does Black display his sense of disbelief in Mercer's answer (in line 35) by not contracting (*You do not recall*). He not only signals disbelief through the noncontracted negative, but also through the stressed partial repetition and expansion of the positive agreement tag – through a doubling up of the tags – the second of which further intensifies a sense of disbelief by incorporating an overt "testimony" tag (*is that correct, is that your testimony here*). Moreover, by mobilizing this second tag, Black bestows a distinct legal identity to Mercer: that she is a witness in a criminal case and her words represent legal evidence (and may well impart a perjury connotation in so doing).

Even so, Mercer's repair request in line 38, *Concerning what,* makes Black repeat a portion of his original question in the *whether-or* correlative – repeating the alternative question – from line 31: *About whether or not you ought to give an interview*. Notice also that the marginal modal *ought* followed by the *to*-infinitive not only refers to a future obligation but also subtly implies information about speaker's authority in making a request (and we will discuss the import of this shortly). In line 41, Mercer responds with the *believe*-mental verb controlling the elided *that*-complement to mark the degree of certainty in her proposition, less than "knowing" but more certain than "suspect" (*I believe I talked to her about that at one point yes*). Notice also in line 41, how the affirmative and unqualified *yes* is pushed back deep into turn-final position. Still, she fails to broach the content of the conversation, the issue of doing an interview, but merely concedes that Bowman and she "talked" about that at one point.

Black assembles a number of remedial practices to ND an answer from Mercer. In line 42, he repeats the issue of talking, *so you did talk with her*, with contrastive stress over the first part of the question and noticeably marked stress on *did*. Emphatic *do* before the base form of the verb generates an emphatic affect, in this case a rejection of Mercer's answer in line 34, and offers an upgraded affirmation of her hedged response in line 41. Moreover, by prefacing *do* with the exclamatory confirmation marker *so*, he not only intensifies the opposition, foregrounding it and revealing it as a "surprise," but also confirms Mercer's statement.[7] By fusing emphatic *do* with the *so*-preface. Black foregrounds and adds emotive meaning to the recycled ND question, revealing Mercer's evasive responses through discursive form. Even so, at this point the question only refers to "talking together" not the relevance of that talk. Black's recycled

---

[7] See Johnson (2002) for an extended discussion of *so*-prefaced questions that both summarize and evaluate the prior statement.

and modulated question in line 35 removes the evaluation topic from line 31, transforms *having a conversation about doing an interview* to *having a conversation*, and recycles to a less evaluative, more factual position that attempts to steer Mercer's response into alignment with agreement. In this regard, he does not say (in line 42) "so you did talk about giving an interview," but *so you did talk with her*: nailing down facts prior to nailing down evaluation and blame.

Resurrecting Evaluation and Blame

```
44  AM:   Yes
45  RB:   And you start- and you made a deal
          with her that you would wait a while
46        before you could[ cash in on your=
47  AM:               [((head shake
                           w/open mouth))
    RB:   =statement isn't that right.
48        I did not make any de::als with Patty.
49        What I do is what I decide to do.
50                      (.)
```

After a 0.5-second pause Mercer delivers a simple affirmative answer (line 44), aligning with the factual issue, and in the next turn Black resurrects the blame proposition from line 26, though this time rather than *had a deal with Patricia Bowman*, Mercer now *made a deal with her* before she *could cash in on* her statement. In this partial repetition of his prior question, Black elaborates why Mercer failed to maximize her profits. Whereas in line 26, we see that Mercer failed to maximize because she had *a deal* with the victim, in line 45 we discover the content of the deal: waiting for a period of time before selling the statement. Whereas in line 27, Mercer *had* a deal, in line 45 Black maintains that she *made* a deal, transforming mere possession via the existence *be*-verb into the highly agentive di-transitive clause (with comitative), in which Mercer is the active subject initiating the *deal* or, at least minimally, escalating her level of agency to a more active role. In fact, *made* suggests that the subject of the main clause possesses coercive power.

The phrasal verb *cash in* indicates that Mercer earned a profit in a crass exploitation of the sexual assault. Before Mercer could *cash in*, however, she had to have permission from Bowman, an unflattering characterization of both Mercer's mercenary identity and Bowman's calculating identity (combining commodification and collaboration). At the precise production of this phrasal verb, Mercer starts to open her mouth and tilt her head to the left (in an almost identical display of visual conduct as in line 29) in a visual pre-display that serves as a preliminary to verbal disagreement (in line 48), which occurs with stress and prolongation of the emphasized *de::als*. What is interesting about Mercer's synchronization of verbal and embodied conduct is how it mirrors the propositions in Black's questions. When Mercer is blamed explicitly (as an active initiator of the collusion), she engages a spontaneous and affective display of embodied conduct at recognition point, but not when she and Bowman are treated as (more or less) equal co-conspirators. Moral reproach and factual evidence parallel embodied and verbal conduct.

Nailing Down Facts Again

```
51  RB:  Well you and Patty had a conversation,
         didn't you? Your friend Patty.
52                                  (2.6)
53  AM:  We might have talked about it yes
54                                  (.)
55  RB:  Well
56         [
57  AM:     But that doesn't mean that we collaborating.
58                                  (.)
59  RB:  Let's- hold it (.) you say "we might have
60       talked." Isn't it a fact that you did talk?
61                                  (3.0)
62  AM:  Probably yes.
63                                  (.)
64  RB:  Well- (.) Not probably. Isn't it true that
         you and Miss Bowman talked about you
         giving a statement.
66                                  (2.3)
67  AM:  Yes
68                                  (1.0)
```

Failing to obtain Mercer's agreement about collaboration, Black retreats from the morally loaded and emotionally charged issue in line 45 and attempts to ND, once again, the mere fact of talking together in line 51. In the to-and-fro rhythms of this recycling, he begins with the discourse marker *Well*, prefacing an oppositional stance to Mercer's prior answer:

Well you and Patty had a conversation, didn't you? Your friend Patty. What is interesting here is that after the reverse polarity tag he designs a relational identity in the second person possessive – *Your friend Patty* – occurring almost as an afterthought in the appended phrase (with a declarative rather than questioning intonation). Moreover, he uses an informal address term (Patty) rather than a more formal "Patricia," or "Miss Bowman," or even "complainant in the case" to index the close personal relationship between the two women, perhaps setting the stage for more important relational work (as we will see).

In line 53, Mercer repeats her degree of uncertainty about the fact of talking through the epistemic modal *might*, but then goes on to address not just the existence of that speech but the blame-relevant content of the speech *We might have talked about it yes. It* refers to the "deal" with Bowman made in Black's accusatory question in line 45.

In line 55 Black begins with the disagreement preface *Well*, but this time his words are overlapped by Mercer's simultaneous speech. As it turns out, Mercer's utterance in line 53 was not complete, only en route to completion, and she expands the turn (in line 57) to designate an implicational distinction between the fact of talking together on the one hand, and the blameworthy issue of collaborating on testimony on the other: talk is not equivalent to collaborating. Ironically, by denying the implicational equivalence, Mercer simultaneously endorses the legitimacy of the legal epistemology of collaboration.

While Black could have accepted Mercer's answer from line 53 (that she had talked to Bowman) he elects to do something else: a cutoff and self-repair on the third person imperative, occurring with emphatic stress and almost as an afterthought (line 59). Although Mercer's *yes* (line 53) indeed agrees with the fact about talking, this is not what Black follows up with in the ensuing question. Instead, he addresses Mercer's epistemological stance (*might*) in the prior part of the turn. Following the cutoff repair on the imperative, Black states that Mercer *did* talk with Bowman, once again retrieving the existence issue, and here an emphatic *do* in the direct quote represents an affirmative contradiction of Mercer's prior qualified statement (her *might* on line 53). It emphasizes and contrasts with her qualified epistemic stance. Black upgrades the oppositional correction first through the *Isn't it a fact* truth clause in the negative interrogative frame, and second through the emphatic *do* in the negative interrogative. *Might* conveys a stance of possibility or low possibility; *did* indexes fact. *Might* is challenged through the negative interrogative + verb *You say you might have talked; isn't it a fact you did talk*? Although Mercer claims that *we might have talked about IT yes*, Black's ensuing question fosters the impression that she actually denied the fact of talking, suppressing her agreement to the fact, even though Mercer concedes that they talked about referential *it* (with turn final *yes*).

Black ignores the collaboration frame and thus does not let Mercer "own" the inference. That is to say, the question in line 59 responds not to Mercer's modulation of blame but to the factual existence of talking in lines 45 and 53. Here we can witness in vivid detail how both attorney and witness select the relevance of a particular element of the prior utterance. In line 57, Mercer produces a contrast over Black's intrusive utterance in line 55, perhaps admitting circuitously to being evasive (but not to collaborating). In line 59, Black partially repeats from the direct quote *might have talked*, with stress on the epistemic modal and emphatic *do* in the second clause. In so doing, he may tip his hand (just a bit) that he is not really concerned with the Mercer/ Bowman collusion but something else, something much more important to the case.

Mercer responds to this form of ND (in line 62) with *Probably yes*, mirroring her answer in 53 (*We might have talked about it yes*), though this time leaving out explicit reference to content and limiting her response to the existence question. The sentence's initial epistemic stance adverb marks the level of certainty or doubt prefacing her agreement: another qualified response. After a cutoff and repair with a slight pause on the clause initial discourse marker *Well*, Black produces stressed negation with partial repetition (*Not probably*) of Mercer's epistemic modal in an almost mirror-image repetition of the preceding sequence (line 64). In the process, he further escalates the oppositional format – not just aggravated but hyper-aggravated opposition.

One of the most powerful resources of ND and for generating the sense of opposition inhering in it, involves repetition operating from turn to turn. In line 64, *Isn't it true* is repetitively expanded from line 59. Lines 59–64 represent an instance of *repeating* repetition, a sequence in which each successive repetition negates the prior qualified proposition, so that "might have talked" becomes "did talk," "probably" becomes "not probably" (with stress on the negative). Black mobilizes this form of hyper-aggravated opposition with negation and partial repetition – including prosodic repetition with contrastive stress in both cases (*not probably* with stress on the negative and on *might* and *did*) – to create a highly animated stance and to display Mercer's evasion in progress (lines 59 and 64). (For example, his repetition and negation of Mercer's epistemic stance adverbial from line 62 *not probably*.)

Just as important, this repetition in ND co-occurs with cutoff on the turn-initial discourse marker *Well-* (line 64) and cutoff plus doubling up on the turn-initial imperatives *Let's- Hold it* (more accurately, the contracted and cutoff "us" in combination with the imperative auxiliary in line 59), to create a sense of urgency in addressing Mercer's evasion and contextualize a state of being "taken aback" by such a brazen denial. Additionally, in lines 59 and 64, notice the repetition between the negative interrogative frames "isn't it a fact" and "isn't it true," which both occur after the discourse marker prefaces *Well* and negated repetition of the stance adverbial *not probably*. These are not merely repetitions of prior answers but recycled forms of ND that employ sequential, lexical, grammatical, and prosodic repetition occurring in crisscrossing streams of relevance. Thus repetition of various sorts plays a prominent role in foregrounding, evaluating, and controlling a witness's answer, as Thomas Mauet mentions in his classic trial text:

Another, and usually more effective, approach to controlling problem witnesses is to let the witness know that you will not be deterred by an unresponsive answer and will insist on a proper one. If the witness then gives a proper answer, you have made your point. If the witness refuses to give a proper answer, you have demonstrated to the jury that the witness is being evasive or unfair, and you have again scored points by discrediting the witness. You can do this simply by repeating the same question, or rephrasing it slightly. (Mauet 1996: 222)[8]

To summarize the points thus far, we have seen the improvisational resilience of Black's questioning in concert with Mercer's resistance as he starts, stops, and redesigns previously affirmed motifs, moving the ND sequence from commodification to maximization, and then to collaboration and combinations of these. As we will see next, the ultimate payoff for these intersecting ideological frames is posed to emerge.

Legal Epistemology in Multimodal Participation

((camera shifts from Mercer to Black on line 74)) B=Beats

```
69  RB:  Was there not an agreement made between
70       the two of you that you would wait awhile
         before you gave your statement.
71                          (1.7)
```

[8] In a similar vein, Hobbs (2003: 491) mentions that "repetition both highlights the repeated information, and encodes the attorney's evaluation of its significance in the truth-finding process. It invites the jury to make sense of the evidence in a way that accords with the attorney's formulations."

```
72  AM:  I do not recall that no
73       (9.7) ((shuffling papers in the background))
74  RB:  You don't reca:::ll having a conversation
75       with Miss Bowman where you said that you
         would wait (.) at least thirty days till giving a
                  (B)          (B)   (B)      (B)        (B)
76       statement.  ((the 2 beats on "thirty days"
         sped up; final beat over entire phrase: "till
         giving a statement))
77                                  (1.4)
78  AM:  No I do not[ remember that.
79  RB:            [ ((head shake w/open mouth
                        and eyes rolled))
80       You don't recall there be::ing a conversation
                         (B)                    (B)
81       between the two of you waiting until charges
         (B)                                      (B)
         were filed for you to give a statement.
                         (B)
82                                  (4.2)
83  AM:  I might have said- (1.3) that I would wa- wait
         (.) yes=
84  RB:  = Because       she        requested
         (B=upstroke)  (B=down)   (B=upstroke)
85       it                 isn't that correct
         (B=down)
86                                  (0.5)
87  AM:  I believe so yes.
88                                  (.)
89  RB:  And so you waited before you gave a
         statement isn't that right
90                                  (1.9)
91  AM:  Yes
```

After nine attempts in progressive/regressive movements, Black finally nails down an affirmative answer to the fact of talking together, and then returns to nail down the substantive implications of that talk. But why does he not address the issue of collaboration from Mercer's turn in line 57 (*But that doesn't mean that we collaborating*)? Why would he pass up an opportunity to claim they were collaborating and focus instead on the fact of talking? As the sequence progresses, we can see that collaboration (like commodification before it) is not the primary issue.

Black asks about an agreement between Mercer and Bowman in line 69: *Was there not an agreement made between the two of you that you would wait awhile before you gave your statement.* He uses the term *agreement*, a more neutral, less morally loaded term, rather than the prior evaluative indexical *deal* from line 45 (which was suggestive of unscrupulous activity).[9] Mercer is no longer positioned as actively making *a deal* but situated more passively (in the passive construction *an agreement was made between the two of you*), which backgrounds her involvement in the legal conspiracy. Black also uses the vague durative (*would wait*) *awhile* to indicate the amount of time Mercer agreed to wait before giving her statement. Consider this hypothetical dialogue: "Bowman: Would you wait awhile? Mercer: Yes I could." Up until this point, the conversation between Mercer and Bowman had dealt with the former waiting to give a statement, but still without any indication of the significance of that time frame.

In her nescient response in line 72, Mercer claims that she does *not recall that no*, through the mental state predicate (*recall*), and utterance final *no*. Black's next question in line 72 repeats the mental verb *reca:::ll* governing the gerund complement with emphatic stress and marked vowel stretching, as if surprised by the qualified reply (and thus escalates the intensity of opposition). His ensuing question on the duration of time Mercer agreed to wait until giving a statement is more precise: from *awhile* to *at least thirty days* (line 75).

But there is quite more going on than Black's verbal component. On line 74, the camera shifts from Mercer to Black and we can see the importance of including multimodal conduct for ND. In Chapter 5 we saw the relevance of rhythmic hand gestures or beats and how, like an orchestra conductor's baton, they hammer out musical time and thereby mark points of speaker emphasis. In Quintilian terms, they contribute to the orator's delivery by making discourse more persuasive. Bearing these points in mind, notice that Black's questions on lines 74 and 80–81 mobilize short, up-down finger beats (bent at the wrist) that land on words and phrases containing significant points of evidence. Notice too how (line 75) the two beats landing on *thirty days* are sped up to synchronize with their speech counterparts – maintaining the integrity of the speech-gesture ensemble in the process (Kendon 2004, see Figure 6.2).

Despite the more precise durative and persuasive beats, Mercer still fails to remember in a flip-flop repetition (in line 78) from her previous response in line 72 (*No I do not remember that*), repetition from utterance final to

---

[9] Wortham (2001) uses the concept of *evaluative indexical* to refer to lexical items and other linguistic constructions that index individuals or groups in highly evaluative ways.

Figure 6.2: (line 75 bent-wrist index finger beat).

clause initial *no*. As soon as Black recognizes Mercer's denial, he produces a lateral head shake (turning his head sideways and back to home position in line 79) and eyebrow flash, in a highly affective display of incredulity: an iconic recoil as if recoiling from Mercer's negative response (see Figures 6.3–6.5). While attorneys cannot comment verbally on the witness's answer during examination, they can display an embodied stance that works just as well, in this instance signaling a strong sense of disbelief in the witness's response. As this occurs he not only assesses her response-in-progress and reveals his stance to it, but also influences her forthcoming answer to his next question, a way of simultaneously assessing a prior, and "tweaking" a next, answer. Put another way, he evaluates the in-progress answer while simultaneously encouraging a more favorable answer in the next, unrealized, yet forthcoming sequence through multimodal conduct. Embodied conduct not only contextualizes an affective stance in a preview of speech but also constitutes a form of embodied epistemology that influences the production of evidence in a powerful ND strategy.

That preview materializes as Black's question in line 80 offers a more precise formulation of time with the temporal terminator *until* (prefacing the gerund with existential *there*, indexing a lack of agency and morally neutral identity for Mercer): *You don't recall there being a conversation between the two of you waiting until charges were filed for you to give a statement.* What is remarkable here is this: *Until charges were filed* indexes a legal identity relevant to Mercer and Bowman's actions in a way that *awhile* or *at least thirty days* do not. These latter phrases lack not only temporal specificity but legal relevance as well.

Once again, we see the use of beat gestures in line 80 to accentuate the legal relevance of collaboration as Black punctuates the pace and rhythm of each phrase with a series of forefinger beats (once again, moving

Figures 6.3–6.5: (line 79 home position to eyebrow flash + open mouth to head turn display of disbelief).

upward and downward as if "beating" out the rhythm of his speech), superimposed over the course of their lexical affiliates. As in line 74, these beats consist of low elevation beats or short up and down finger movements from the bent wrist platform. He relies heavily on such gestures to enhance his emphatic stance and build a dramatic tension into the questioning. Just as words become more precise, the coordination between gestural forms and their lexical affiliates become precision tuned to nail down Mercer's next answer in a persuasive display of legal oratory. That nailing down is accomplished, at least in a qualified sense, in line 83, when Mercer indicates *I might have said* (1.3) *that I would wa- wait (.) yes*. Her extreme display of reluctance in betraying her friend – even in the face of precision-tooled and finely discriminating forms of control – is vividly marked through evasive form (line 83): (1) the 4.2-second interturn silence (the longest in the whole segment); (2) epistemic modal *might*; (3) cutoff on *said-* and the ensuing 1.3-second pause; (4) cutoff repair on *wa- wait*;

(5) micro-pause; and (6) turn final agreement. Notice even the epistemic stance verb *believe* and turn final agreement in line 87, and this is what we mean by the ideology of collaboration being marked through discursive form. *Mercer simultaneously displays the cabalistic interaction as she is denying it – not only in the past but in the current speech event as well.*

Black's response takes an unexpected turn after Mercer completes her turn final affirmative response. Rather than reject and recycle Mercer's epistemic modal preface *might* (from line 83), as he had done previously, and exploit the qualified segment as a platform to launch the ND sequence (such as for example, "not might," etc.), he accepts her response through an elliptic and immediately latched *because*-clause (heavily stressed in staccato-like fashion) that functions as a type of collaborative expansion (line 84).

Whereas Black had initially portrayed Mercer as an active and co-equal collaborator, on occasion as even initiating the collusive scheme, he now repositions her as a more passive figure in a reconfigured participation structure; she withheld giving her statement to the mass media because Bowman requested it. The reference to the Bowman and Mercer scheme becomes a request from the former to the latter, a request that Mercer, as it turns out, merely grants. Mercer is repositioned in the narrated dialogue as follows: "Bowman: Would you wait till charges are filed; Mercer: Yes I could."

As it turns out, the historical dialogue was neither just a conversation nor collaboration between Mercer and Bowman, but an impression management scheme engineered by the latter to help obtain a more favorable outcome in a criminal case. In the indirect quote (line 83) Mercer positions herself as a recipient of a request from Bowman: *I might have said that I would wa- wait (.) yes.* This represents the climax of the sequence running from lines 69–83, the final ND sequence in which Black foregrounds the legal relevance not of collaboration (which has turned out to be not that important), but of a transposed form of participation in which *who* initiated the request is crucial (not collaboration but the form of participation in it). It contextualizes distinct forms of co-participation in the intertextual circulation of historical events and gears those differential forms into interpretive prominence. If we consider Mercer's role in the intertextual dialogue in lines 69, 74, and 79 we can see that she is, to varying degrees, represented as a co-equal conspirator with Bowman. But the preliminary part of line 83 does not indicate that Mercer would merely "wait." Nor does it merely refer to a conversation between the two. Much more prominently, it indexes a specific speech act with a differentially weighted and evaluated participation structure in which the active

Bowman makes a specific request to the passive Mercer. In a more symbolic vein, Black's immediately latched collaborative expansion (in which he appears to complete Mercer's answer) constitutes an iconic representation in which Mercer appears passive, just as she was with the victim, her friend, a recipient of someone else's action. Together, *I might have said that I would wait* and the ensuing *because*-clause, fragment the form of co-participation in both the narrated and current speech events, a process that unfolds as follows.

First, the narrating event (or current speech event with Black and Mercer) describes the historical collaboration between Mercer and Bowman in the narrated event. Second, Black fragments collaboration in the narrated event into an utterance event indexing a form of participation in which the active Bowman makes a request to the passive Mercer, showing the extraordinary lengths that Mercer went through on behalf of her friend (to the tune of $110,000), and the extraordinary influence that Bowman wields over her. Third, Bowman's power over Mercer historic-ally, in turn, reshapes the form of participation in the current speech event, so that Black not only deals with Mercer but the absent Bowman too, as she speaks and evades through Mercer. That is to say, impression man-agement in the historical event constitutes an indexical icon of impression management in the current event: an emergent parallelism across historical (or represented) and enacted dialogue (Wortham 2001). This implicated dialogue (what Irvine 1996, refers to as the "implicated event") with its intricate lamination of participation bears the principal and authorial voice of Bowman in the midst of Mercer's qualified responses. All this is designed to foster the impression that Mercer is indeed evasive, but on behalf and at the behest of Bowman, a type of ventriloquistic voicing, an intertextual projection of power, in which Black and Mercer project – indeed *enact* – Bowman as speaking (and of course withholding) through Mercer. In so doing, Black constructs a victim identity actively engaged in impression management (concealing his own role in its construction), as if this amounts to a manipulation of evidence (when it in fact does not), and thus generates the ultimate ideology in the case: *Rape victims are expected to be passive and innocent not only in the physical assault but during legal prosecution of the case as well.*

Over the entire segment, Black makes minute adjustments and readjust-ments about the historical dialogue to maneuver Mercer into an evasive stance – just enough to give up Bowman – and thus fragment the current form of participation in a dynamic and mutual elaboration of intertextual relationships. Both currently and historically, forms of participation include not only Black versus Mercer but, first, a separate axis of oppos-ition between Bowman and Mercer against Black and, second, another layering of opposition in which Bowman requests Mercer's assistance in plotting against the defendant. Bearing these considerations in mind, question control may be less crucial than intertextual projections of participation and the power relations implicated in these. This is doubtless why Black does not reject, recycle, and ND Mercer's final modal qualification (from line 83, as he had done previously); the immediately latched *because*-clause indicates his interest in Bowman. It is not collaboration, not just ideology, but the form of participation and the mutually elaborative interpretive frames embedded in it.

At a finer level of granularity, Black's *reason*-clause continuation, *Because she requested it* in line 84, expands and makes explicit the issue of responsibility implicit in Mercer's indirect quote. It indexes a more passive role for Mercer in the now reformulated plot, opens a space for a favorable route out of the double bind and her morally degrading predicament, but at the cost of "giving up" her friend (of course, it also completes the ND sequence). Mercer's indirect quote complement followed by Black's recipient collaboration (in lines 83 and 84) – in the syntactically synchronized and immediately latched clause – constitutes an indexical icon of the collaboration between Mercer and Bowman. Mercer appears as the passive recipient of collaboration practices, one sequential, the other legal epistemological. As this happens, legal epistemology is delicately superimposed onto sequential form in a stunning display of collaborative coordination: sequential expansion and ideological closure fused in the same utterance.

A crucial part of that display is achieved through the emphatically marked forefinger beats in line 84, both possessing much higher elevation on the upswing (on *Because* and *requested*) and accelerated pace on the downswing (on *she* and *it*) (see Figures 6.6 and 6.7). These are not index finger beats moving up and down from the bent wrist platform as we saw in lines 75–76 and 80–81, but gestures launched from the bent elbow platform that reach elevation peak at the head level, incorporating the head and upper torso (along with the index finger) for added delivery affect as he builds toward the crescendo. In this instance, we see how beats simultaneously foreground semantic information and visualize pragmatic aspects of the utterance. As mentioned in Chapter 1, metaphoric gestures involve the interpretation of a mapping between the source (more concrete) and target (more abstract) domains. Applied to this instance, the exaggerated delivery marks the crescendo of Black's nailing down strategy. However, the pragmatic effect of ND is only intelligible through an understanding of how metaphoric "nailing" impacts the totality of his multifunctional delivery. ND as a legal phenomenon – as the prescriptive culture of trial advocacy – is not part of the semantic content of his speech.

Figures 6.6 and 6.7: (line 84 upstroke and downstroke bent-elbow beats with head and upper torso moving forward *Because she*).

Nonetheless, as a legal tactic this is not only apparent in verbal questioning but through the manual modality. Rather than functioning as discretely organized categories, the verbal attempt to nail down an answer is visualized in the gestures as the pragmatic and metaphoric functions mutually elaborate one another in a creative moment, creating dense clusters of co-improvisational harmony to make an overall picture. In the process, Black's collaborative completion of the collaborative ideology completes Mercer's utterance, concludes the disagreement, and exits the collaboration ideology via sequential collaboration in a powerful ND crescendo.

Was Mercer Being Evasive?

In the ND finale, one gains a sense that Mercer sacrificed a lot for Bowman, so why should she take the blame for something Bowman initiated? Why suffer the indignity of Black's moral reproof and the courtroom degradation ceremony? Why not let Bowman take the "heat" as it were? Black's strategy is not just to control Mercer (at least in the long run as witnessed at the end when he lets her "off the hook") but make her defensive enough to display Bowman's control over her (and show more generally how "easy" she is to control). In fact, both Bowman and Black control her. But not exactly. Black only wants to control Mercer to the extent he can position Bowman as controlling her both historically and now. *Black uses ND and the exaggerated blame tokens in it as a strategy of control not just to extract an unmitigated answer but to engineer a performance of Mercer as passively evasive; evasiveness is embodied in the ND process itself.* In more general terms, attorneys may design questions to encourage defensive responses from witnesses and thus activate nailing down strategies in an effort to portray them as evasive, whether or not they actually are. For example, Black's face-threatening questions exaggerate Mercer's role in hatching the collusive plot as a way of manipulating her defensiveness and thus steering an impression of her as evasive. (In this regard, Mercer's "didn't make any deals," for instance, is just what she described: an altruistic response to, and granting of, her friend's request).[10] Still more generally, while the explicit propositional meanings of Black's questions are true, the moral presuppositions embedded in those questions are not. Thus, on the one hand if Mercer agrees with the proposition, she implicitly accepts the inferences embedded in those propositions (talking as equivalent to collaboration). On the other hand, if she rejects the proposition, she is seen as lying ("we didn't talk"). And if she questions the false assumptions in the proposition, she is seen as evasive ("we might have talked but that doesn't mean we collaborating," followed by Black's "you say we might have talked"). Although cross-examination (and ND more specifically) is regarded generally as a method for exposing or uncovering the truth, it is just as felicitous to consider it as a technique for manufacturing the truth (Hobbs, personal communication).

Conclusion

Nailing down is depicted typically as a method of control the questioner mobilizes to extract a preferred answer from a witness, and evasion is usually portrayed as something the answerer does to "weasel out" of the moral difficulties posed by the question. But, at least on occasion, they are not only or even primarily about that. Additionally, evasion and control may function as micro cultural practices that ground belief and legitimate knowledge, communicative practices unfolding incrementally, interactively, and multi-modally in the improvisational epistemology of trial discourse.

Of special interest is how these questions encode and set into motion intertextual participations of power. While power may indeed be the ability to prevail in overt contests, one way to covertly contextualize it is to endow a physically absent participant with the power to shape the current interaction – to shape participant as both author and principal of words spoken and, even more importantly, words evaded. Such multidimensional forms of participation and the intricate laminations of voices

---

[10] And that defensiveness (and difficulty in responding to his distortions) is also revealed in the lengthy pauses before answering his questions (lines 13, 17, 21, and especially 61), a point we owe to Pamela Hobbs.

embedded in these generate parallel laminations of power: Black over Mercer, Bowman over Mercer, Bowman/Mercer against the defendant, and Bowman/Mercer against Black. Black fragments the participation roles and reconfigures them to create a discursive space for the physically absent, yet interactionally relevant Bowman to accomplish distinct strategic work. He manages to tacitly demonstrate (rather than explicitly reveal) the extraordinary influence that Bowman wields over Mercer not only in the narrated event, but much more importantly, in the current speech event also. Just as Mercer "withheld" giving a statement at the behest of Bowman, so too does she "withhold" straightforward answers and truth to Black's questions. This is not just power to nail down an answer or merely represent history, but power to improvisationally and symbolically enact a parallelism across historical dialogue and the current speech event: not abstract power to represent history but power enlivened in the indexical and multimodal details of communicative practice. ND involves not just controlling the witness's resistance, but just as crucial, performing intertextual participations of resistance.

7   Exhibits, Tapes, and Inconsistency

In this part we have discussed key trial techniques such as motivation and nailing down an answer. We conclude our analysis of the prescriptive culture of trial advocacy by focusing on another key trial technique, perhaps the most important in the attorney's arsenal: impeaching credibility through exhibits and tape recordings. In the adversary system, the most common strategy of impeaching the credibility of a witness is by pointing out prior inconsistent statements. In so doing, the truthfulness, reliability, and accuracy of the witness's testimony may be undermined and discredited. We demonstrate in vivid detail how the integration of language and material conduct like artifacts, audio recordings, and transcripts figure in the co-construction of inconsistency. We show how disparate streams of multimodal resources converge in an incremental buildup of suspense and intertextual escalation of testimony that circulates around the manipulation of a crucial material object of evidence.

Material Conduct

We mentioned that Heath and Hindmarsh (2002: 117) introduced the "local ecology of objects and artifacts" to refer to the role of material conduct and how it integrates into the semiotic stream of embodied and verbal action: how participants utilize material objects to accomplish distinct interactional tasks. In a similar vein, Streeck (1996: 366) mentions that meaning "is not just contextualized by the material environment; rather the environment, through the interpretive use that participants make of it in their situated activities, becomes a component of the process of communication." In reconfiguring Heath/Hindmarsh and Streeck a bit, we show how features of the material environment figure as dynamic and strategic resources in the *evidential ecology of material conduct*.

While relatively neglected in language and law research, material conduct constitutes a crucial modality in the law, especially the trial. As an imprecise gauge of their legal significance, consider the role of exhibits in the prescriptive culture of trial advocacy, where major trial textbooks typically devote an entire chapter to their use (see Tanford 1983; Haydock and Sonsteng 1990; Mauet 2010). In his classic textbook on trial techniques, for example, Mauet (2010: 170) notes how exhibits "grab attention" and "become the center of attention. They make an immediate and lasting impression on the jury." Later in the same chapter he (Mauet 2010: 224) states: "Good trial attorneys ... know that objects – drugs, weapons, appliances, machinery – have a dramatic impact. To heighten that impact, they usually keep the object out of sight, then introduce it into the courtroom with a dramatic flair."

In this chapter, we examine how material conduct integrates with language and other multimodal resources to "grab attention" in an interdiscursive escalation of narrative suspense and incremental amplification of evidential intrigue. We explore how a legal exhibit functions as a situated communicative resource and becomes the "center of attention" as multimodal elements mutually elaborate one another in the transformation of evidence and impeachment of credibility through inconsistency. Part of that multimodal transformation occurs as the center of attention shifts from the exhibit to audio recording/transcript, and then back to the exhibit. As we will see, the exhibit does not possess meaning as an autonomous artifact; its evidential significance emerges in the multimodal ensemble in which it is reflexively situated. Yet, rather than introduce the exhibit with a dramatic flair in a single movement, attorney and witness "heighten the impact" of the exhibit in a suspense injected progression to make a "lasting impression on the jury." In the process, we will see how the exhibit becomes endowed with interpretive significance and epistemic relevance in the legal order. Most importantly, we will see how the multimodal integration of different semiotic resources offers an additional dimension of meaning in the trial process – especially in the production of inconsistency – not captured as vividly if we look at speech alone.

Data and Ethnographic Background of the Excerpt

Shaken and unable to drive because of the sexual assault, Bowman called her friend Ann Mercer (who had been with her at Au Bar earlier that evening) to pick her up at the Kennedy residence. Mercer arrived with her boyfriend Chuck Desiderio at around 4:30 A.M. to collect Bowman and take her home. Fearing that no one would believe she was raped at the Kennedy home (or that she had even been there in the first place), Bowman took a notepad and small picture frame as proof that she had been at the estate and, inexplicably, instructed Chuck to take (or carry) an urn. However once in the parking lot, Bowman started her car and drove alone to Mercer's home, where the two women discussed the traumatic and unsettling sweep of events that had just transpired at the Kennedy estate. During the trial, the urn became "real" evidence of considerable intrigue.

In what follows, we show how trial participants integrate speech, written transcripts, bodily movement, gaze, audio recordings, gesture, and exhibits to organize the evidential ecology of material context. In so doing, we will see how they not only negotiate legal identity but also transform evidential status of the exhibit to accomplish the strategic task of producing inconsistency. The first segment analyzes how the exhibit is introduced, while the second considers a heightened cumulative effect surrounding its historical movement. The third segment recruits a puzzle about fingerprints on the urn, and the final segment shows how the fingerprint puzzle reaches a rather "puzzling" crescendo, as the center of attention shifts from the urn to a police audio recording and transcript. In each segment, we will consider how material conduct figures prominently in layering legal identity and evidential intrigue.

Once again, the focus on the exhibit and recording is not meant to suggest that discursive action and material conduct co-exist merely as autonomous semiotic resources pressed into the service of the interactional task at hand. Following Goodwin (2000), Heath, Hindmarsh, and Luff (2010), and Streeck (2009), members of the multimodal ensemble mutually elaborate one another in the co-construction of legal context. Consider an analogy from jazz music. In a jazz piano trio each musician brings a different instrument with different properties into play (piano, drums, and bass), but in their subsequent coordination as an ensemble, something novel – something greater than and different from the sum of the individual instruments – emerges in their co-improvisational interplay: a stirring rhythmic performance. As we will see, the same synergistic analogy grounds material conduct and situated meaning in the courtroom.

Lines 001–034: Introducing the exhibit

Exhibit transcript (5 minutes and 52 seconds total; DA = defense attorney; AM = Ann Mercer)

```
001   DA:   On the questioning (.) by (.4) the prosecutor
             (1.1) that when you got back to the kitchen
             (.) after being with Will (.) you saw
003          Chuck carrying an urn is that right?
004                            (3.6)
005   AM:   When I walked through the kitche:::n (.)
006          uh::: (3.0) I sa::w (.) I believe Patty
006          carrying the picture frame and (1.3)
```

```
007          note pad (.7) I did not see Chuck with
             the urn until (.5) I was in the parking lot.
                                  (2.9)
009   DA:    So when you were out in the driveway
             you saw him with the urn?
010                               (1.4)
011   AM:    Uh::::: (2.5) I believe it was in the driveway.
012          Maybe it was in the car (.8) either one of
             those places I saw him with the uh::: urn.
013                               (.)
014   DA:    OK but your car was in the driveway wasn' t it?
015                               (0.8)
016   AM:    Yes.
017                               (6.4)
018   DA:    ((carrying box to witness stand))
019          ((reaches witness stand))
020          [
021          While we' re asking you about it (.) let me
022          show you what it looks like
023          [ ((sits box on table))
024          ((takes urn out of box))
025          [ ((places urn on witness stand))]
             ((lines 23-25 7.9 seconds))
026          [
027          This is the- uh:: (.) urn that we' re talking
             about is it not
028          [
029   AM:    Uh yes=
030   DA:    =that you saw that night=
031          [ ((places lid on urn))
032   AM:    =Yes.
033                               (8.0)
034          (DA returns to podium during 8 second pause))
```

As we saw from Mauet, attorneys should project a "dramatic flair" when they introduce an exhibit, heightening evidential value and fore-grounding its relevance for their case. But in lines 18–31, rather than introduce the exhibit with "dramatic flair" the defense attorney offers little more than a subtle introduction executed in a rather nonchalant manner. Moreover, since the prior three sequences (lines 1–16) have already engaged its topical role, displaying the exhibit afterwards would hardly meet Mauet's dramatic impact recommendation.

In line 001, defense attorney Roy Black initiates a line of questioning by asking Mercer when she saw Chuck carrying the urn, and in response (line

Figure 7.1: (line 018 Black carries a large box toward the witness stand).

Figure 7.2: (line 030 *that you saw that night*).

005–007) she first provides unsolicited information about Bowman carrying the *picture frame and notepad* and second indicates that she only saw Chuck with the urn when she was in the *parking lot*. After two sequences to confirm temporal location of the urn (lines 009–016), Black carries a large box toward the witness stand with his back arched slightly to indicate that the box is heavy and awkward to handle (Figure 7.1). When he reaches the witness stand, he resumes questioning – still holding the box in transit – with a theatrical gesture (for the overhearing jury) that functions on-record as a type of "recognitional courtesy" (line 021), so that the object of reference materializes in embodied form (*While we're asking you about it let me show you what it looks like*). In lines 023–031, he takes the urn out of the box, places it on the witness stand directly in front of Mercer, and then puts the lid on top (Figure 7.2). As he places the urn on the witness stand, he simultaneously produces a second metapragmatic utterance with turn initial demonstrative to secure referential verification from Mercer (*This is*

the- uh:: (.) urn that we're talking about is it not that you saw that night), a
question that inherits overlap agreement from Mercer in the tag, and a
second agreement in the clear after the turn-final relative clause increment.
At a finer level of granularity, notice how positioning of the urn coordinates with utterance construction in the form of slight delays in utterance
progressivity: the cutoff on *the-*, vowel prolongation on the delay marker
uh::, and the short untimed pause.

While certainly not fulfilling the dramatic flair prescription recom-
mended by Mauet, Black's multimodal actions still raise a host of puzzling
questions. If the evidential value of the urn consists of its referential sense
and recognitional significance, as indicated in lines 021–032, then why not
just show it to Mercer, obtain her agreement, and put it away? In more
detail, while Black introduces the urn under auspices of confirming object
recognition and/or verifying reference, he could have managed the same
task more economically from the other side of the courtroom by merely
taking it out of the box and having Mercer confirm evidential identity at
that location (as we can see in Figure 7.1, it is a big object). And finally,
why does he leave the urn on the stand directly in front of the witness
instead of putting it back in the box?

In a theoretical sense, we can witness how the urn and accompanying
multimodal conduct bequeath an aura of evidential sense and narrative
significance to the unfolding legal activity, and in the process reveal an
additional dimension of meaning not captured as vividly or accurately by
looking at speech alone. In more concrete terms, although the attorney's
metapragmatic utterances project referential identity, the urn and its
accompanying physical movements recalibrate the meaning of talk in a
reflexive interplay among the different modalities. Even though Black's
explicit metapragmatic introduction imparts a parenthetical afterthought
of the urn's fleeting insignificance (in lines 021–022), his material conduct
signals a hint of more looming prominence.

First, his movement with and positioning of the urn direct visual
attention to handling of the exhibit. We will see in the next section that
this multimodal activity generates an iconic representation of forensic
importance concerning Chuck's conduct with the urn during the historical
event. Second, leaving the urn on the witness stand not only channels a
momentary focus of joint attention but sustains that attention over the
course of questioning, an augury of things to come. Third, when this
occurs the urn can be mobilized as a material object continuously available
for use in the multimodal network. As we will see in the ensuing segments,
Black places the urn directly in front of Mercer and leaves it there
throughout her testimony, like contraband for the jury to ponder. There
is no way for courtroom participants to look at Mercer without seeing the

urn, making the two inseparable. In a more theatrical sense, when Black puts the urn on the stand it becomes, for all practical purposes, a witness in the trial. By manipulating the proxemic distance between Mercer and the urn, Black puts them in an intimate relationship, and she acknowledges that relationship via gaze as it is placed in front of her (but ignores it in a type of civil inattention during the remaining part of questioning). By placing the urn directly in front of Mercer, Black makes it part of her "personal front" that – for Goffman (1959: 22–30) – consists of props as well as other "expressive equipment" like clothing, insignia of rank, and so on. But, at least in this performance, that expressive quality is not merely selected by the performer but co-constructed interactively by participants.[1]

In sum, although Black indeed fails to introduce the exhibit with that dramatic touch, his metapragmatic utterances pull against a subliminal multimodal counter current to implicate something much more imminent for the defense case: the unraveling of suspense over identity of the urn. In just this way, the urn, embodied conduct, and speech recalibrate one another in constructing evidential ecology.

Lines 035–64: Holding, putting, and taking – a progressive buildup of suspense

```
035  DA:   Chuck had it? tu::h >is that correct<. ((tag
           sped-up))
036              (2.7)
037  AM:   Chuck (.) yes had it in his possession.
038              (.)
039  DA:   Was he holding on to it when you saw him.
040              (3.0)
041  AM:   I believe he was holding on to it
042              (2.5)
043  DA:   OK (1.1) and uh did he put it (.) put it into
           the jeep.
044              (2.2)
045  AM:   Yes.
046              (0.5)
047  DA:   And then (.) you got into the jeep.
048              (.)
049  AM:   Yes.
050  DA:   And the two of you drove home?
```

---

[1] According to Goffman (1963: 84), civil inattention occurs when "one gives to another enough visual notice to demonstrate that one appreciates that the other is present ... while at the next moment withdrawing one's attention from him so as to express that he does not constitute a target of special curiosity." Here of course the "other" refers to the urn.

```
051  AM:  Yes.
052              (.)
053  DA:  And he took it out- was he holding it while
          you were driving.
054              (3.2)
055  AM:  Uh:::: (.) I don't remember that no.
056              (0.8)
057  DA:  Did he take it out of the jeep and bring it
          into your home.
058              (1.2)
059  AM:  Yes.
060              (.)
061  DA:  Where was it placed in your home?
062              (3.2)
063  AM:  Uh::: (.) in the living room.
064              (15.0)
```

In line 035 Black begins a litany of factual questions about putting, taking, and holding the urn. At the very outset, however, he suggests something more imminent than denotational facts about its movement. After the eight-second pause and return to the defense podium, he asks Mercer if *Chuck had it*? In particular, notice the pronoun contains both stress and questioning intonation that contextualizes a sense of doubt about Chuck holding the urn (or some other type of doubt).

Still, he withholds any development of that doubt and addresses Chuck's various movements with the urn. The questions in lines 039, 043, 053, and 061 execute discretely synchronized and progressively foregrounded motion questions, in which each successive increment draws more attention to Chuck and the urn (Figure 7.3). Each question encodes embodied and material aspects of activity through causative verbs,

Figure 7.3: (line 063 *in the living room*).

agentive control, and source/path/ goals of motion deictics. That is, the urn circulates around an intertextual organization of putting and taking verbs with Chuck holding, putting, taking, and placing the urn into the jeep, out of the jeep, into the home, and so on. As an indication of the delicacy of question design in the series, notice the cutoff repair in line 053 (*he took it out- was he holding it while you were driving*) to include the omitted increment in the ongoing litany, aborting the question in progress to revise movement of the urn. Such delicate care in crafting questions in the series appears iconic of the delicacy and care required of anyone handling the urn, a large yet fragile object with a removable lid that would require two hands when being transported. Moreover, it would need to be balanced or stabilized in an upright position to keep the lid from falling off and perhaps breaking. Finally, it would also have to be handled with some degree of care when being placed in and removed from the car. Transporting the urn would require a good deal of manual-hand involvement that would leave forensic residue – that is to say, fingerprints.

Just to add another layer of iconicity, Chuck's transport of the urn would mirror Black's multimodal conduct with the urn during the introduction phase of the exhibit. As it turns out, Black's questioning not only refers to Chuck's material conduct with the urn but also retroactively *enacts* that conduct from the prior introductory segment, such that *what we are saying becomes what we are doing now in the questioning* (or what we *were* doing in the questioning).

Just as complex is how the material aspects of legal discourse figure in the construction of coherent courses of unfolding legal action, and how intertextual and multimodal resources weave a prospective and retrospective texture of evidential intrigue. Notice how Black's questioning about the spatio-temporal sequence of unfolding historical events in lines 035–063 interacts with his prior exhibit introduction segment in lines 001–033. The level of precision in crafting each movement question interacts with the delicacy of positioning the urn on the witness stand to suggest something more than mere evidential identity; something much more menacing looms on the evidential horizon. Referential identity of the urn in lines 001–033 becomes transformed into movement and possession of the urn in lines 035–063, signaling something novel is imminent as both segments mutually elaborate one another. Black and Chuck's handling/ movement of the urn contextualizes across cross-examination en route to an evidential crescendo. In this final iconic layering, escalation of suspense portrayed in the represented event mirrors the incremental and progressive questioning about movement and handling of the urn in the current speech event. Here again we see how speech and material aspects of conduct reflexively construct evidential ecology.

Lines 65–86: The puzzle – what happened to Chuck's prints?

```
065  DA:  Are you aware that tuh only your
066       fingerprints are found on the urn?
067                         (2.4)
068  AM:  Uh:::: (.) I had read that (.) a:::nd I assumed
069       that's because I had given it to the police.
070                         (1.1)
071  DA:  But Chuck's fingerprints are not on the urn
          (.2) are they.
072       [ I mean-
073       [((extends left arm palm up to witness/retracts))
074       [
075  AM:  That is very odd to me.
076                         (0.5)
077  DA:  Do you have any idea why Chuck's prints
078       uh:::: were not on the urn?
079                         (1.8)
080  AM:  That's very odd to me.
081                         (.)
082  DA:  I mean=
083       [((extends left arm with transcript to witness
            and retracts))
084       =did anybody clean the urn after it was in
          your house?
085  AM:  No.
086  DA:  OK.
```

As we have seen thus far, Black transforms the relevance of the urn across more or less distinct episodic boundaries in a multimodal layering and unraveling of the evidential puzzle. At the end of the introduction episode we saw a lengthy pause as he returned to the podium to resume questioning about Chuck's movement with and handling of the urn. At the end of the second episode we see another lengthy pause, but this textual boundary grounds a quite different interpretive effect: a more puzzling shift in focus about evidential identity. After the fifteen-second pause in line 064, Black asks Mercer about fingerprints found on the urn. Here we can see in vivid detail the relevance of the first two episodes, especially the prior emphasis on the putting and taking verbs. Given Chuck's manual handling of the urn, his prints should be on it – just as Black's prints would be on the urn via the introductory (re)enactment. But the only prints found on the urn belonged to the witness – to Mercer. What happened to Chuck's fingerprints?

Figure 7.4: (line 072 *I mean-*).

In line 065, Black asks Mercer if she was *aware that only your finger-prints are found on the urn*, mobilizing the predicative adjective that describes her state of mind. After the lengthy pause and other delays, she offers a possible candidate solution to the puzzle based on the fact that she had given the urn to the police. In line 071, Black uses her response to implement the turn-initial *but*-prefaced contrast that not only illuminates the inadequacy of her response but highlights the anomaly of the missing prints: *But Chuck's fingerprints are not on the urn are they*. The contrast adds a poetic layering of affective suspense and recruits an evaluative stance about this "fact" of evidence. However, as Mercer begins her answer, he adds two interesting increments in line 072 that overlap her response, one verbal, the other visual. First, turn-initial cutoff on the discourse marker *I mean* signals something important about the prior issue of the missing prints and that the hearer needs to maintain focus on that prior point (Schiffrin 1987: 309–310). Second, the discourse marker co-occurs with a *gestural intensifier*, what Kendon (2004: 264) calls a "palm up" or "open hand supine" gesture, which contextualizes a "readiness to receive something." Indeed, the gesture itself appears noticeably marked because the hand has to move downward from its "home" position of touching the left ear to the stroke position with the arm outstretched toward Mercer (Figures 7.4 and 7.5).[2] Together, gestural and verbal increments indicate Black's "readiness" to receive a plausible resolution to the puzzle.

Instead of resolving the puzzle, however, Mercer's overlapping response in line 075 reveals her as puzzled as Black about the prints. She matches

---

[2] As mentioned previously, according to McNeill (1992, 2005) the stroke phrase represents the meaning-bearing component of the gesture that generally, though not invariably, co-occurs with its speech counterpart.

Figure 7.5: (line 082 *I mean did anybody clean the urn*).

Black's multimodal intensifier with an adverb intensifier and affective
adjective to mark her own sense of surprise: *That is very odd to me*. Rather
than provide a reply to the question or solution to the puzzle, Mercer
expresses an affective evaluative stance on the missing prints. In the
ensuing sequence Black produces a more explicit question about the prints
but once again receives a repeat of the intensifier plus affective adjective
(lines 077–080). After Mercer's response, Black repeats the *I mean* marker
co-occurring with the gestural intensifier (actually a variant form of repetition as he switches the transcript from right to left hand, to gesture with
arm plus transcript extended), but here we see retroactively how the prior
aborted marker in line 072 appeared en route to a candidate solution that
materializes in line 082 – *I mean did anybody clean the urn after it was in
your house*? (Figure 7.5). That Black offers Mercer several chances to
explain the missing prints before providing his own not only escalates
the aura of suspense but holds Mercer normatively accountable for knowing their whereabouts. Even so, his candidate solution inherits an immediate rejection from Mercer in line 085 (which is interesting because this is
one of her few responses that occur with no delay).

 Thus, the depth of affective interplay between Black and Mercer and the
escalation of explicit questioning over the prints allows us to further gauge
the significance of the urn and its contingent relevance to the co-
construction of evidential context, a dynamic context pulsating with a
robust sense of perpetual motion from referential identity to agentive
control, and now to forensic puzzle. However, there's no puzzle about
one thing: Mercer's forensic residue is embodied in the material exhibit in
front of her, linking them in the unfolding drama. Thus, the significance of
and suspense over the urn is not just momentarily relevant but continuously layered in the integration of multimodal, affective, and intertextual

resources even as its evidential status transforms over the unfolding sequence. As we will see in the next episode, Black uses the missing prints as the interactive and evidential platform to launch a puzzling resolution to the puzzle, a resolution that furnishes a key justification for using a multimodal approach in the analysis of legal credibility – of inconsistency.

Lines 087–136: Puzzling resolution of the puzzle

```
087  DA:   Well le[t me ask you uh:::: (.) if you recall=
088           [((turns and gazes at defense table))
089        =these statements (.) from uh:: April fifth
090        of your police statement on page seven.
091        ((looking at transcript as tape plays))
```

Taped police interview (47.1 seconds)

```
Detective:   You came back from the beach area,
             went outside, out into the kitchen and
             then what happened?
AM:          Uh:: I ran through the kitchen area and
             went out to the- to the- to the to the
             driveway
Detective:   (Patty) (transcription doubt)
AM:          I don't remember
Detective:   OK. Was Chuck holding anything?
AM:          I didn't see him holding anything.
Detective:   Alright.
             ((tape stops))
```

```
092                            (1.2)
093  DA:   Now that's uh::: detective Rigolo
094        questioning you (.) on April fifth is it not?
095                            (1.1)
096  AM:   Yes.
097                            (0.5)
098  DA:   She's a detective on this case.
099  AM:   Yes.
100                            (1.5)
101  DA:   And she questioned you? about this urn- (.)
102        or excuse me she questioned you as to whether
103        or not Chuck was holding anything didn't she?
104                            (1.4)
```

```
105  AM:   Yes she did.
106                              (.)
107  DA:   And you said (.) I didn't see him holding
108        anything isn't that right.
109                                 (2.0)
110  AM:   I said that at that point when she asked me
           yes.
111                                 (0.5)
112  DA:   That was a lie wasn't it
           ((markedly lowered volume))
113                                 (3.4)
114  AM:   Tha- tuh:: (1.4) I wouldn't call it uh lie=
115  DA:   =It was not true.
116                                 (5.0)
117  AM:   I was afraid maybe to answer that question
118        uh::: (.) that she may say that we were
           stealing.
119                                 (1.0)
120  DA:   Well my- my question is Miss Mercer when
121        you said I didn't see Chuck holding anything
122        ((staccato)) that wasn't true was it.
123                                 (2.6)
124  AM:   That is true.
125                              (.)
126  DA:   In fact- (.9) to be blunt (.) you were lying
           weren't you.
127                                 (4.1)
128  AM:   I- I don't like (.) you to say that to me.
           [                    ]
129        ((closes eyes+looks down))
130                                 (31.7)
131  DA:   Well who took the urn?
132                                 (3.5)
133  AM:   You are going to have to ask Patty or
134        Chuck that question (.) because I wasn't
           there.
135  DA:   You weren't there?
136  AM:   I wasn't there when that event took place.
```
((urn stays on the witness stand for the rest of Mercer's
  cross-exam))

We see thus far that the urn does not possess autonomous meaning as a passive aspect of context but rather its evidential sense and interactional relevance emerge dynamically in a delicately choreographed, yet

Figure 7.6: (line 087 Black gazes at the defense table to play the tape).

thoroughly improvised multimodal ensemble of which it plays a crucial role. The interplay among verbal, material, and other modal resources contextualizes the significance of legal evidence and amplifies the intrigue that circulates around the urn. In this regard it is neither a theatrical "splash" nor just an incremental buildup of facts that evoke the exhibit's "dramatic flair." Rather, the poetic layering of suspense on top of those facts orchestrates the drama necessary to make Mauet's "lasting impression on the jury" a work of verbal art.[3]

A major facet of that layering occurs in line 091 with a shift in the center of attention from the urn to a tape recording of Mercer's prior police statement, a recording organized around *prospective and retrospective instructions* that channel interpretation and evaluation. In line 087, Black begins with turn initial *Well* to introduce the intertextual recording. According to Schiffrin (1987: 102) the discourse marker *well* in this turn environment is multifunctional and may operate as a preliminary to disagreement or challenge, as a contrast to a prior utterance and as a change of direction/boundary marker. All of these functions converge and merge when Black glances at the defense table for one of the attorneys to play the tape (see Figure 7.6).

By inserting the tape into the intertextual field Black not only adds another layering of suspense but also activates another lamination of participation – detective and witness – and multimodal organization into the unfolding narrative that instructs the jury how to interpret and evaluate the electronically mediated speech. More specifically, his pre-tape instructions trigger strong expectations that the tape will yield a resolution to the ongoing puzzle by foregrounding the recording against the routine

---

[3] This is, of course, in reference to Jakobson's (1960: 356) "poetic function of language" or a "focus on the message for its own sake."

stream of speech in a figure-ground relationship. As this happens, the tape *appears* to naturalize its own relevance – reified and fetishized as an objective source of knowledge and further augmented by his reading of the written transcript as the tape plays.[4]

Still, although the instructions promise an imminent resolution via the tape, it is not clear what the resolution is. Black's preliminary work could refer to Mercer's affective sentiments that only her prints were found on the urn, or Chuck's missing prints, or cleaning the urn (or all these) – or it could refer to something else. As the tape plays, the resolution to the puzzle turns out to be that *something else*, a process that unfolds as follows.

While the tape appears to "speak for itself" as we hear Mercer impeach her credibility in her own words, it only fosters such an impression because multimodal laminations of participation and linguistic ideologies naturalize a continuity between historical and current speech events. On the audiotape we hear the detective ask Mercer *Was Chuck holding anything*, and Mercer responds with *I didn't see him holding anything*, a transparent inconsistency in her testimony in both direct and cross-examination. After the brief *Alright* acknowledgement, Black stops the tape and transfers gaze from the written transcript to Mercer. In so doing, he promotes a linguistic ideology in which the interview (and interviewer) functions as a passive vehicle for "harvesting" information from the active interviewee. That is, he constructs a multimodal layering of voices by positioning himself and the detective in a neutral relayer footing: someone who merely plays the tape or interviews the subject to harvest historical information.[5] Stopping the tape and glancing away from the transcript at that moment naturalizes Mercer's final statement about Chuck as the focal topic. Thus, rather than being interview participants who actively shape the interviewee's response, Black in the current speech event, and the detective in the historical event, appear in neutral mediator footings, erasing any hint of involvement or responsibility for shaping Mercer's speech, bleaching out any indexical particulars on the tape, and fostering the impression of

---

[4] In this respect, the tape and transcript constitute what Komter (2006: 202) refers to as an "authoritative document" that the police produce with an eye toward their future interactional work. As she notes in her extensive studies, these documents are always accomplishments. Similarly, Hodges (2016: 38) notes how this "tape fetishism" functions as a "supposedly objective and self-evident record of the past while erasing the interpretive dimensions involved in those recontextualizations."

[5] We have seen how Goffman (1981) developed the concept of footing to refer to the speaker's relationship to his or her utterance. The relayer footing just mentioned builds on his initial discourse roles of animator, author, and principal.

iconic transparency.[6] For instance, why does the detective question Mercer about Chuck carrying anything in the first place – a mystery within a mystery in the tape lamination? Why does Black start and stop the tape at just those precise moments? Why would Mercer lie in the first place? Under the taken-for-granted guise of projecting a passive footing for himself and the detective, Black coordinates multimodal laminations of participation to naturalize a continuity across historical and current speech events, a continuity that generates the inconsistency in Mercer's testimony.

After stopping the tape, Black resumes questioning in line 093: *Now that's uh::: detective Rigolo questioning you.* Notice in particular how the turn-initial discourse marker *Now* contextualizes and foregrounds a shift in topic or reorientation from description to evaluation (Schiffrin 1987; Aijmer 2002). Moreover, as both Aijmer (2002) and Schiffrin (1987) note, *Now* signals the subtle development of an argument, and in this instance it retrospectively instructs hearers how to interpret and evaluate the final tape increment; it contextualizes a new – rather unexpected – development in Black's argument about Mercer, Chuck, and the urn. That is, rather than solving the puzzle about the missing prints, the voices in the tape reveal a stunning inconsistency in Mercer's current testimony compared to her historical comment on the tape.

Black exploits the inconsistency immediately while simultaneously recalibrating expectations about the puzzle, from fingerprints to credibility. On line 102 we see him read from a written transcript of the tape, and during his reading he produces a cutoff repair on the urn. Even though the repair provides a more accurate representation of the detective's question on the tape, it also highlights the referents being repaired (that is, the urn). Relatedly, given the referential distance from *And she questioned you about this urn-* to *or excuse me she questioned you as to whether or not Chuck was holding anything*, how could he have made such a glaring error when reading from the transcript? One point to consider is this: Although the urn possesses immense presence in the courtroom, it is noticeably absent in the tape interview, and the repair keeps attention riveted on it, even though the detective never mentions it on the tape. The repair could be designed to replicate as closely as possible the detective's question, or it could be a methodical resource designed to keep attention riveted on the urn, smuggling in its relevance under auspices of doing the repair (or

---

[6] Could the lack of light on a dark evening have played a role in her perception? Precisely when did she see Chuck "not carrying anything?" See Matoesian (2000) for an in-depth analysis of how audiotapes function in testimony as reified and fetishized communicative objects.

both). Thus, we see the strategic significance of the repair and how Black gets in two major points, first sustaining attention on the urn as the center of attention shifts to the recording/transcript, and second, constructing the inconsistency. Moreover, error-correction demonstrates how the urn becomes not just part of the multimodal context but relevant to and oriented by participants during the course of legal action. More theoretically, this is how speech, recording/transcript, and material conduct recalibrate the evidential significance of one another – progressing from an object of reference to a buildup of facts, and then to the fingerprint puzzle and finally, to impeaching Mercer's credibility.

Although the tape promises a resolution to the fingerprint puzzle we see that it only creates another puzzle layered on the missing prints – transforming one puzzle into another. Instead of seeing the looming resolution materialize we see it evaporate into multimodal impeachment of Mercer's credibility. As mentioned previously, that alone constitutes a key justification for using a multimodal approach.

Why did she tell the detective that she didn't see Chuck holding anything? In line 107 Black's question includes a direct quote drawn from Mercer's final statement on the tape, and in line 110 she admits to the statement, but the lengthy two-second inter-turn pause, temporal adverbial *at that point*, and backloaded *yes* signal some impending qualification or account without further elaboration in the current turn. In the ensuing question, Black delivers a face-threatening question – *That was a lie wasn't it* – concerning Mercer's taped statement in line 112, an accusation occurring with a noticeably marked shift in pitch register (notice the modulated volume), for emphasis and effect that sets into motion a lengthy sequence as both sides negotiate the meaning of her taped statement.

The negotiation begins in line 114 with several distinguishing features in Mercer's turn. First, her response occurs only after a 3.4-second gap or inter-turn silence. Second, her turn consists of a cutoff on turn initial *That-* followed by two additional delay components, the first a vowel prolongation on *uh::*, the second a 1.4-second pause or intra-turn delay. Third, her *wouldn't call it uh lie* response neither agrees nor disagrees with Black's accusation while simultaneously withholding mention of what she would call it. And before she can propose a candidate solution, Black's immediately latched next question (with no delay) preempts that possibility by downgrading accusatory force from *lie* (line 112), to *not true* (115), a downgrade designed to elicit agreement from Mercer.

Mercer's response to the downgraded accusation occurs only after a lengthy five-second gap, yet rather than align with an agreement, she delivers on the promissory note alluded to previously in line 110, providing an account for the inconsistency (line 117). Notice how her justification invokes a rather delicate maneuver loaded with affect, indirect speech, and epistemic stance. *Afraid* is an emotion adjective. The epistemic adverb *maybe* and modal verb *may* encode uncertainty in the account. The referential object of her affective and epistemic components unfolds in the hypothetical indirect speech attributed to the detective: *she may say that we were stealing*. Through plural *we*, she underscores not just a selfish concern with protecting herself but the loyal act of protecting her friends, a crucial point we will return to shortly.

Although Mercer's account attempts to preempt further progression of the accusation sequence (even in the downgraded version), and perhaps steer questioning in another direction, Black merely recycles the question, first by frontloading contrastive *Well*, and second by re-mobilizing the direct quote (though in staccato this time) from the tape and his immediately prior *was not true*, ignoring her account in the process. After three recycled questions he finally receives an agreement from Mercer.

Consider the logic of the negotiation at a finer level of granularity. Black attempts to steer Mercer into a state of alignment with his question – to elicit agreement – by downgrading the accusation. One way to conceptualize this process would be in terms of polar extremes and variations on a gradational scale. A "lie" refers to intentional agency and invokes reference to moral character: that one is a liar. On the other hand, "not true" refers to a proposition being true or false, and even though "lie" and "not" true in this instance are doubtless related (e.g., via indirection) – one being inferred from the other – the distal demonstratives (e.g., "that's true, that wasn't true," etc.) distance Mercer's personality trait from the proposition (as we have seen something could be "not true" for any number of reasons, such as memory, misperception, obstructed view, etc.). Put simply and stipulatively, *wasn't true* fails to ascribe the same dimension of deliberation, agency, and intention that *lie* does, and it promotes different modulations of blame on the gradational scale. When Mercer agrees with *That is true* in line 124 she may expect that both have reached a conciliatory end to the negotiation. Both have conceded ground to the other, as it were. He has "backed off" the more face-threatening position with its embarrassing implications, and she has moved into alignment – her truth about the untruthful statement – with the downgraded accusation.

One other observation, a rather delicate one, perhaps merits consideration in this regard. If we look at the less threatening preliminary questions in lines 093, 098, 101, and 107, notice that we see short inter-turn gaps (silences) between the questions and Mercer's answers (1.1, 1.5, 1.4, and 2.0 respectively).[7] As the intensity of the accusations escalate in 112, 115, 120, and 126, notice the gap (and pauses or intra-turn silence) length between the accusations and responses increase to 3.4 (and 1.4 within-turn pause), 5.0, 2.6, and 4.1 (with the short within-turn pause), increases that index Mercer's heightened reluctance to respond to the face-threatening questions. We can also see that both the *lie* and *lying* questions inherit considerably lengthy combinations of inter- and intra-turn silence (as well as other delays such as repair, pausing, and vowel stretching of considerable length in 114 and 128). More speculatively, the "stray" 2.6 pause in the pattern (line 123) occurs after Black repeats his final downgraded accusation, perhaps an indication that Mercer (mis)perceives that the negotiation has culminated at this less threatening level.

However (and doubtless unexpectedly for Mercer), once Black nails down an agreement he resurrects and recalibrates the original formulation in line 112, frontloading the epistemic and style of stance adverbials to deliver an upgraded accusation: *In fact- to be blunt you were lying* (with emphatic stress on the latter stance marker). In this contingent and incremental – to-and-fro – negotiation he uses her agreement as the sequential platform to launch a direct accusation (with Mercer in the subject position from "that was a lie" to "not true x 2," and finally "you were lying"). The nailing down negotiation develops not progressively but by circling around and expanding its initial impulse (going two steps backward to move one step forward, as it were). In terms of the gradational modulation along the sequential axis, this last accusation is the most face threatening of all four versions. Put in more prosaic terms, Black "sucker punches" Mercer by getting her to agree to the downgraded version and then uses her agreement not to end the negotiation but to escalate the accusation beyond the original *That was a lie wasn't it* in 112.

Perhaps it is too threatening, for just as Black escalates the intensity of his accusation in line 126, so too does Mercer escalate the intensity of her response, not by upgrading her prior account, however, but by constructing a multimodal affective stance. By intensifying the accusation into a personal attack, Black perhaps goes a question too far. After the 4.1-second gap, Mercer mobilizes cutoff, short pause, and negative affective verb (*don't like*), augmented by the closed eyes and

---

[7] On the flip side, notice how Black's most threatening accusations in line 112 and 126 occur with very short gaps post Mercer's response.

Figure 7.7: (line 128 *I don't like you to say that to me*).

downward glance to assemble an intense emotional performance, a negatively charged affective stance (Figure 7.7).[8]

Mercer does more, however, than encode affective stance through the emotion verb (plus *to*-infinitive) augmented by the multimodal display of withdrawal. She recalibrates the accusation sequence and reconfigures participant roles from impeaching credibility to an emotional frame, so that she almost looks like a "victim" herself! In this case we can see how her metapragmatic answers recalibrate the meaning of questions and reconfigure participant identities in the discursive division of labor. In a strikingly astute maneuver, Mercer deploys multimodal affect as a strategic interactional resource to modulate the topic and shift legal identities.

More speculatively, the micro-social organization of withdrawal in this sequence may involve more than legal identity. For Black, a lie rests in the objective nature of rules and possesses a public meaning. Mercer personalizes the inconsistency and relativizes it via the relationship in her account (as mentioned previously, protecting her friends via the *we*). Black's final upgraded accusation once again objectifies, especially in the two stance markers. In response she personalizes the attack through the emotional frame of hurt feelings. Thus, we see a clash between two different underlying presuppositions or ideologies for conceptualizing the sequential negotiation, one based on rules, the other on relationships. And according to the classic study by Conley and O'Barr (1990), the

---

[8] According to Goffman (1963: 40), closed eyes may convey a "deep emotional involvement in the proceedings." But here they seem to convey what Jaworski (2000: 125–126) refers to as a type of "withdrawal," or symbolic exiting of the accusation or conflict sequence (see Jaworski 2000: 125–126 for an uncanny resemblance to this, though in a quite different context).

former indexes males and professionals in the legal system, the latter females and minorities more generally.

In this sense, Mercer's affective response *may* project a discursive fracture of participation from attorney-witness to male attorney versus female witness along with bullying/hurt feelings superimposed onto a more dynamic and multiplex lamination of participation – perhaps indexing gender identity in the process. That Black switches from who "carried" to who "took" the urn after the thirty-two-second silence, *may* indeed warrant such an interpretation (as he appears to back off of the "carry" accusation to avoid such a conspicuous display of male power).[9]

Of course, the negotiation could warrant still another interpretation, a legal strategic rather than gender-infused performance. Although Black fails to resolve the puzzle and withdraws from the accusation after Mercer's response, we might consider another point. What if his goal is not to resolve the mystery but to construct and sustain it? What if failure to resolve the fingerprint mystery is the resolution, for as Goffman (1959: 70) notes, "The real mystery behind the mystery is that there is no mystery. The real problem is to prevent the audience from learning this too." Hence switching the questioning from "who carried" to "who took" the urn, creates another mystery with no resolution in sight. Just as the urn on the witness stand and puzzle about the fingerprints are left suspended, so too is talk suspended in the lengthy thirty-two-second pause.

Still more puzzling, while participants fail to resolve the print mystery, let me entertain the possibility of a *took* and *we* mystery embedded in the mystery, one like a shadow wafting across the multimodal landscape. Let us return to Black's *took* in line 131 and then move to the plural *we* in Mercer's account (line 118). What is most ingenious about the attorney's theatrical performance is this: Black is interested in neither Mercer nor Desiderio. Nor is he interested in the urn per se and/or what happened to

---

[9] As Ochs (1996: 418) notes, however, things are rarely that simple. Discursive forms rarely index one sociocultural context. Rather, discursive forms intersect with multiple situational dimensions to index sociocultural context. For instance, we may consider how Mercer's relational stance in the historical event interacts with a "cooperative" dimension of femininity in the here and now speech event, and how the rule-oriented perspective that Black adopts interacts with a more aggressive and asymmetrical masculine identity. In this regard, she seeks a conciliatory stance in the negotiation while Black projects a type of "one-upmanship" power relation. Moreover, the heightened affective intensity of her multimodal response (hurt feelings) intersects with his callous indifference (in the upgraded accusation) to project a dynamic gender performance. On the other hand, one could certainly attribute these characteristics to the adversary system with its winning-at-all-costs culture, and how this may interact with gender identity along certain lines (see Komter 2000 for a discussion of this).

the fingerprints. This entire spate of testimony constitutes a thoroughly unveiled allusion about exposing – better yet – co-constructing the victim's backstage machinations about manipulating testimony to make a more convictable story in court.

Throughout Mercer's testimony thus far, and in opening comments (and later, the entire defense theory), Black has gone to some lengths to portray the victim as a man-hater, mentally unbalanced and a woman scorned, strongly motivated by revenge against the defendant. Black's theatrical performance insinuates that the missing prints are part of the same cabalistic performance engineered by the victim.[10] Bowman manipulates Mercer and Desideria just as she manipulates the legal system to pursue her unscrupulous scheme.

Consider *took* in who *took the urn*. *Took* encodes a removal event in which the agent causes an object to move from its original place. Mercer did not take the urn, nor did Desiderio – at least not of his own accord. Black suggests that only the victim would have instructed Chuck to take the urn and/or directed Mercer to lie about it. Such a strategy displays how "ghost" or "shadow" participation roles (Irvine 1996) in the form of the victim's backstage involvement in the winning-a-conviction scenario constitute a supra allusion that hovers over the entire puzzle sequence, one that draws the urn into its gravitational orbit, stimulating further confusion about what happened and the victim's state of mind. In terms of legal strategy, the following quote is analogous to Black's objective. "The task of both the prosecution and defense is to present the jury with the more convincing story. The problem is that too conspicuous an orientation to 'winning the case' might undermine the persuasiveness of their stories" (Komter 2000: 42).

Thus, confusion about the urn and fingerprints – as well as the victim's motivational conspiracy and conspicuous orientation to winning the case – conveys iconic representations and allusive images of confusion about the sexual assault, instructing the jury of reasonable doubt in and through the mystery (not to mention the mystery about the mystery). Just as the urn persists and alternates with the recording as the focus of attention, and becomes a permanent fixture on the evidentiary landscape, so too does the

---

[10] In Chapter 6 we discussed Black's construction of the cabalistic plot hatched by the victim and how Black constructed a collusive scenario where the victim instructed Mercer to delay a statement to a popular TV talk program until charges were filed, etc. Moreover, Mercer's credibility has already been demolished in this second day of cross-examination, so Black needs no further "mileage" from her. He has a much more important agenda to pursue here (as any good defense attorney would). In a more allusive vein, recall Black's question using the indefinite *anybody* in line 84. Why not ask if Mercer or Chuck cleaned the urn? *Anybody* would include Bowman under its referential auspices.

puzzle or mystery about who took and carried it persist and evolve into
new directions. Did the victim take the urn? Did she possibly wipe the
prints or instruct Mercer or Chuck to? Why did she take the objects in
the first place? If Chuck took and carried the urn under the direction of the
victim where did his prints go? Was Mercer lying on the tape or in
courtroom examination? If she lied in either case was it at the behest of
the victim? Who does the "we" refer to in Mercer's account (*we were
stealing*) and is that Mercer or Bowman's voice?[11] Is this a case of collusion between the victim and her friend? And if the jury is confused about
issues surrounding the urn and unsavory motives, then they may be just
as confused about the sexual assault – confused enough to acquit the
defendant!

Conclusion

We have witnessed how legal realities like inconsistency and credibility
emerge in the concrete details of material conduct, and how the urn and
other modal forms recalibrate the meaning of the unfolding verbal drama
as the defense attorney orchestrates an ensemble of disparate resources
into a reflexive unity. Indeed, the urn anchors shifting contexts of legal
evidence as it transforms its own identity across current and historical
discourses. What this suggests is that the urn is not so much relevant
momentarily to a particular sequence of speech or utterance or lexical
item, as it is to the incremental and progressive buildup of suspense about
itself within and between the narrative segments – retaining its physical
presence even in the midst of significant evidential transformations. It
indexes the illogic of the victim and Mercer's actions and promotes a
dynamic representation of confusion, not just in the current speech, but
even more importantly, during the historical event as well.

   A useful way to theorize this verbal drama is to re-specify (slightly) the
classic framework on communicative skill designed to engage and move an
audience – here the jury – and how trial strategies like impeaching credibility go beyond establishing the facts. Jakobson (1960) and later Bauman
(1986) turned our analytic gaze to the poetic function of language, language as an aesthetic performance "above and beyond referential content"
(Bauman1986: 3). But there is no reason to limit the poetic function
to language or verbal artistry. Consider the multimodal fusillade of

---

[11] Black may be trying to show that Mercer is not clever enough to come up with *we were
stealing* on her own. Here too we can see how *took* links back to *anybody* and *we*, to
suggest Bowman's involvement. Of course, by switching to *took*, he keeps the allusive
reference to Bowman in continuous play.

movement, props, gesture, gaze, civil inattention, silence, and speech co-constructed by Black and Mercer in the improvisational density of court-room performance. Layering allusion upon allusion, both escalate the aura of evidential suspense and narrative intrigue – circling like an obsessive ceremony – that moves toward a moral crescendo ever beyond its reach. This microcosmic infrastructure of legal order emerges not only through the drama of spoken performance, but theater of material artistry as well.

Part III

Integrating Gestures and Material Objects in Closing Argument

8 Material Mediated Gestures

In Part II, we saw how multimodal conduct featured in trial tactics like resistance, control, and credibility in direct and cross-examination of witnesses. In the final part we explore the poetic organization of multimodal conduct in the attorney's closing narrative. We investigate the micro-organization of beat gestures and how they integrate with material objects to mobilize participant alignment and reinforce significant points of evidence for the jury. The current chapter examines how *material mediated gestures* figure in the production of speaker positioning, epistemic stance, and evidence. Evidence of the assault must be inscribed not only *on the body* but also *in the mind* of the victim. The ensuing chapter analyzes the multifunctionality of beat gestures as they work through the hands and fingers to not only accentuate rhythm and foreground points of evidential significance, but also, at specific moments, to invoke semantic content as well: *how* and *why* evidence of the assault should be visible on the body. Both emphasize closing as an oratorical performance with a sophisticated rhythmic sensibility and refined sense of evidential imagery, one that attempts to do things: persuade the jury.

Closing argument represents the most crucial part of the adversarial system of justice, the most dramatic moment in the adversarial trial – the "main performance event" (Heffer 2010: 212). It is the attorney's final chance to convince the jury that his or her account is the most complete, coherent, and plausible; it provides the attorney an opportunity to showcase persuasive skills through the full range of multimodal resources at his or her disposal. Closing argument takes disparate strands of testimony and weaves them together in a persuasive and coherent narrative, summarizing previous points and evaluating the position of both sides.[1]

According to Rosulek (2010: 218) closing argument takes the "same people, events and evidence and creates two opposing representations for

---

[1] For example, in response to the cross examination of Dr. Good (Chapter 2), Black stated in his closing: "Dr. Good was attacked in every way imaginable but not once was his scientific theory attacked."

the same audience." She also concludes that closing argument is "understudied," and future research should analyze its "extralinguistic features" (2008: 549). In his classic text on trial techniques, Mauet (2010: 387) states that closing represents the "chronological and psychological culmination of the jury trial," a culmination that *should* include "forceful" and "persuasive" gestures, and "exhibits" to highlight major points of argument (2010: 394–400).

In this chapter, we examine this understudied – perhaps totally neglected – extralinguistic feature of closing argument: hand gestures and the incorporation of material objects into gestures and their role in persuasive oratory. Indeed, we show that the most forceful and persuasive gesture in court may be these rhythmic and object-mediated hand movements. In the first part of the chapter we explore speaker positioning and hearer engagement during closing argument, and demonstrate how an attorney can reduce social distance between himself and jurors through the use of impersonal and exclusive pronouns. In so doing, the attorney brings jurors into the event in question and projects his biased and unilateral interpretation of evidence as a product of joint co-construction. The next section analyzes how speech, gesture, and material objects integrate along the aesthetic dimension of communicative practice to emphasize and evaluate testimony, paying particular attention to the manner in which gesture as material conduct – photo evidence – encodes features not contained in speech. After that we show how epistemic stance emerges through a poetic flow of gaze, objects, and coding practice. The final section explores how the attorney brings transcripts into play and integrates them into his gestural action as he argues that there were ulterior motives for bringing the charge of rape, which he argues, was fabricated.

Beats and Materiality

We have seen that *beat* gestures (in the orthodox view) do not depict an object of reference but, like an orchestra conductor's baton, beat out rhythm and provide visual structure that mark specific parts of speech as significant (Streeck 2008). This represents the acoustics of speech in movement. In McNeill's (2005: 40) gesture classification scheme, beats are:

among the least elaborate of gestures ... they are mere flicks of the hand(s) up and down or back and forth that seem to "beat" time along with the rhythm of speech ... They signal the temporal locus in speech of something the speaker feels is important with respect to the larger discourse ... the equivalent of using a yellow highlighter.

While most gesture studies focus on representational gestures or gestures that depict semantic or propositional content, few in-depth studies have been conducted on beats, perhaps because they are thought to merely beat out "musical time" rather than convey substantive information (McNeill 1992: 15). Even so, beats perform crucial gestural functions in persuasive oratory (Ferre 2011). Krahmer and Swerts (2007: 396) found that speech-synchronized beats increased the persuasiveness of the message compared to words, phrases, and clauses without them. Maricchiolo et al. (2009: 244) found similar results: "Experimental design with control groups show that beat gestures have an important effect on receiver's perceptions of communicative effectiveness, and persuasiveness of the message." As we will see, beats are more than McNeill's mere flicks of the hand or finger carried out to the rhythm of speech, and offer quite important yet more subtle contributions to semantic meaning than traditionally conceived.

We have also seen how material objects figure prominently and actively in the production of emerging forms of legal activity, and how they are embedded in and relevant to the construction of legal context and plausibility (or weight) of evidence. In the case here, we illustrate the active contextualizing role of *material mediated gestures* in persuasive oratory and how they organize the epistemicity of legal narrative in concert with speech and gaze. More specifically, the defense attorney mobilizes photos and transcripts as expressive vehicles for the assembly of gestures, orchestrating objects for rhetorical and evidential affect.

Speaker Positioning and Impression Management

Research on impression management in court addresses how lawyers portray themselves when appealing to their interlocutors. Fuller (1993) and Hobbs (2003) find that lawyers present a "multiplicity of partial selves" (see Ochs and Capps 1996: 22) by shifting styles to negotiate favorable alignments or relationships with their interlocutors (often jurors). We show how speakers not only shift alignment through talk, but also take up multiple alignments or positions simultaneously through the finely synchronized interplay among gesture, gaze, and objects.[2]

---

[2] Deppermann (2015: 370) conceives of positions as situated achievements that are "tied to the social actions by which they are made relevant," while Bucholtz and Hall (2005: 592) define position as "temporary and interactionally specific stances and participant roles." We use them along similar lines though with a more Goffmanian emphasis on forms of involvement, alignment, and engagement among participants.

In a closely related sense, epistemicity refers to the source and status of knowledge, the authority to make a given claim, and to the participant's commitment to their words. States of knowledge are dynamic and can range from circumstances of absolute knowledge, to no knowledge of the topic. For example, Goodwin (1994) examined how objects of knowledge, such as coding schemes, were constructed and shaped in the discourse of a profession. This "shaping process" creates objects of knowledge that are then used to reflexively define and evaluate evidence. That is, knowledge is distributed through the very practices used to organize the perception it establishes.

In a similar vein, epistemic stance refers to the grammatical-lexical encoding of a speaker's degree of commitment to or level of certainty about their words through, for example, stance adverbials like "in fact" or "actually." However, we move from a narrow consideration of linguistic encoding of stance, and demonstrate how participants encode epistemic stance through gaze, gesture, and objects. In particular, we explore how multimodal conduct functions as a sociocultural practice in speaker positioning, and the constitution of epistemicity. For example, as lawyers attempt to convince an audience that his or her account is the most plausible, they mobilize subtle discursive maneuvers like confirming assertions and evaluating evidence under the guise of directing jurors to merely "look" at a particular piece of evidence. In the ensuing section we see how positioning and epistemicity emerge through gesture, gaze, and material objects as these semiotic modes come together "in the moment" to persuade the jury.

Excerpt 1
What follows is an analysis from a 1:02-minute excerpt of closing argument by defense attorney Roy Black. In the transcript, Black argues that bruises on the victim's body were not recent but old, which would refute the prosecution claim that they came from a recent collision in which Smith tackled Bowman on the lawn.

```
01  Take a look at- (3.1)
                [((reaches with right hand for photographs
                 on table to his right and grabs a small stack
                 and removes paper clip during 3.1 pause))
02  what they say are bruises (.)
    [((brings photographs to mid torso while maintaining gaze
    on photos))
03  Take a look- (.) at
    [((selects top photo and directs it and gaze to jury))
04  any red (.)    or purplish    type        marks
        [((beat))    [((beat))    [((beat))  [((beat))
        ((vertical photo beats w/right hand))
```

05 on this arm (.)
    [((moves photo horizontally closer to jury))
06 Take a look
    [((Black directs gaze toward photo))
07 and see if you can see **anything** there (imploring intonation)
    [((redirects gaze at jury and pushes first photo even closer
    to jury members))
                              (6.3)
08 ((sets first photo down, looks at the second, and
    sets it down while holding the pile of photographs
    in his left hand during 6.3 pause))
09 Take a look (.) here is:: (.)
                        [((directs gaze to stack of photos; grabs
                          third photo from stack in left hand))
10 the *bruise* (1.5)
        [((maintains gaze while turning the photo upside
        down and twisting it counter-clockwise))
11 State's exhibit seventeen they say is on the
                        [((flips the photograph in his right
                          hand while gazing at it))
12 *shoulder* (1.4)
    [((directs photo and gaze at the jury and takes step
    forward with right foot while pushing photo
    forward to jury))
13 Is this a   *reddish*   bruise?
    [((beats photo)) [((beats photo)) [((beats photo))
    [((takes another step toward jury))
14 Is this *purplish*
            [((beats photo))
15 Is this an *ugly*   *nasty*
                [((beats photo)) [((beats photo))
16 *bruise*   that   one
    [((beats photo)) [((beats photo)) [((beats photo))
    gets (.)
    [((beats photo))
17 for   falling   down with
    [((beats photo))   [((beats photo))   [((beats photo))
18 three hundred
    [((beats photos in left and right hand))
    pounds of
    [((beats photos in left and right hand))
19 **weight**?
    [((beats photos in left and right hand))
20 *on the lawn*?
    [((beats photo))

```
21                                  (1.6)
   [((sweeps photo from right to left laterally across jury))
   [((sweeping occurs after the 1.6 pause for 1.1 seconds))
   [((Black maintains gaze on jury from line 011 to present))
22                                  (6.2)
   [((sets photos down, sifts through photos during 6.2))
23  When
   [((beats photos in left and right hand))
24  you
   [((beats photos in left and right hand))
25  go
   [((beats photos in left and right hand))
26  back
   [((beats photos in left and right hand))
27  there
   [((beats photos in left & right hand))
   look at- (.) what they say is a bru::ise (.)
   [((gazes at photo in right hand))
28  on the foot(1.1)
   [((turns photo in right hand toward jury
   and redirects gaze toward the jury))
   [((takes a step toward the jury with
   photo elevated in right hand during pause))
29  Do                          you
   [((another step to jury))    [((beats photo))
30  see:: a                     reddish bruise (.)
   [((beats photo))             [((beats photo))
31  a purplish
     [((beats photo))
32  a nasty                bruise
     [((beats photo))    [((beats photo))
33  that you're going to get (.) from
   [((micro beats on every lexeme in line 033))
34  the actions       that             they've- (1.0)
   [((beats photo)) [((beats photo)) [((beats photo))
35  described                in this case?
   [((beats photo)) [((redirects gaze from photo
                       to jury))
```

Speaker Alignment and Hearer Engagement

A rather unremarkable aspect of any civil or criminal trial is the introduction of different forms of evidence to address relevant issues in the case. Idealizing the phenomenon somewhat, we may say that direct evidence points to the facts pertaining to the ultimate issue in the case, such as a contract or testimony that person X witnessed person Y shooting person Z and so on. On the other hand, circumstantial evidence does not point directly to a fact but creates an inferential link to the fact that the party is trying to prove. In the example just provided, while the photos may show bruising on the victim's body they do not reveal the cause or age of the bruises.

The police took photographs of bruises on Bowman's body at the hospital. The prosecuting attorney argued that the defendant caused the bruises during the sexual assault based on direct evidence from the victim's testimony. In response, the defense offered a coding scheme for bruising based on those very same photos, creating circumstantial inferences that the bruises were old and thus not caused by the defendant. Black stated that the most important aspect of bruising was the age, and that age followed a color encoding sequence from recent red and purplish-blue colors (with blood under the surface of the skin), to older green, yellow, and tan colors before fading away. Bowman's own orthopedic surgeon testified that the bruises found on her body could be as much as ten days old. If the defense could prove that the bruises were old, yellow, or tan colors, then objective physical evidence for the prosecution's case would fade away, much like yellow/tan colors would disappear from the body in the final stage of the encoding sequence.

In lines 01, 03, 06, and 09 Black attempts to shape those circumstantial inferences about the age of the bruises with directives to the jury to inspect the photos. Put simply, directives steer the recipient to some objective for the speaker. As Hyland (2002: 217) notes, "Pragmatically, directives are often seen as a way in which status differences are both marked and constructed in interaction, with choices depending on an assessment of social relationships along the dimensions of social distance and relative power ... directives can steer readers to certain cognitive acts, where readers are initiated into a new domain of argument, led through a line of reasoning, or directed to understand a point in a certain way." Although Black's directives implore them to inspect the photos, his multimodal conduct with the photos transforms his speech act in distinct ways. Rosulek (2015: 32) mentions how attorneys may position themselves relative to jurors in ways that go beyond the transmission of referential text through what she calls "interlocutory voice": "lawyers tell jurors what they should currently be thinking or how the lawyers themselves are feeling." One way Black positions himself relative to jurors is through the use of impersonal *you*, projecting jurors as active interlocutors and co-constructors of evidence rather than passive recipients – as more than mere rhetorical objects of persuasive language use.

That is, while deictic *you* refers to the addressee(s), impersonal or non-deictic *you* – as in lines 07, 16, and 33 – makes a general statement about what anyone knows or could see (and is not necessarily referential). According to O'Connor (2000: 116) non-deictic *you* is "double-positioning, simultaneously self-distancing and other-involving." In this regard, good attorneys know that they have to accomplish two things to win a case: first, personalize their argument for the jury and, second, distance themselves as a biased source of information.

A legal-strategic way to think about this is that even though the jury in the adversary system understands that parties will only select evidence that best supports their case, they also expect attorneys to present an objective argument based on the facts brought before them. As mentioned previously in Chapter 3, attorneys must manage the impressions of the jury by projecting an appearance of objective neutrality rather than presenting an argument that appears too explicitly biased.

As we saw from Komter (2000: 420), if persuasion appears too persuasive – too oriented to winning at the expense of truth – it undermines the facticity of the legal narrative and "spoils" the impression management performance; the attorney has to find the seam between coherence and fracture to cultivate the threshold of objective neutrality for the jury. How does Black modulate the overt and exposed evaluative thrust of his narrative?

When Black looks at the photos (line 06) on the *Take a look and see if you can see anything* directive, he becomes a "virtual" juror, simultaneously instructing jurors to look while maintaining an allusive authoritative stance and fragmenting legal identity into a neutral animator or relayer footing as an evidential and oratorical strategy. Hypothetically, Black could have said, "This is not a red bruise" but he poses the question to the jury instead, involving them in the decision-making process rather than instructing them overtly and unilaterally on what decision should be made. However, this is not a mere neutral instruction. By fracturing his animator role, Black's *Take a look* directive becomes an implicit metapragmatic evaluation on how to perceive images in the photo, instructing the jury to question the alleged bruises on the victim's body (as we will see in greater detail later).[3]

Along similar lines, consider impersonal *you* (line 33) and its more formal variant *one* (line 16) (*Do you see a reddish bruise, a purplish, a*

---

[3] As Thompson and Hunston (2000: 5) state, "evaluation is the broad cover term for the expression of the speaker or writer's attitude or stance towards, viewpoint on, or feelings about the entities or propositions that he or she is talking about." For Labov (1972: 366) evaluation refers to the "means used by the narrator to indicate the point of the narrative."

nasty bruise that you're going to get from the actions that they've described and *is this an ugly nasty bruise that one gets from falling down*). In the former, Black engages the jurors through the verb of perception and then impersonal *you*, placing them into the domain of color perception based on the action description from the prosecution. In the latter, he recruits an evaluative perceptual category with the formal *one*, using the impersonal variant in a hypothetical event construction. In both cases, Black uses the impersonal pronoun to place the jury directly and actively into the situation, making them participants in the current discourse, allowing them to understand the outcome by juxtaposing what they know to be probable with what he is showing and telling them. He coordinates a joint focus of attention toward events and evidence, an evaluative and agential strategy that not only permits jurors to reach a conclusion through their own volition but also portrays Black as similar to the jurors' opinions and evaluations. While Black does not use inclusive pronouns, he nonetheless reduces the social distance between himself and the jurors through the personal use of impersonal pronouns.

Even more interesting, if we look closely at lines 01–07 we gain a glimpse of how impersonal *you* and multimodal conduct integrate to engage the jury. As we have seen, the impersonal pronoun involves the jurors by placing them directly into the discourse, creating distance between Black and the juror's version on the one hand, and the alleged victim's version on the other. In line 05, after asking the jurors if the photo depicts the type of bruise described by the prosecution (*Take a look at any red or purplish type marks on this arm*), Black steps toward the jury box and sweeps the photograph from right to left laterally (several feet) along the jury box (line 005 that co-occurs with *on this arm*), a virtual attempt to involve all jurors in evaluating the (im)plausibility of the prosecution's claims (see Figures 8.6 and 8.7). In so doing, we see how impersonal *you* (line 07) and the personal sweeping motion coordinate not only a joint focus of attention but an engaging instruction on how to evaluate the evidence.

Black not only reduces the social distance between him and the jurors through the use of impersonal pronouns, but also increases the distance between the jurors and the prosecution through the use of exclusive third person. On lines 02, 11, 27, and 34–35 each utterance includes a reported speech parenthetical on the source of information contained in the photo, one that contests either depiction of a bruise (lines 02 and 34–35), or precise location of the bruise on the body (lines 11 and 27) through the third person and verb of saying (*they say/they describe*). In a very transparent sense, he creates a dynamic opposition between exclusive third person (excluding Black and the jurors while including the prosecution), and impersonal pronoun (including Black and the jurors), that gets super-imposed onto a second opposition: the epistemologically privileged status of observing evidence. He designs a "what they say" versus "what you see" opposition that frames the supremacy of observable evidence over argu-ment – reality above words in the sense that the prosecution may have "said it," but you, can "see it."

In sum, Black's role as animator to and relayer of, objective photo-graphic evidence, removes the relevance of speaker intention and bias. The photos speak authoritatively and independently about the age of bruising. He merely animates or passes on inanimate information contained in the photo, allowing the inanimate object to author its own inanimate message. His strategy attempts to foster the impression that both he and the jurors will reach the same conclusion, a conclusion that emerges as a joint construction instead of a unilateral decision; once the jurors look at the photos they will see what Black sees. As we will see shortly, Black uses multimodal polyrhythms – or repetitive parallelisms in speech that co-occur with repetition in gesture and motion – as a persuasive device to drive his instructions to the jury on how to interpret the bruises.

Rhythmic Integration of Gesture and Speech

Whether in politics, religion, or law, poetic repetition represents a distin-guishing feature of persuasive oratory. In Jakobson's (1960: 356) classic formulation, the poetic function differs from other functions such as refer-ence, phatic, emotive, etc. and elevates the aesthetic dimension of language to a position of discursive prominence, highlighting language form over content to "focus on the message for its own sake." Along similar lines, conversation analysts using experimental design discovered that famous orators used metricalized patterns in the form of three-part lists to "strengthen, underline and amplify almost any kind of message" (Atkinson 1984: 60) and that such rhythmically recurring segments were much more persuasive than speech delivered without them (Heritage and Greatbatch 1986). Repetition or repetition with variation – metrical organization like parallelism – in phonological, morphological, or syntactic structure consti-tutes a major mechanism for emphasizing significant points of evidence in legal argument, as in the following lines from our example (more refined transcription from Excerpt 1 here to include all the relevant gestures).

```
13   Is this a          reddish              bruise ?
     [((beats photo))  [((beats photo))  [((beats photo))
     [((takes another step toward jury))
     [((vertical/forward focus movement starts))
```

```
14  Is this purplish
            [((beats photo))
15  Is this an ugly                        nasty
               [((beats photo))        [((beats photo))
16  bruise      that           one          gets (.)
    [((beats    [((beats ))    [((beats     [((beats
       photo))   photo))          photo))     photo))
17  for                   falling              down with
    [((beats photo))      [((beats photo))   [((beats photo))
    [((arm recalibration))][((vertical forward focusing
                             ends after "falling"))
18  three hundred              pounds of
    [((beats photos in left  [((beats photos in left
       and right hand))          and right hand))
19  weight?
    [((beats photos in left and right hand))
20  on the lawn?
    [((beats photo))
21                              (1.6)
    [((sweeps the photo from right to left laterally
       across jury members))
    [((sweeping occurs after the 1.6 second pause))
    [((Black maintains gaze on jury))
```

In this transcript, Black uses syntactic, morphological, and phonological repetition to develop the color coding sequence and emphasize its significance for the "collision" between Smith and Bowman. He does so along several dimensions. First, he recruits three *yes-no* polar interrogatives (*Is this*) with inverted copula and deictic in clause initial position (lines 13, 14, and 15) to create a parallel structure consisting of rhythmic reduction (*is this a reddish bruise, is this purplish*), followed by rhythmic expansion (*is this an ugly nasty bruise*), and its NP complement. Second, his rhythmic fluctuations include embedded repetitions that evaluate the significance of the color scheme. Repetition of the bound morpheme (*reddish, purplish*) in lines 13 and 14, and close front vowel in line 15 (*ugly, nasty*) projects a symbolic parallelism in the recurring couplets, a reflexive logic that intensifies epistemic stance and increases evidential weight. Finally, the shift from color modifiers to twin adjectives results in a shift from color encoding of the bruises to their evaluation, with the evaluative adjectives double functioning as rhythmic intensifiers modifying the NP (*bruise*) in a logical syllogism. If the bruise is *reddish/purplish* then it would be *ugly/nasty*, and if ugly/nasty, then it would be recent and thus caused by the defendant. On the other hand, if the bruise is not reddish/purplish then it would not be

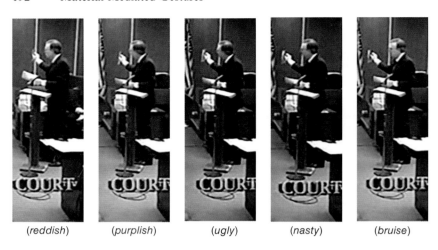

(reddish)   (purplish)   (ugly)   (nasty)   (bruise)

Figures 8.1–8.5: (lines 13–16)

ugly/nasty, and if not ugly/nasty, then it would not be recent and thus not caused by the defendant.

But Black's narrative reveals much more than patterns of recurrence in similar linguistic forms, more than a metricalized poetics involving just language. When considered in more detail, Black's oratorical strategy brings multimodal polyrhythms to bear on the construction of legal evidence, creating a dense harmonic stream in the process. Notice how a repetitive progression of photo beats accompanies his repetitive signs, reinforcing the regularity of the rhythmic pattern. That is to say, Black does not merely point out the object of deictic reference – the bruise in the photo – but uses the photo to beat out its own evidential relevance. His photo beats consist of recurring vertical up-down movements of the photo in the right hand (and displayed toward the jury) that synchronize with turn initial copula, color modifiers, evaluative adjectives, and clause final noun (*bruise*). In line 13, beats co-occur with *reddish* and *bruise*, in line 14 with *purplish*, and in line 15 with both evaluative adjectives and *bruise*. (See Figures 8.1–8.5). In all three lines, the beats emphasize the main points of bruising and instruct the jury to visualize them implicitly from Black's viewpoint.

However, Black's gestures are not mere vertical up-down movements of the photo. Each vertical movement in lines 13–16 is accompanied by a forward progression of incremental fragments toward the jury to convey a powerful focusing effect. The gestural phrase starts with the arm bent at the elbow and photo projected toward the jury box. With each minute gestural increment the arm is progressively expanded in a forward motion until almost fully extended. In fact, by the time the contrapuntal motion decays and splinters into the *that*-clause expansion, the photos are only a few feet from the jury box, well past the speaking podium. Notice how the Figures in 8.1–8.5 inch ever closer toward alignment with the flag and move past the vertical line in the wall partition.

Consider the level of delicate and precise synchronization of the gesture-speech ensemble as his arm unfolds. On the activity verb (*gets* in line 16), Black's arm appears fully extended, yet with more to say he runs into a problem. How can he continue progressive movement of the photo after reaching full arm extension? As a solution, on *for falling* he retracts and recalibrates the arm to re-extend it and prolong the focusing effect (which ends on line 17). In a masterful display of harmonic nuance, he thereby continues forward progression of the photo to foreground the progressive color encoding sequence, a dynamic parallelism in the twin motifs! By the time the photo display decays and reaches *bruise* in line 16, the photos are only a short distance from the jury box. Thus, just as the text expands horizontally (over the clause) and vertically (across narrative lines), so too does the gestural incorporation of material objects vary and expand along the visual axis. This shows how such object incorporation not only highlights but also modulates the significance of evidence by varying its form and intensity in the speech-gesture ensemble.

After Black terminates the multidimensional beats he resurrects vertical beats that synchronize with the *that*-complement in line 16. But toward the end of the clause he modulates intensity of the beat gestures once again in lines 18 and 19 with two-handed vertical beats that build a crescendo on *three hundred pounds of weight*. In this beating form, he holds the dormant photos in the left hand with the arm bent at the elbow, while the right hand directs the "active" photo toward the jury, such that both move up and down simultaneously to land on constituents of the quantifier (*three hundred, pounds,* and *weight*, with increased stress and loudness on *weight*), and thus emphasize the force directed at Bowman. According to Ferre (2014: 48), this shift in gesture "focalizes" the shift in the main point of emphasis, thus linking photo evidence to the representation of the collision. In line 20, he returns to the solo photo beat but here it possesses higher elevation on the upstroke, and increased acceleration and intensity on the downstroke, to foreground the point of spatial contact (*on the lawn*) and expected embodied outcome. He then sweeps the photo laterally along the jury box after a 1.6-second pause as if to engage each individual juror and further personalize the photo evidence. (See Figures 8.6 and 8.7).

More theoretically, if gesture functions in both language production and listener comprehension, then it may also aid in argument construction and

Sweep 1 (occurs during 1.6 second pause)   (Sweep 1 continued)

Figures 8.6–8.7: (line 21)

evaluation by making significant points of evidence more memorable than descriptions without them. Although beating of the photo may not neces- sarily convey propositional meaning or semantic content, it does encode features not expressed by speech alone, such as the manner, degree, and intensity of actions or events. As Kendon (2004: 176) shows, gestures contribute to how the recipients experience the utterance, "allowing it to be apprehended in a more enriched, vivid and evocative way than it would have been without the gesture." In this regard, Black's photo beats not only operate as rhythmic accompaniments to speech but function simul- taneously as a communicative platform – a discursive tool – for organizing and conveying semantic content in a salient succession of sound, imagery, and motion.

Combined with prosodic intensity and tonal variation in speech, these emphatic photo beats foreground the absence of recent bruising based on Black's coding scheme and thus provide a dynamic evaluation of the prosecution's direct evidence testimony about bruise causation (cleverly using the prosecution's claims against them).[4] Moreover, using the photo as an in-motion interpretive template adds to its epistemological facticity while simultaneously projecting Black as a mere animator and relayer of objective facts. Impersonal and formal *one* (line 16), and third person

---

[4] In Labov's (1972: 378–380) classic formulation, gestures along with syntactic, phono- logical, and morphological repetition function as internal or embedded devices that inten- sify the evaluation component of the narrative. More substantively, in lines 13–21 (as well as lines 01–07) these devices converge and merge in polyrhythmic laminations of crescendic energy that build to the main evaluative point in Black's narrative.

exclusive *they* (referring to the prosecution), bounds off the personae of the speech event, selecting jurors as agents of evaluation.

The "yes-no" prefaced interrogatives and final rising intonation limit the jurors' internal response to Black's instructions on how to interpret the coding scheme in such a way as to bolster the facticity of what the photograph displays. The response, then, cannot be one of degree but of certainty. Posing a question to the jurors portrays Black as a mere neutral interlocutor, a relayer footing, further diminishing his legal voice. While the prosecution may *say* what caused the bruising (direct evidence), the jurors have the opportunity to actually see the bruising itself (circumstantial evidence that infers the cause), marking the epistemological and ontological supremacy of observable facts of evidence over subjective impressions.

Another way that these multimodal polyrhythms organize participation roles is by reducing the social distance between interlocutors. Linguistic style may index social status and structure social relations through grammatical, stylistic, and phonological features – contextualization cues – that release indexical meanings of equal access to discursive resources, and thus equal position relative to one another. Most relevant here is the choice of register: language style linked to the legal setting. Just as a lawyer can shift into legalese, reaching a scale-level (Blommaert 2010) inaccessible to lay persons, so too can he or she reduce social distance and renegotiate ratified participants to include him or herself. By choosing a style from the more informal end of the discursive repertoire, one minimizes hierarchy and social distance, signaling egalitarian social relationships even when the participants are positioned asymmetrically in the formal institution (Cameron 2003: 30). In this regard, when Black selects *reddish/purplish* and *ugly/nasty*, synchronizing them with multidimensional photo beats, he produces evidence accessible to all participants and signals that he is in the same knowledge territory as his recipients. Just as germane to these points, Black not only reduces the social distance between him and the jurors, but simultaneously and more literally, reduces physical distance via the focusing effect. More symbolically, the balanced symmetry between Black and the jury mirrors not only the repetitive symmetry in the bound morphemes and close front vowels, but also the balanced alignment between those paired couplets (if the bruises are *reddish/purplish* then they are *ugly/nasty*), a more provincial, less formal description.

Using photo beats, Black coordinates a multidimensional and multimodal integration of sound, space, and motion to display a crucial intertextual leitmotif in the case, pushing it forward and toward the jury as if presenting it to them in a type of polyrhythmic pointing gesture.

Impersonal "one" and reified photos further personalize Black's argument to the jury while simultaneously distancing him as a biased source of information. Creating a subtle tension between the rhythms subliminal urgency and "scientific" objectivity, his virtuosic performance integrates a dialogic interplay of speech, gesture, and object to forge a mutually reinforcing co-construction of participation with the jury, instructing them to see the photos as he sees them.

More generally, we see how gestural rhythms incorporate complex variations and object inflections synchronized with metric modulations of language form. If language includes gesture and language possesses an aesthetic function then gesture – as part of language – also possesses a poetic function, at least in concert with speech. Indeed, it may be problematic to speak of the aesthetic dimension of language without including the integration of speech with gesture in the production of these richly layered and intricately synchronized polyrhythmic textures. We develop this in more sociocultural detail shortly.

Epistemic Stance and Multimodal Conduct

Reconsider the first seven lines of the original example (once again, a more refined transcription from Excerpt 1 to incorporate the relevant gestures).

```
01  Take a look at- (3.1)
                    [((reaches with right hand for photographs
                        on table to right and grabs small stack and
                        removes paper clip during 3.1 pause))
02  what they say are bruises (.)
    [((brings photographs to mid torso while maintaining
        gaze on photos))
03  Take a look- (.) at
    [((selects top photo, then directs it and his gaze at
        the jury members on at))
    [((gaze at top photo))
04  any red (.) or purplish    type        marks (.)
      [((beat))  [((beat))   [((beat))  [((beat))
      ((vertical photo beats w/right hand))
    [((focusing movement starts)) [((focusing movement stops))
05  on this arm (0.7)
    [((sweeps photo horizontally across jury box
        while gazing at photo))
06  Take a look
    [((Black maintains gaze at the photo))
```

```
07   and see if you can see anything there (6.3)
     ((imploring intonation))
     [((gazes at photo on first see then redirects gaze to
     jury and pushes first photo even closer to jury members))
     [((lateral head nod))
```

In lines 01, 03, and 06 Black mobilizes another form of rhythmic organization, repeating the directive phrase (*Take a look*), balanced by a new element consisting of the object of the directive: *what they say are bruises*; *any red or purplish type marks on this arm*, and *see if you can see anything there*. Building off the color coding scheme, Black first directs jurors to *look at* (one of the prototypic directives in English, see Hyland 2002) *the bruises* (in line 02), then employs the quantifier (*any* in lines 04–05), and demonstrative determiner (*this arm*) to ground specific shades of bruising (*red or purplish type marks*) on the victim's arm. Finally, in line 07, he delivers the directive with an embedded challenge consisting of the modal verb, indefinite, and spatial deictic (*can see anything here*). While the *Take a look* phrase means to direct one's attention to the evidence, the directive in line 07 becomes a directive to not merely look, but challenge the prosecution's interpretation of the evidence. That is, the modal signals the (im)possibility of seeing anything resembling the injury described by the prosecution while the perception verb (*see*) recruits more of an instruction to see something specifically compared to *look*. In and through this aesthetic arrangement, Black delivers a fluid transition from directive to challenge and finally to evaluation, decreasing the plausibility of the prosecution's argument in the process.

Moreover, the aesthetic qualities of Black's narrative embed an epistemic coding scheme of considerable interdiscursive (the circulation of different speech events across space and time) and evidential significance. As Goodwin (1994: 606) states, "Coding schemes transform the world into categories." To begin that transformation, Black delivers a metrical pattern organized around the idiomatic directive (*Take a look*) (lines 01–07). Less spectacularly, each segment in the recurring pattern possesses a noticeable ambiguity. The segment in line 01 seems to propose that although there are marks on Bowman's arm, those marks are not necessarily bruises. On the other hand, the marks could be bruises but not those that fit into the red-purple recent bruising category. In line 003, Black becomes more specific. The photo reveals *marks* on the arm but these do not fit into either the *red* or *purplish* category. Finally, the indefinite (line 07) alludes, first, to the absence of any marks or bruises on the arm and, second, to marks or bruises that cannot be classified as red or purplish in the coding scheme. Although Black's coding scheme is quite ambiguous, it takes on immense intertextual significance by transforming colors into categories, a sociocultural process that turns signs on the body into legally relevant events and identities – into evidence.

In terms of epistemicity, Black's coding scheme constitutes an interpretive template for shaping and evaluating evidence – for organizing and distributing legitimate knowledge. Just as impressive, while the template emerges as a unilateral product of adversarial partisanship and epistemic asymmetry, Black naturalizes it as objective, modulating his institutional status and reifying the scheme as an evidential substrate for categorizing colors on the body.

But this process accomplishes more than mere color categorization; it contextualizes legally relevant events and identities associated with those colors (such as the alleged collision on the lawn). As the lines unfold, Black produces a reflexive relationship between each *Take a look* token in the recurring pattern and the coding scheme, a relationship in which each token directive reflexively recalibrates the next as each then reprises the coding scheme, a relationship that reduces the plausibility of the prosecution's evidence while increasing the case for the defense. The marks could be bruises but not evidentially relevant ones; these only emerge from Black's coding scheme.

In a more provocative vein, Black's coding scheme forecloses and preempts other possible schemes and trades on a linguistic ideology of coding that stipulates a determinate algorithm for inclusion of tokens into the type category (Silverstein 2005). How *reddish* must different shades be to count as an instance of red, especially when one considers the fuzzy nature of their non-focal boundaries (in contrast to basic focal colors)? How close a fit must exist before we classify the token instances under auspices of Black's coding scheme? Perhaps he selects only the least purplish or reddish photos? What if the color shades are less conclusive than he indicates? Moreover, while he focuses on the evaluation of the color as *ugly* or *nasty*, which implies age, this erases other descriptions beyond coloration such as the shape, size, and location of the bruise. In essence Black's coding scheme constitutes an epistemic engine for producing the legitimacy of evidential claims, an underlying technique of power that sets the criteria for determining what counts as evidence of recent bruising. And for coding to work persuasively, jurors must assume the legitimacy of Black's scheme as it percolates from one speech event to the next.

One method through which that raw data works up to categorial status occurs when Black synchronizes multidimensional photo beats with the main evidential points in line 04 (*red, purplish, type*, and *marks*) – beating

Figure 8.8: line 04 (beat with photo on *type*) (same as Figures 8.1–8.5, lines 13–16).

the photo up-down and forward in a polyrhythmic progression of short focusing increments toward the jury (see Figure 8.8; these are the same focusing beats we saw in Figures 8.1–8.5, lines 13–16). Just as each up-down beat moves forward in progressive increments, so too does each recurring unit in the syntactic pattern intensify its epistemological and metrical drive toward an evaluative crescendo. This demonstrates in vivid detail how multimodal and transitory polyrhythms figure prominently in organizing the coding scheme.

As we have seen, Black modulates his beating gesture (line 05) with a lateral sweep of the photo across the jury box, along with a gaze shift in the same direction to engage virtually each individual juror – synchronizing gaze, photo beats, and the sweeping motion. But notice something else about Black's gaze, something just as crucial to the status of his utterance. When he directs gaze to the photograph on *Take a look* (lines 03 and 06), he indexes epistemic stance by projecting a lesser degree of certainty about the photos, a process that transforms the multimodal environment as follows.

Like other multimodal resources, gaze contextualizes a distinct organization of participation. Black's gaze to the photograph on *Take a look* (lines 03 and 06) signals that he does not possess existing knowledge or information that is being discussed. In Goodwin's (1981: 149–166) terms, Black marks himself, as well as the jury, as "unknowing recipients" with less knowledge in this epistemic balancing act. His gaze at the photograph signals the relevance of a topic-invoked participation framework: that is, those who have access to information. Indeed, epistemic stance can be dissembled by a person to appear more or less knowledgeable than s/he really is to accomplish a given strategic task. Through his gaze, Black fosters the impression of a lesser epistemic stance, one that simultaneously privileges the epistemologically informative and arguably objective power of the photograph. Epistemic stance recalibrates the status of both the interlocutor as well as the photograph. Further, gaze partitions the relevant division of participant labor to those who have knowledge of an event – those with more or less certainty – and those who do not, reorganizing participation and reconstituting the local order not as epistemic asymmetry between attorney and jurors, as one might expect in a courtroom, but as symmetrical with co-equal epistemic domains. As Goodwin (2007) demonstrated, the structure of situated activity organizes and orchestrates social roles, with the categories of person and their position relative to one another marked in the theater of storytelling. Here we see how multimodal resources push against structurally endowed positions, placing relevant participants in an equal epistemic domain.

Additionally, just as gaze indexes epistemic stance, so too do objects in the multimodal ensemble. When Black gazes at the photo on the directive (see Figure 8.10) he orients to its evidential and interactional relevance, increasing epistemic stance and evidential status by deferring to the epistemological privileged status of the photo over subjective impression.[5] When gaze at the photo co-occurs with the subsequent beating gesture – with the photo held up in the display mode – we see how speech, gaze, gesture, and object reflexively elaborate one another in the production of evidential weight. Gaze at an object shows it deserves special evidentiary status by drawing attention to it; speech-synchronized gestures sweep participants along in a trance-like aura of involvement through multidimensional polyrhythmic movements; and materiality moves evidence from

---

[5] Goodwin (1994) observes how "seeing" and analyzing events in the domain of professional scrutiny is socially organized relative to a particular social group, constituting what he terms "professional vision." "All vision is perspectival and lodged within endogenous communities of practice" (ibid: 606) whereby the object of analytic focus emerges through a set of discursive practices. And de Jorio (2000: 72) writes "when someone wishes to call attention or another to some object, if he looks at it, he will explain his ideas to him with his eyes." Black's gaze shift to the photograph in his hand allows the photo to speak authoritatively, rendering Black a mere animator/relayer of the objective information contained in the photo. His gaze, then, positions him to see the same information contained in the photograph that is made available to the jury. His discursive (or more accurately multimodal) maneuvering erases his partisan role as well as any perceptual ambiguities held by jurors – organizing and controlling the perception of events favorable for the defense. His redirection of gaze and relocation of the photo toward the jury, however, positions Black to see how the jury is taking into account what he has just vocalized for them. This joint attention takes structurally different actors and reconstitutes them as they carry out joint courses of action – seeing the photograph together and reaching a conclusion as a projection of joint construction.

Figure 8.9: (line 01 reaches for photos and grabs small stack during pause).

Figure 8.10: (line 03 selects and gazes at top photo on directive).

subjective impression and biased intent to an impression managed object of party neutral facticity.

At a finer level of granularity, in lines 01, 03, 06, and 09, Black begins each utterance with the *Take a look* directive that co-occurs with movement to fetch a stack of photos from the evidence table (line 001), followed by gaze at the photos (lines 06, 09, and 10) (see Figures 8.9 and 8.10). Moreover, the movements in lines 01, 03, and 09 possess distinct implications for turn trajectory. In line 01, Black's utterance consists of a cutoff on *at* and an ensuing 3.1-second pause as he retrieves the photos; in line 03, it contains a cutoff and prosodic intensity on *look* and short micro pause as he selects the relevant photo and maneuvers it into position for inspection; and in line 09 it

Figure 8.11: (line 07 redirects gaze and pushes photo even closer to jury).

co-occurs with two micro pauses and vowel elongation on the copula as he gazes at and picks up the relevant photo. Each perturbation in speech delivery displays how objects as communicative action intrude on turn construction and design, delaying, shaping, and recalibrating the utterance to coordinate a joint focus of attention that directs the jurors to the object.

The cutoff in line 01 delays and extends the speech segment until the proper photograph is selected, with his speech resuming once the proper display is chosen. When Black directs his gaze at the photographs at strategic times it allows him to fracture participation and signify epistemic stance. Consider the hypothetical question: Why would Black look on the directive *take a look* if he already possesses certain knowledge about what the photo displays? His speech perturbation in the form of a cutoff fosters the impression that his utterance is informed only through the objective information contained in the photo. Black's gaze, as we have seen, marks him as a recipient of the speech, which, of course, is his speech. The interaction of speech and gaze with the photo allows him to take multiple alignments simultaneously – as animator and relayer as well as a partici-pant in concert with the jury. Just as Black synchronizes a delicate inte-gration of speech, gaze, and photo gesture, so too does he simultaneously synchronize a relational position with the jury as an unknowing recipient.

Black employs one other rhetorical device to signal the shift from directive to evaluation. On the directive (line 06 *Take a look*), he thrusts the photo toward the jury in a fast motion (with arm extended) (*see* Figure 8.11). On the first perception verb (*see*) he delivers a series of micro lateral head nods that continue to the second perception verb (*see*). The head nods intensify his evaluation in the challenge, a negative assessment emblem or conventionalized gesture that co-occurs with transition from *look* to *see*. The lateral head nods and beat gestures function to frame speech and contribute to the significance of the utterance of which they are a part by showing a kind of move being undertaken by a turn at talk (see Kendon 2004: 281 on the performative function of gestures). In this instance, the lateral head nod functions – in concert with gaze and speech – not as a conversational device to elicit a response from a recipient (as in a vertical nod), but as a metapragmatic instruction on how to interpret bruises on the victim's body (see McClave 2000; Aoki 2011), an injection of crescendic energy that signals the climax of the parallel structure.

In this section we have seen how epistemic stance and evidence converge and merge in and through a polyrhythmic and multimodal cascade of coding practice, gaze, and photo beats. Indeed, by anchoring the photo in this metrical design, Black produces a rhetorical practice of considerable complexity, an evidential fusion of legal and persuasive action designed to shape the perception of the jury. More substantively, the sociocultural shaping occurs in the intertextual and interdiscursive circulation of the photographs from the police at the hospital to the prosecuting attorney and defense attorney in the trial. The coding scheme not only links different speech events together but critically evaluates them by placing Black's version in a position of epistemological prominence while leaving only an impoverished evidential residue for the prosecution. As this happens, we observe that evidence does not merely interpret itself. Evidential sense only emerges as the attorney foregrounds its significance through synchronization of the coding scheme with the multimodal ensemble, letting jurors infer circumstantial evidence but only after he steers their interpretation in a particular direction.

Transcript Gestures

An ironic aspect of the Kennedy Smith rape trial, at least from a legal perspective, involved the quantity and quality of Bowman's police statements. There were five taped police statements, and their content provided the defense with material to construct ulterior motives for fabricating the charge: that Bowman hated men because of a prior relationship with an ex-boyfriend and father of her child. In an interview with Black after the trial he stated: "We were very fortunate to have five taped statements. They sounded like a session between a psychiatrist and patient more than a police officer and a witness to a crime" (see Matoesian 2001: 21).

In this final part of the chapter, we analyze how Black constructs ulterior motives through an interdiscursive balance of speech, gaze, and material mediated gestures, and how the relevance of putative mental predicates emerges in and through multimodal conduct.

Excerpt 2   56 seconds total

```
01   Look at what she sa::ys (.) about men (4.3)
            [((gets transcript during 4.3 pause))
02   In trying to understand her motivation (1.2)
     you have to take a look at- (0.5)
     [((thumbing through transcript))
03   some of the things that she said (.)
     [((thumbing through transcript continued))
04   On April first (1.5) she was asked questions (.)
     about that (1.2)
     [((thumbing through transcript continued))
05   And she sai:d (3.0) that her last relationship (.)
     [((holds transcript in right hand/rests left hand on podium))
     [((gaze to transcript))  [((gaze to jury))
06   she felt abandoned (.)
        [((gaze to transcript))
07   that it was a pretty harrowing experience (2.1)
08   that- anger built up
     [((hand off podium/grips transcript with two hands))
09   I
     [((gaze to jury))
     [((material mediated gesture or mmg with 2 hands))
10   didn't   feel    I         could    trust    men
     [((mmg*))][((mmg))  [((mmg))  [((mmg))  [((mmg))][((mmg))
                              (1.5)
                              [((gaze to transcript))
11   and that I was pretty a::ngry at them (1.0)
                      [((turns page on transcript))
12   I actually didn't see              what    wo::rth
                      [((gaze to jury))  [((mmg))    [((mmg))
13   (.) that          they         had
        [((mmg))      [((mmg))      [((mmg))
     (1.4)
     [((gaze to transcript))
```

```
14   They really didn't do::: that much (1.1)
                 [((removes left hand from
                 transcript/places it on podium))
15   I don't trust men
           [((mmg with right hand only))
                 [((lowers transcript in right hand
                    to side/redirects gaze to jury))
                 (2.1)
                 [((brings transcript up to mid torso,
                    gripped with both hands))
16   Look to see (0.9)
            [((dg*=deictic gesture))
17   what- (.)      what         he::r   (0.8) mental status is (.)
     [((dg))        [((dg))      [((dg))        [((dg))
18   See            what's       in her mind (8 second pause)
     [((dg))        [((dg))      [((dg))
```

((each gesture in 16-18 is a left hand deictic gesture with fingers spread
and tensed that lands on the top of the transcript. Transcript is held flat
and facing upwards in the right hand palm up))

In the previous sections we demonstrated how the attorney sets the
aesthetic coordinates of speech by using photo beats to simultaneously
engage the jury and point out features of evidential significance. We
analyzed how these interwoven gestures shape the relevance of material
objects as contingent pieces of legal knowledge. In this final segment, we
will see how the attorney uses transcript beats to display how evidence
of assault must be inscribed not only on the body (as we will see in
Chapter 9), but also *in* the mind of the victim. In a much more allusive
vein, Black needs to link Bowman's words to false motivation for the
charges, such as a woman scorned or an enduring disposition as a man-
hater, etc. Why? Her negative sentiments about men might be warranted after being sexually assaulted by a man just a few hours prior
to the interview. How does Black channel the interpretive frame to
motivation for fabricating the charges instead of, for example, rape
trauma syndrome?

Black's initial utterance in line 01 starts with the prepositional verb
(*Look at*) that directs the jury's attention *to what* [Bowman] *sa::ys about
men* and uses the lengthy pause to fetch the police transcript from the other
side of the courtroom. Movement to retrieve the transcript signals something out of the ordinary, something significant enough to read verbatim,
and thus enhances its epistemological value. Lines 02 and 03 unpack the

puzzle in line 01 by linking "men" to motivation, and deploy second person generic, partitive, and expository directive to allow the jury to imagine the statements from a particular frame and guide the interpretive process (*you have to take a look at some of the things she said*) (see van der Houwen and Sneijder forthcoming: 32–33).

While leafing through the transcript in lines 02–04, Black asserts that Bowman was *asked questions (.) about that* but it is not clear what the demonstrative "that" refers to: men or motivation or some of the things she said, or perhaps all of these? Just as puzzling, did the police detectives ask questions about men and/or motivation for fabricating the charges? And if they did pose such questions, then why? For if the police did question Bowman along those lines, it could lead to the inference that they were suspicious of her claims. On the other hand, if Bowman volunteered the information it might lead to questions about her mental status either before or after the incident. We will return to these interviews and Black's comments about the psychiatric speech event later.

For now, he begins a litany of unsavory statements attributed to Bowman from the written transcript, and on line 05 he reaches the page containing her sentiments about men. He synchronizes the indirect quote with gaze at the transcript followed by a quick gaze shift to the jury on the *that*-complementizer, and return gaze to the transcript on the affect verb (*felt*). Notice his selection of emotionally charged fragments to embed in the narrative – noun, phrasal verb, affective adjectives (*abandoned, harrowing, anger, built-up*), and intensifying adverb (*pretty*) – and signal her negative stance toward men.

In line 08, Black grips the transcript with two hands and on line 09 changes from indirect to direct quotes of Bowman's speech, a transition accompanied by gaze to the jury and a noticeably marked shift in pitch register superimposed over the quote: *I didn't feel I could trust men.*

There's something else that accompanies the transition. In line 09 Black synchronizes a series of two-handed gestures while holding the transcript over each word in the direct quote (see Figures 8.12–8.15). These *object-mediated gestures* consist of low elevation peaks, increased acceleration, and micro distance between elevation peak on the upstroke and nadir of the downstroke, to animate the sense and punctuate the significance of each word in the quote. Put more prosaically, he beats out the importance of her words with her words.

If we consider the buildup to the material mediated gestures, notice how the indirect quotes on lines 05, 06, and 07 consist of a repetitive sequence of *that*-complementizers, or what van der Houwen (2013; van

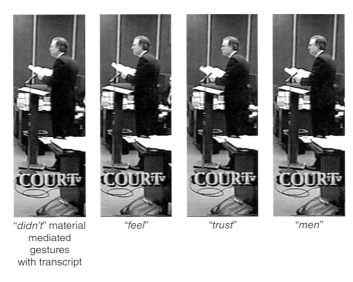

"*didn't*" material mediated gestures with transcript   "*feel*"   "*trust*"   "*men*"

Figures 8.12–8.15: line 10

der Houwen and Sneijder, forthcoming) refers to as a "pre-quote sequence." Modifying her concept slightly to fit this case, the repetitive *that*-clauses constitute an iconic buildup representing Bowman's *build-up of anger* (line 008) that culminates in the direct quote and accelerated (fast tempo) material mediated gestures. That is, build up in sequential intensity to the direct quote(s) and transcript beats appears iconic of Bowman's buildup of anger toward men – a buildup that explodes in an ulterior motive for fabrication of the rape charge (*I didn't feel I could trust men*). At that moment, distribution of gaze, buildup of sequential intensity, and unfolding material conduct intersect in a dynamic performance of motivational symbolism.

During the 1.5-second pause Black shifts gaze from the jury to the transcript and continues the second clause of the direct quote, turning a page of the transcript over the intensifier and attitudinal stance adjective (*pretty* **a::ngry** in line 11). Turning the page and "reading" gaze shows that Black has to reference the transcript for (author-principal) Bowman's words, and thereby augment the facticity of his argument by not just saying but reading her words, branching off into the even more passive animator footing in the process or just reporting her words. Here we can see in vivid detail how actions incorporating material objects, in concert with gaze and motion, build emergent forms of participation in Goffman's (1981) sense.

In lines 12, 14, and 15 the moving litany of direct quotes continues with the epistemic stance adverbs (*actually* and *really*), and *do*-copula plus contracted negative (*didn't see, didn't do:::*,and *don't* **trust**) that ground Bowman's emotional state. Notice in particular how *actually* (*I actually didn't see what* **wo::rth** *(.) that they had*) is used emphatically to indicate "something which is in sharp contrast with expectations" (Carter and McCarthy 2006: 28). On the perception verb (*see*) in line 12, Black returns gaze to the jury and begins the second series of object-mediated gestures synchronized over the *wh*-clause. The material mediated gestures here, as well as lines 09–10, synchronize with distribution of gaze and prosodic stress over the quote to mark affectively charged passages of evidential significance. In both instances, the gestural incorporation of material objects synchronizes with distribution of gaze, prosody, and direct quotes in an arrangement of emphatic rhythm.

At the 1.4-second pause he returns gaze to the transcript while in line 14 he removes the left hand from the transcript. In line 15 he concludes with the final element of the repetitive arrangement (*I don't* **trust** *men*) with a single right hand material mediated gesture (on **trust**), and then lowers the transcript in the right hand to his side, and redirects gaze to the jury.

We mentioned previously that we would return to Black's comment about Bowman's psychiatric speech event. After the flurry of direct quotes, Black pauses for 2.1 seconds and then moves the transcript to mid-torso level in front of the body to contextualize an evaluative summary. The summation materializes in lines 16–18 with two directives that implore the jury to inspect Bowman's *mental status* and **mind**. The first directive mobilizes two perception verbs, *look to see*, the second repeats *see* in clause initial position. While gazing at the jury, Black's left hand points to and beats on the transcript (held flat on the right hand palm) during both directives (*Look to see (0.9) what- (.) what he::r (0.8) mental status is (.), and See what's in her* **mind** in Figures 8.16–8.19). Each hand-hitting-the-transcript gesture consists of accelerated movement (once again consisting of micro spacing between elevation peak at the upstroke, and nadir of the downstroke) repeating over both lines. What is most interesting, however, is not just the repeating movement but also the repeating shape of the hand in the movement. The palm faces downward with the fingers spread slightly in a tensed shape for hyper emphasis. The rhythmically organized "stressed" fingers emphasize the "stressed" point, demonstrating how the form of the hand signifies the function.

In so doing, Black integrates pointing with rhythmic gestures to simultaneously locate and emphasize Bowman's mental status. More theoretically,

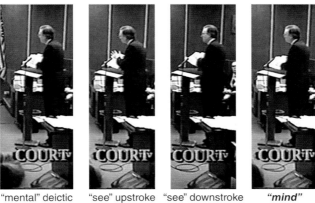

"mental" deictic   "see" upstroke   "see" downstroke   *"mind"*
gesture

Figures 8.16–8.19: lines 17–18

pointing to and beating on the transcript displaces Bowman's mind as the
focus of the discourse and recalibrates the transcript as the emphatic object
of deictic reference, that is, as the locus of Bowman's mental status. This
demonstrates in vivid detail how gestures can be embedded in and fused
with improvisational forms of the discourse use of objects. As deictic
rhythms converge and merge at point of contact with the transcript, they
ground Bowman's psychological state – her mind in the transcript – and
Black's speech in the material world.[6]

Relating this to imagistic gestures, Lakoff and Johnson (1980) argue
that ontological metaphors like "the mind is an entity" afford us a way of
viewing or conceptualizing experiences, emotions, and events as entities or
substances, transforming the abstract into the concrete. Similarly, Müller
(2008: 75) refers to "in the mind" as a metaphor in which "non-physical or
abstract objects are containers." In this regard, ontological metaphors
locate or ground abstract entities in the physical domain through the
imposition of spatialized boundaries. Here, the mind is bounded by a
surface and located in the transcript. Viewing her mind as an entity that
can be seen, identified, and referenced enables Black to assign an artificial
location to an abstract concept. That her mind exists in the transcript

---

[6] Hindmarsh and Heath (2000) also discuss how speakers coordinate gaze, gesture, and
speech as resources to locate an object and guide interlocutors toward the object of deictic
reference, similar to Black locating the "mind" in 8.16–8.19.

allows him to refer to her mind as a tangible and enduring object, one that provides visual structure to the jury's experience.

Still, more is displaced and objectified than the mind. As the mind materializes in transcript and gesture, we see motivation to fabricate the charge as a socially organized and emergent phenomenon, rather than some inner springboard of social action, a process we can summarize as follows.

First, he channels her motivation into a personality trait by using present tense (lines 16–18): *Look to see (0.9) what- (.) what he::r mental status is (.)* and *See what's in her **mind***. There is no way he could use the past tense and say, for example, "Look to see what her mental status was" or "See what was in her mind," because this could support the rape trauma argument. Consequently, her negative sentiments toward men were present before, during, and after the rape incident as an enduring personality trait.

Second, he conceals an interdiscursive construction of identity and textuality by picking out epistemic and affective stance markers (*pretty a::ngry*, *pretty harrowing*, *actually*, *really*, *feel*, *felt*) to index her state of mind. However, the mind in the transcript emerges in the first place from the way he decontextualizes fragments from police statements and re-contextualizes them selectively in the narrative.

Third, his gestures point to and beat out displacement of mind to transcript, giving it a corporeal quality that he can reference as an object. In a "case study" of impression management, Black's reading of the transcript not only erases the police questions that elicited Bowman's sentiments about men, but also conceals any reason the police would pose motivational issues in the first instance (assuming they did), yet leaving intact the unsavory inferences triggered from such questions. That is to say, Black bleaches indexical particulars from both the historical speech event and current courtroom event, a process that leaves only an entex-tualized residue – turning talk into text and then back into talk – in the "animated" transcript.

More fundamentally, like survey and other forms of interview, the police interviewer is treated as a passive harvester of information com-pared to the active, cognitively rich interviewee, which erases the inter-viewer's dynamic role in co-constructing the interview. As Komter (2006: 222) notes, the interviewer's questions are "noticeably absent in this text." Hence a "double" erasure occurs when Black superimposes the same linguistic ideology of interviews as reference in the courtroom: that is, erasure in the historical interview speech event and erasure in the current here and now courtroom.

Finally, all the direct and indirect quotes appear on the same page, except the line where Black turns the page. This fosters the impression that Bowman's statements in the police interview consisted of monologue (see Komter 2006: 222), even though in reality Black took disparate fragments of a fragmented text (the transcript) from a fragmented police interview, and laced them together in a seamless stream of motivational monologue – and not just any monologue but one that resembles a psychiatric or therapeutic speech event. In this strategic maneuver, he fosters the impression that his monologue is iconic of Bowman's speech in the historical speech event (the police interview), insulating his own voice and evaluation in the process. That is, Black not only does something with Bowman's speech through direct and indirect quotes, but also bleaches out any difference in his construction of the police interview, psychiatric session, and current here and now courtroom narrative. Just as Black orchestrates embedded forms of participation in a seamless monologue, so too do the repetitive pointing gestures orchestrate a seamless rhythm for emphasis: that Bowman is an unstable man-hater. The material mediated and repetitive pointing gestures authorize the circulation of interdiscursive speech events in a way that supports the attorney's evaluative stance.

Conclusion

Closing argument represents the culmination of the legal case in the adversary system of justice. For attorneys, it provides an opportunity to showcase their oratorical and persuasive skills, and to manage the dilemmas of objectivity versus partisanship. We have shown how an attorney mobilizes pronouns, poetic repetition, and epistemicity as persuasive strategies of inclusion, exclusion, and involvement to instruct the jury on how to interpret objects of legal evidence while simultaneously managing those discursive dilemmas in a delicate impression management performance.

That performance involves much more than the verbal dimension of language. Poetic eloquence in multimodal performance – the temporal synchronization of speech, objects, and gesture – attempts to instruct the jury on the significance of medical and motivational evidence for the crime of sexual assault. Indeed, we have shown that beat gestures involve much more than simple "flicks" of the hand or finger. As Ferre (2011: 11–12) discovered, beats play "different roles at different levels," and here they anchor the circulation of photos and transcripts across variant speech events and set powerful coding and motivational schemes into interdiscursive motion – moving across space, time, and motion in the rhythms of sociocultural practice. In fact, it may be misleading to speak of beats as an autonomous and distinct gestural entity, for the gestures here appear as part of a multimodal and multidimensional delivery system consisting of objects, gaze, and motion in a temporally synchronized and rhythmically integrated oratorical performance.

9   Rhythmic Gestures and Semanticity

In this final chapter we continue our explorations of rhythmic gestures in closing argument and raise an issue posed by Kendon in Chapter 1. In his critique of McNeill, he (Kendon 2004: 103) stated: "it is sometimes quite difficult to decide whether a given unit of hand action should be considered a 'beat' or a gesture with some imagistic features. Often it must be considered to be both."

How do speakers invest certain hand movements with "both" properties, as Kendon notes? How do speakers not only mark speech rhythms but also convey imagistic content – and do so simultaneously? In the previous chapter we saw how evidence of the assault, for the defense, should be inscribed both *on the body* and *in the mind* of the victim. In this chapter, we investigate how lexico-syntactic parallelism in speech co-occurs, first, with finger movements, and second, with gestures in which one hand pounds the palm of the other hand in a fist-hitting gesture to explain *how* and *why* evidence of the sexual assault should be found *on* the victim's body. We show that the latter gestures not only mark significant points of evidence with staccato-like movements, but simultaneously convey semantic imagery, augmenting content through incisive visual actions.

Finger Movements

In our first segment, the defense attorney recounts crucial aspects of evidence and testimony from direct and cross-examinations: that the victim was running away from the defendant and then tackled on the lawn.

(Segments 1–3 =62 seconds total)

*vc = parallel vertical chop

ig = interdigital gesture (tip of right index finger lands on and ascends up the fingers of the left hand)

^ig = intradigital gesture (right hand index finger latched onto the little finger of the left hand where rhythm is beat out with latching motion)

Segment 1

```
01  She's running across the lawn at full tilt (0.6)
        [((vc*))                        [((vc))
02  She's being chased by a man (0.5)
            [((vc))      [((two open palms in front of
                                body))
03  who is six foot two and uh half (0.8)
    [((ig on little finger))
04  a hundred and ninety- five      pounds (0.9 )
     [((^ig))    [((^ig))[((^ig))[((^ig))
     ((^IG on index finger still latched on little finger))
05  who has-
    [((downstroke to unfurled ring finger abort))
06  as Miss Lasch                   brought out
    [((right hand lateral gesture))   [((ig onset on ring
                                            finger))
07  size eleven and a half shoe (0.9)
        [((ig downstroke on ring finger))
08  who tackles her (0.6)
    [((ig on middle finger))
09  and hits the ground. (0.8)
        [((two handed vc))
10  She is on the      bottom (.) and absorbs
        [((hitch))   [((vc))          [((vc))
        ((the "hitch" or perturbation above is a
         resynchronizing gesture))
11  all the force (1.0) of that event. (1.1)
    [((vc)) [((vc)) ((post-stroke hold))
```

In line 01, the defense attorney initiates his argument with *She's running across the lawn at full tilt*, which co-occurs with two right-handed vertical chopping gestures on both the stressed verb and sentence final adverbial, the main points of emphasis. At the beginning of line 02, he begins a much more complex construction that continues to line 09: *She's being chased by a man*. Once again, we see a right-handed chopping gesture align with the action verb *chased*, but he then switches to a two-hand, open palm gesture (at an oblique angle) on the phrase *by a man*. Here, it is held horizontally at mid-torso and with palms facing upward (at a 45-degree angle), depicting a "man/woman" in which the "male" hand is introduced to accompany the given female hand used in the single-handed chopping gestures. In other words, when talking of a single person, a single hand is deployed. Upon introduction of a second person, a second hand appears to accompany the other – depicting aspects of the two-person imagery contained in his speech. In the process, the defense attorney first offers this evidence to the jury, and second (and most importantly), encodes a socially organized and distinctively gendered description through the pronoun and masculine noun.

We see the significance of social organization develop in line 03. Here the attorney selects the passive construction as the syntactic platform to launch a succession of markedly stressed *wh*-relatives, listing the size, weight, and actions of the defendant: *who is*, *who has-*, and *who tackles* (lines 03–09). Moreover, each relative co-occurs with an ascending progression of finger movements (transcribed as "interdigital gesture") in which the tip of the index finger on the right hand lands on the tips of the unfurling (from a closed fist) digits of the left hand to accompany the verbal listing of facts (little finger to ring finger, and then middle finger).[1] Moreover, the gesture upstroke occurs on the relative; the downstroke hits the finger on the verb. To reiterate a point from Quintilian (2001: 143), this is "how we tell off arguments on our fingers," what Bulwer (2003: 184–186) refers to as the "dialects of the fingers," or how skilled orators employ digital computations when counting off numbers. More recently and theoretically, Cienki and Müller (2008: 491) mention how "using the fingers of one hand to point to successive fingers on the other hand while listing ideas or making different points represents the metaphor *ideas as objects*." That *listing* is crucial for engaging the jury and involving them in the interpretive process.

Lists represent one of the poetic devices of language, or a "focus on the message for its own sake" (Jakobson 1960: 356) and generally, though not invariably, occur in a rhythmic three-note phrase repeated in different forms (Jefferson 1991). As Atkinson (1984: 60) notes, speakers use lists "to strengthen, underline and amplify almost any kind of message" and indeed Heritage and Greatbatch (1986) found that such devices are much more persuasive than an ordinary sentence (which is why they are characteristic of charismatic speakers). Along similar lines, Tannen (1987: 576) emphasized the role of sound and sense repetition and how it generates a state of persuasive involvement with the hearer – how the circulation of repetitive motifs and patterns "sweeps the hearer or reader along." Still, while researchers have examined lists and repetitive modulation for their persuasive and emotive effect, few studies include how bodily rhythms co-occur with these communicative practices to enhance charismatic effects: how repetitive

---

[1] Lempert (forthcoming, and Lempert and Silverstein 2012:187–189) refers to these as "enumerative" beats.

gestures highlight important evidence to "sweep the hearer along" (see Streeck 2008: 166 and 174, for a notable exception).[2]

With this theoretical point in mind, gestural position moves (in line 03) from open palms to a series of finger movements organized over the *wh*-relatives, the first of which lands on the little finger to emphasize the defendant's height: *six foot two and uh half* (see Figures 9.1 and 9.2). But instead of ascending to the ring finger next, the defense attorney maintains position with the index finger latched on the little finger to construct a pattern of *intradigital* movements, highlighting the defendant's weight (Figure 9.3). Notice how each of the four intradigital movements lands on an explicit point of emphasis (by pressing this finger down each time he mentions a feature): *hundred, ninety, five*, and *pounds*. Just as the attorney's complex clause delivers several embedded *wh*-relatives, so too does the first finger movement launch several intradigital movements governed under its auspices (before ascending to the ring finger). To summarize the difference: Intradigital movements occur with index finger of the RH latched on to the little finger of the LH and beat out rhythm with this latching motion. Interdigital finger movements occur with the index finger of the RH ascending from the little finger to the ring finger, and then to the middle finger of the LH.

But why background such important evidence on a single digit rather than ascending finger by finger up to the ring finger? Intradigital movements disclose the defendant's weight and height in discriminating detail that expands the gestural phrase as the clause is expanded syntactically, expounding an entire idea unit in the process (that is, maintaining height and weight as a unit). At the same time, they preserve the metrical integrity of the impending rhythmic triad (the cardinal arrangement of "threeness") for both the *wh*-relatives and finger movements, synchronizing bodily and verbal conduct in the process.

The second *wh*-relative (line 05) co-occurs with a finger movement ascending from the little to ring finger. However, as this second finger movement reaches its elevation peak prior to the onset of the downstroke, the defense attorney aborts descent and produces a cutoff on the *wh*-relative *who has-*, leaving both the just unfurled ring finger and relative momentarily stranded to accommodate the off-kilter parenthetical in line 06. Notice the delicate online adjustments to forge speech-gesture

---

[2] As Silverstein (1985: 183) and Lempert (2012: 184) note, text-metricalization as poetic organization applies to any linguistic form, not just phonological or prosodic structure. As we have seen and will see, such similarity-driven and perceptually salient patterns of recurrence apply to co-speech gestures as well as speech.

003 "*who*"
interdigital upstroke

003 "*is*" interdigital
downstroke

004 "*a hundred and
ninety-five pounds*"
intradigital x4

006 "as Miss Lasch"
parenthetical or PP

Figures 9.1–9.4

alliance, how both modalities calibrate and recalibrate pace to manage precise synchronization. While progression of the speech-gesture litany is momentarily suspended, it is not abandoned. On the parenthetical, *as Miss Lasch brought out*, the defense attorney produces a lateral open palm motion to the side with the right hand: a side comment and gesture that sweeps it to the side. Simultaneously, the unfurled ring finger on the left hand waits to receive its beat from the right index finger post the parenthetical (see Figure 9.4).

That said, the parenthetical constitutes more than a mere tangential aside. Black recruits prosecuting attorney Lasch's speech to add objectivity to the unfolding list tokens and epistemological weight to his argument. Kendon (2004) refers to this open hand supine gesture as a "palm presentation" or "PP," which shows some spatial inflexion to the side of the speaker's transactional space, a deictically inflected PP referring to Ms. Lasch in a virtual space in which Black is working within. Ironically, Lasch brought out not only shoe size but also weight, height, and athletic prowess at the very outset of her cross-examination of the defendant. Moreover, the objectivity of the parenthetical augments the facticity of the other list tokens since she first brought out this important evidence.

Near the end of the parenthetical, the right hand index finger touches the ring finger of the left hand (on *brought out* in line 06), but the finger movement does not materialize until a push-down on *eleven and a half shoe* in line 07 (see Figure 9.5).

The relative construction culminates with a third finger movement landing on the middle finger in line 08 (the third relative *who tackles her*) and a two hand parallel gesture in line 09 (*hits the ground*), both co-occurring with action verbs (see Figures 9.6 and 9.7). In this instance,

007 "*eleven and a half*   008 "*who tackles* her"   009 "*hits the ground*"
shoe" interdigital   interdigital downstroke   two hand chopping
downstroke   gesture (same gesture
in 010-019)

Figures 9.5–9.7

Black calibrates his utterance so that increased intensity in the historical event coincides with prosodic emphasis synchronized with a more forceful chopping gesture in the current speaking event, adding a level of affective intensity to the narrative not available through speech alone.

The points we can extract thus far reveal that the gesture-speech ensemble creates a polyrhythmic delivery of factual evidence building up to a crescendo. By polyrhythmic we merely refer to first, the repetitive stressed relatives and their co-occurring finger movements, and second, the embedded relatives, intradigital movements, and parenthetical. Notice, in particular, the repetition of stressed relatives that coincide with both intra- and interdigital gestures as they ascend incrementally up (and within) the ladder of the hand, paced by intervals of temporal spacing (the pauses between the relatives in lines 03, 04, 07, and 08). In terms of evidential function, we can see how the speaker accumulates type-token relations by means of these bodily and discursive rhythms. The defense attorney recruits the type "man" along with token (and sub-token) listing of attributes organized around height, weight, and shoe size. With each increment of verbal and gestural listing, he escalates the magnitude of force directed at the small, petite victim who hits the ground, force that culminates in line 09 as the finger movements evolve into two-handed vertical chopping gestures. In this regard the inter- and intradigital movements along with the words associated with them, convey a finer layering of discriminating detail about the type, all with an eye toward the evaluative summary in lines 09–11: *She is on the bottom and absorbs all the force of that event.* That is to say, inter- and intradigital lists cumulate facts of evidence – unfurling digit to digit from the closed fist like the unfurling of hidden facts of evidence – that contextualize forthcoming evaluative inferences, in this instance orchestrated by the two arm vertical gestures superimposed upon the phrases (*on the bottom* and *all the force*), and by shift from passive to active. In more detail, the verb *absorbs* means "integrates a substance into a fabric" (Allerton 2002: 226), and here it emphasizes how Bowman receives all the force between the large defendant on top, and ground on the bottom, as she gets tackled while running at full tilt. Put another way, just as the index finger ascends up the digits of the opposite hand, so too should the force absorbed by the victim increase (later we will see that the consequences of that intense force should be embodied also).

As a further appreciation of its evidential significance, consider the gesture-speech alignment in more detail (in line 10). As Black starts a two-handed chopping downstroke on the locative complement, notice an abrupt stop or hitch – a resynchronizing movement (starts, stops, retracts, and then re-starts) – that recalibrates the downstroke so that it co-occurs precisely with (not before), *bottom*. With these points in mind, we see gesture-speech alignment, and that these gestures vary structurally relative to narrative function: The digital listing gestures accumulate facts of evidence; the ensuing two hand chopping gestures begin to evaluate those facts. Moreover, alignment of stress on the *wh*-relatives and verbs in lines 03, 05, and 08 creates a type of rhythmic balance that is punctuated with gestural emphasis – what Bulwer (2003) refers to as a dialect of the fingers.

In the next segment, we turn to the evidential development and significance of absorbing all this force in the collision.

It's Not a Freeze Frame

In lines 12–16 the defense attorney elaborates the dynamics of absorbing force from line 11. In the process, we can see that the movement of intra- and interdigital gestures (segment one) up the ladder of the hand foreshadows the folk-physics of collision in the ensuing segment.

*vc = parallel vertical chop

Segment 2 (continuation of segment 1)

```
12   Now there' s not uh                    freeze frame here
         [((vc* upstroke))                    [((vc downstroke))
13   You don' t                             just stop (1.1)
         [((vc upstroke))                      [((vc downstroke))
```

```
14  You're going to           sli::de along the ground
        [((vc upstroke))       [((vc downstroke))
15  You're going to           hit that ground with great force
        [((vc upstroke))       [((vc downstroke))
16  There's gonna be          force from both sides (1.4)
        [((vc upstroke))       [((vc downstroke))
```

Line 12 starts with the turn initial discourse marker *Now*, that as Schiffrin (1987: 240) notes, initiates a shift in stance (and a new idea unit), a shift into a full-blown evaluative mode from the accumulation of facts in the prior segment. Black synchronizes the clause using the two-handed vertical chopping gesture (refer back to Figure 9.7) with the upstroke occurring on the existential *There's* and downstroke on the *freeze frame* alliteration.[3]

In line 13, he repeats a fragment of the motif (*stop* replaces *freeze frame*) from the prior clause accompanied by the same chopping gesture. But line 13 involves much more than mere repetition. First, he uses the impersonal pronoun to invite the jury to participate in the collision event and, more importantly, share his version of events to naturalize, conceal, and authorize the facticity of his partisan claims (Siewierska 2004: 212). Second, the discourse particle *just* signals epistemic stance (in addition to its meaning "only"). As Aijmer (2002: 157–159) notes, emphatic *just* "intensifies one's commitment to the proposition" and "tones up an argumentative strategy." Third, and most important, the downstroke that lands on *just stop* reaches to the high mid-torso level (the upper limit of the mid-torso region), and there is a halting motion or marked recoil, as it hits this level, followed by a lengthy clause final pause to convey a quick stopping imagery (see Figure 9.8). Together, multimodal signal streams – rhythmic halting at high mid-torso, recoil at bottom of the downstroke and lengthy pause – represent an iconic imagery of stopping, lending *rhythmic semanticity* to the gesture in addition to and simultaneous with its orthodox rhythmic function.

Such imagery in speech-gesture interplay grounds an intricately balanced opposition of tension and release between lines 12–13 on the one hand, and 14–16 on the other: juxtaposition of negative and positive clauses. As it turns out, the former not only add negative balance to the imminent contrastive structure but also build suspense for a positive resolution. The

---

[3] Non-stressed existential or nonreferential *there* with contracted copula is quite interesting in its own right. As Sasaki (1991) and Huckin and Pesante (1988) found, the existential, among other functions, summarizes and signals new information and/or a series of items forthcoming; all of these unfold in lines 014–016. Along similar lines, the uncontracted negative particle in line 012 also makes the clause more emphatic.

positive component of the contrast – in the parallel clauses – explicates and emphasizes the magnitude of collision under the listing conditions witnessed in lines 01–11. That one does not merely *stop* as if it were some *freeze frame* derives, as we have seen, from the given negative clauses. How does the collision happen? What are the "folk-physics" of tackling?

The second half of the contrastive opposition contains a second impersonal pronoun – once again allowing the jury to stretch out and imagine the event – with the contracted copula, "going-to" future, and vowel stretching on the manner of motion verb (*sli::de*), which in this case would be iconic of "sliding." The second line of the parallel structure repeats with variation and expansion from its predecessor, so that after sliding Bowman *hits that ground*. Notice, in particular, how the expansive component (line 15) includes the evaluative or affective adjective; Bowman does not merely hit the ground as in line 09 but hits *with great force*. And, finally, rhythmic modulation in the third line (line 16) contains the existential, consonant cluster reduction (*gonna*), and resumptive repetition with expansion using the clause final noun from line 15 (*force*) and adverbial (*from both sides*), tweaking the last line with a modulated motif to maintain continuity with the initial pulse of the rhythmic triad. Notice also how lines 14–16 contain repetition of the contracted copula (*You're, You're,* and *There's*). Indeed, we can see how the assault involves not just a collision of mere sliding and hitting. Bowman hits the ground with such great force that she is squished between the ground on the one hand, and the rather large defendant on the other.

Consider the repetition of the two-handed chopping gestures that accompany the emerging parallel lines. Each gesture begins its upstroke on the contracted copula and lands on the stressed verb in lines 14 (*sli::de*) and 15 (*hit*), and noun in 16 (*force*). In line 14, we encounter repetition along both horizontal and vertical axes, as the gesture lands on the *freeze frame* alliteration in a finely articulated interplay of speech and gesture. However, something interesting happens in line 15 with the gesture synchronized with *hit*. This gesture occurs noticeably marked off from the other two-handed vertical gestures, foregrounded against and nestled between the gestures in 14 and 16. To be more precise, it possesses higher elevation on the upstroke, and much greater acceleration on the downstroke, as it reaches depth at the lower torso level. Moreover, there is greater intensity of gestural movement with not only the hands and arms, but also head and upper torso moving forward. Morris (1977: 61) refers to such gestures as head and body batons that possess a "slightly attacking quality" used in "forceful, aggressive statements" (see Figure 9.9).

Here we think of such "batons" rather differently and expand Morris' observations. The defense attorney leans forward to convey another instance

13 *"just stop"*   15 "You're going to *hit*"

Figures 9.8–9.9

of rhythmic semanticity, that is, to visualize "hitting with great force." Although words describe hitting the ground with great force, they fail to visualize what that force looks like. In this sense, the motion of hitting is not conveyed as vividly in language via the contact verb as in gesture. To put this another way, while it is one thing to describe an event occurring *with great force*, it is quite another for recipients to see it visualized at the same time that it is expressed verbally. Gesture multifunctionality picks up the slack on this point in the fine-tuned interplay of speech, gesture, and bodily movement. While rhythmic beats may appear as simple flicks of the hand that merely orchestrate the metapragmatic rhythm of utterances, a concrete analysis reveals much more complexity than prior research has considered, more complexity in both form and function. Indeed, in line 15 we see a poignant illustration of *how rhythmic gestures may, at specific moments, operate simultaneously as both accentuating rhythm and emphasis on the one hand, and capturing imagistic content on the other, demonstrating the relevance of fine-grained analysis of naturally occurring data for the study of rhythmic hand movements in particular and gesture in general.* Following Morris (1977) and Quintilian (2001), the force embodied in the gesture makes the attorney's argument more forceful and conveys a depth of emotion without compromising the sense of objectivity necessary to persuade the jury.

To summarize, in the first segment the defense attorney sets the scale such that the magnitude of the collision can be appreciated, with a detailed listing of facts about weight, height, and size, using gestures to enhance the foregrounding and distinctiveness of each of these features. The second segment explores the "folk-physics" of collision, in which his hand actions are coordinated with his speech in such a way as to provide physical illustrations of sliding, colliding, and hitting with force. In the next segment, the defense attorney turns to the consequences of that collision.

What Happens When Bodies Collide

As we move to the final segment in the progression, we see how the prior two segments contribute to a final crescendo on the consequences of the collision: what *should* happen after such impact.

*vc = parallel vertical chop

fh = horizontal fist hitting gesture where the right hand fist hits the left hand grasping palm

rh = residual hitting gesture where the form of the last hitting gesture is maintained to form two up-down vertical gestures in the hitting gesture position

Segment 3 (continuation of segment 2)

```
17  Now                    you've    heard (1.8) from
    [((vc* upstroke)) [((vc)) [((vc))
    numerous               people (1.7)
    [((vc downstroke))     [((vc))
     ((in the 1.8 pause the upstroke for the next gesture is
       suspended at the elevation peak))
18  this (.8)              principle in science of transfer theory
      [((vc upstroke))[((vc downstroke))      [((vc)  [((vc))
     ((in the .8 pause the upstroke is suspended at the
       elevation peak))
19  What        happens when bodies collide (1.3)
    [((vc))    [((vc))      [((fh))
20  or when a body collides with  other   items  (1.7)
            [((fh))                [((rh)) [((rh))
21  There has to be some evidence of that.
            [((open left hand to the side; open palm
                supine))
```

In line 17, the clause initial discourse marker (*Now*) contextualizes a new progression in Black's narrative, one dealing with the consequences of the collision. He galvanizes the quantifier plus plural noun to signal an interdiscursive connection with prior testimony from *numerous people* who have introduced the scientific theory about the folk-physics of absorbing force from the collision. But these people are not just people. Much more impressively, Black marshals the voices of scientific and forensic experts who have testified about *transfer theory*, or what happens *when bodies collide*. In Goffman's (1981) classic scheme, Black animates the voices of scientific experts who are authors and principals of the scientific theory. In this interdiscursive maneuver, he uses words in the scientific register to confer expertise, and ground his narrative with epistemic authority (*science*, *principle*, and *theory*).

Looking back to include segments 1 and 2, we see how he regiments the narrative into progressively stratified forms of identity and knowledge: First, the prosecuting attorney – eliciting facts that set the scale of magnitude for the collision; second, the impersonal pronoun – inviting the jury to imagine/evaluate the dynamics of the collision; and third, scientific expertise – predicting the embodied consequences of the collision. Each segment reflexively augments the other in the constitution of legal context, producing an objective framework for understanding the consequences of the collision and infusing it into closing narrative.

He unpacks the theory in line 19 and reformulates it in line 20, first from what happens *when bodies collide*, which refers to Smith and Bowman, and second *when a body collides* with *other items*, which refers to Bowman, Smith, and the ground. In the process, he magnifies the physical consequence one should expect from the collision. As usual, Black never fails to miss a "beat" in merging elements of the current speech event with the sequence of physical details in the historical event.

Notice, in particular, the coordinated interplay between speech and gesture as Black fractures space with the hands. In lines 17 to 19 he delivers a series of two-handed vertical chopping gestures that we have seen previously. In lines 17 and 18 he suspends the upstroke on *Now* and *this* at the elevation peak for a marked duration of time to calibrate and recalibrate precise synchronization of the downstroke, so it lands on *numerous* and *principle*, respectively. *This illustrates how research must look at the dynamic process of gestures – here the pacing of upstrokes and downstrokes – in empirical detail rather than merely code or conceptualize them.*

Black continues with the two-handed vertical gestures until they evolve into horizontal fist or "beating" rhythmic gestures during the temporal adverbial (*when bodies collide*) in lines 19 and 20 (see Figures 9.10 and 9.11). In these two gestures, the fist on the right hand collides with, and cradles in, the open grasping palm of the left hand, with the thumb of each hand in an upwards-touching position. This also demonstrates that gestures may not only have upstrokes, but sidestrokes as well. On the clause final phrase (*with other items*) in line 20, the beat evolves further into two

19 *"bodies collide"* two   20 "when a   20 *"other items"* x2
hand fist hitting gesture   *body collides"*

Figures 9.10–9.12

vertical (up-down) clasping gestures, with the left thumb interlocked over the right in the fist-hitting position (maintaining the same fist hitting position in line 19 and 20) (see Figure 9.12).

The segment concludes in line 21 with the main point of the narrative: *There has to be some evidence* of the collision. Sentence initial unstressed existential *There* is also used to summarize and/or introduce new information, and arrives just before the gesture, contextualizing the relevance of *evidence*. That relevance develops when Black produces an open palm supine gesture co-occurring with the stressed infinitive, which, as Kendon (2004: 266) mentions, is used "when a conclusion or summary with regard to something that has just been said is being given."

Bearing these points in mind, just as Black's fist-hitting gesture demonstrates the collision, so too must there be an embodied consequence of the collision between Smith and Bowman: some embodied proof absorbed from the impact.[4] Relatedly, the increase in intensity, velocity, and force in the rhythmic gestures – the folk-physics of reaction on the fist-hitting gestures – provides kinesically an image of the force and collision that *should* have occurred in the sexual assault. That is, if we consider the *science of transfer theory* (as Black refers to it in line 018, or action-reaction), we see how rhythmic gestures provide a kinesic illustration of what happens when one body collides with another.

---

[4] Ehrlich (2001), in her discussion of the representation of rape in rape trials, notes how defense attorneys organize their side of the rape trial around what she refers to as the "utmost resistance" ideology. Utmost resistance – a once codified legal hurdle for the allegation of sexual assault – required the victim to physically fight off the attack until all resistance was overcome by overwhelming male force. Attorneys continue to use it as a cultural resource to impeach victim credibility. We find here that the defense attorney not only enacts the utmost resistance ideology, but *embodied resistance ideology* also.

By the same token, while *collide* describes the action, it does not show the magnitude of reaction in the same manner as the fist-hitting beats. The motion verb describes the manner of contact; beats visualize the intensity, shape, and consequence of objects coming into contact (see McNeill 1992: 129). Together, they yield a rich unity of meaning to visualize the physics of collision. *Once again this shows the multifunctional versatility of gestures and how they can craft iconic imagery as they simultaneously fracture space into rhythmic episodes.*

In more detail, repetition in the temporal adverbial (*when bodies collide*) synchronizes with both stress and repetition in the horizontal fist gestures to highlight crucial evidence. These repetitive rhythms co-occur at regular intervals in the metric pattern, even though in modulated form. The bodily repetition in the clause final phrase (line 020 *with other items*) branches off into vertical (fist-shaped) gestures, but still maintains the initial impulse of the horizontal beat gestures as it continues, expands, and elaborates the twin motifs. By repeating a fragment of the initial motif, the residual (beating) gestures maintain reflexive continuity with the form and substance of the recurrent pattern: generating poetic pulse and investing gestures à la Kendon with both iconic and rhythmic properties simultaneously. *That one hand gestures the other both imagistically and rhythmically, underscores our desire to demonstrate this empirically using naturally occurring data.*

Why does Black mobilize the subtle shift in gesture phrasing? The first and second *when bodies collide* involve one person hitting another symbolized by the beating movement and thumbs in an up and touching position. But residual gestures (in the clause final phrase) consist of interlocking fingers with one thumb closed over the other (slight variation on the fist-hitting position), a symbolic representation of one body on top of another directed vertically toward the ground (or toward the curled interlocking digits as the virtual ground). The gesture illustrates how, as Smith collides with Bowman who is falling down, he falls on top of her.

More theoretically, the beating and reaction movement represents a gestural imagery of the collision, semantic content that delivers a powerful rhetorical punch to the attorney's narrative. In the process, the interplay of language, gesture, and motion instructs jurors that the evidence of rape must be embodied; it cannot be an issue of private feelings or private language.

Conclusion

In this chapter we have developed Kendon's proposition that discrete taxonomies separating one type of gesture from another may be difficult to sustain. The varied forms and functions of the different hand movements we have analyzed reveal the inadequacies of earlier gesture classifications and, following de Jorio (2000: 59), the importance of detailed analysis of the multifunctionality of gestures. By keeping our analysis close to the data, we have seen that rhythmic, iconic, and deictic functions are not empirically isolable at certain moments in the unfolding interaction. Rather than appealing to some sort of gesture typology, we have seen how beats may simultaneously accentuate rhythm and emphasis on the one hand, and capture imagistic content and/or deictic reference on the other, demonstrating the relevance of fine-grained analysis of naturally occurring data for the study of beats in particular, and gesture in general. In so doing we have called into question the idea that beats and other related taxonomies that are found in gesture studies today, necessarily constitute a "type." Occasionally, one type of gesture may integrate not only with speech, but also with another gesture and thereby fuse into emergent – multifunctional – gestural forms to manage the interactional task at hand.

For the study of legal oratory, this section has followed Rosulek's recommendation to study the neglected extralinguistic dimension of closing argument, and translated Mauet's prescriptive advice on forceful gestures into empirical analysis of how communicative resources in various modalities function in the production of persuasive oratory. Each segment in the narrative consists of an incantatory ensemble of gesture, sound, and space that builds to an oratorical crescendo, one that reveals the persuasive force of closing argument.

10   Conclusion

In conclusion, we wish to summarize some of the more salient points in the book and explore the relationship between law and multimodal conduct along more theoretical lines. As the universal emblems of drama and theater (from the front cover) symbolize, the criminal trial, like all trials, is not about truth or falsity but winning and losing, and that, in turn, depends on which side can best manipulate multimodal conduct as a persuasive resource for engaging the jury. Ignoring this crucial semiotic resource leaves researchers with an impoverished understanding of law and legal proceedings. Omitting multimodal conduct is to ignore a good part of what goes on in the law in action, the law as a sociocultural performance. Indeed, we have demonstrated throughout the book how gesture, gaze, and materiality function as part of the message, often signaling meanings that are not available from words.

Part I examined the multimodal construction of identity and participation. In Chapter 2 we saw the expert recalibrate participation roles during questioning. But his words only convey propositional or denotational content. It is his co-speech head movement, facial expression, and gesture that show the absurdity of the prosecutor's question and naturalize his recalibration of her question and his response. In Chapter 3 we demonstrated how the prosecutor's words indicated what Lynn would have done in response to a stranger, but not *how:* only the prosecutor's metaphoric *brush off* gesture conveyed how she would have brushed off such an advance. On Chapter 4, we saw how the witness's shifting body movements and gaze contextualized interactive meanings in a dynamic negotiation involving multiple laminations of participation: how the organization of participation emerged only from the attorney's linguistic ideology in concert with the witness's multimodal actions. In a striking oratorical maneuver, Black's metapragmatic response exhibited an alert spontaneity tempered by a sophisticated legal-interactional intelligence to recalibrate Mercer's narrative: a reflexive multimodal alignment emerging with both "fully in the moment." In Part II, we illustrated how the prescriptive culture of trial advocacy could be displayed in real time, not by making up examples or relying on intuition but by examining the unfolding organization of multimodal conduct.

In Part III, we emphasized not only how the study of legal performance could benefit by including multimodal conduct, but also how the study of gesture and multimodal conduct could benefit by including legal performance. We wish to explore this mutual contribution further by developing and expanding our analysis of interdigital beats from Chapter 9.

We begin with a quote from Goffman's *Presentation of Self*: "one finds that the performer can be fully taken in by his own act; he can be sincerely convinced that the impression of reality which he stages is the real reality. When his audience is also convinced in this way about the show he puts on ... then only the sociologist or the socially disgruntled will have any doubts about the 'realness' of what is presented" (Goffman 1959: 17).

In a closely related sense, Mauet's classic text on trial advocacy (or what we have referred to as the prescriptive culture of trial advocacy) claims that jurors often decide the case on the basis of "which lawyer *really believes* his side should win" (Mauet 2010: 398). But how do we determine *realness*, or if an attorney *really believes*, and how can we demonstrate this in empirical detail? Consider the following extract and ensuing pictures (not all lines illustrated in photos).

Extract 1 Interdigital Beats (11 seconds)

B1 = One hand vertical/up-down beats/chops; ig = interdigital gestures/beats

```
01   They looked at everything with a microscope
                              [((B1+hold))
     (1.2) n found absolutely nothing
     [ ((B1))
                                   (2.1)
02   Not a single              grass stain (.)
     [((gaze at finger))       [((ig starting with little finger))
03   no abrasion (.)
        [((ig ring finger))
04   no cuts (.)
        [((ig middle finger))
05   no rip (.)
        [((ig index finger))
06   no mud (.)
        [((ig on thumb))
07   no dirt (.)
        [((ig on index finger on down slope))
08   no soil
        [((ig on middle finger on down slope with 1.4
           second post stroke hold on soil))
09   Nothing.
     [((vc=two hands open palms vertical parallel gesture))
```

Figure 10.1: line 02 ((gaze at and downswing on the little finger)).

Figure 10.2: line 02 ((interdigital beat on little finger)).

Figure 10.3: line 5 ((interdigital beat on index finger)).

Figure 10.4: line 6 ((interdigital beat on thumb)).

Figure 10.5: line 8 ((interdigital beat on middle finger on downslope)).

Residual Semanticity

Consider an aspect of gesture not easily, or even possibly, encoded in speech. We have seen in Chapter 9 how interdigital beats recruit the index finger of the right hand to hit and push down the digits of the left hand in the action-reaction imagery (or embodied resistance ideology). We also mentioned in the same chapter that beats may, at certain moments in the discourse, not only foreground key strands of evidential significance but also evoke aspects of propositional imagery – of semantic content. In the example, expert scientists should have found forensic residue on Bow-man's clothing because of the "tremendous impact" between her and the defendant. That no evidential residue showed up under microscopic scru-tiny, exposed, according to the defense, a serious inconsistency in the prosecution's case. During the interdigital beats, the friction of two fingers colliding signifies the impact between one force hitting another and projects how there should be some visible consequence as a result. More explicitly, just as the interdigital beats represent a symbolic residue of touching (contact), so too should the collision between Smith and Bowman be revealed by evidential residue of the collision on her clothing. Put another way, Black shows how one force impacts another in the pushdown part of the stroke or stroke intensifier, and how, by analogy, there should be residual effect on Bowman's clothing. In this action, referential text maps onto the here and now interactional-multimodal text in a dynamic process of what we refer to as *residual semanticity*: how what we are saying becomes what we are doing through the integration of text metricality and rhythmic beats. *Beats, in this instance, not only serve a pragmatic function but convey residual semanticity, or aspects of content as well.*[1]

Counting Off Inconsistencies

In the adversary system, the weight of evidence refers to the weight or significance of facts necessary to tilt the burden of proof to one side or the other, and such proof rests on the persuasiveness of the evidence. Which attorney *really believes* his side should win? Who counts off the most facts and thereby creates the most favorable impression on the jury? And, most importantly, how does one attorney make their account *count, make it appear real*?

Consider counting in metaphoric terms as we discussed in Chapter 9 – as *more of form is more of content* (Lakoff and Johnson 1980) and *ideas as object* (Cienki and Müller 2008). In the aforementioned example, the items Black counts off with the interdigital beats could suffice semantically at the type or category level (such as "There's nothing on her clothing," etc.). Moreover, the interdigital beats accompany synonyms or noun phrases similar, if not identical in meaning, at the conversational level: *grass stains* equals *dirt* equals *mud* equals *soil* and so on. What interactional work does such redundancy accomplish in the law?

The interdigital beats make each individual piece of evidence stand out, just like each individual digit stands out from the others. The beats carve up or dissect a unity into discretely layered and distinct items of significance: a microscopic division of referential detail that counts off and

---

[1] Along similar lines, the ascending and descending movements on the hand (which show increase and direction of the inconsistencies) are not something as easily conveyed in speech as in gesture.

expands inconsistencies in the prosecution's case. That is, the defense attorney not only magnifies the prosecution's inconsistencies but also shapes and quantifies them in embodied forms of harmonic density and rhythmic complexity. In the spatio-temporal conversation among the fingers, he allows the jury to visualize that counting and cumulative process in motion.[2] This conversation demonstrates that counting is not merely a mathematical operation but a sociocultural resource in the construction of legal context.

More theoretically, we are claiming that counting, cumulating, and differentiating are more richly conveyed through gesture than speech. According to Goldin-Meadow (2015: 73), "Because the representational formats underlying gesture are mimetic and analog rather than discrete gesture permits speakers to represent ideas that lend themselves to these formats (e.g., shapes, sizes, spatial relationships) – ideas that ... may not be easily encoded in speech." Just as important, touching the individual digits of one hand with the finger of the other hand, encodes and individuates objects more effectively than other types of gesture. As Alibali et al. find (2001: 52), "Touch is closer to the tagged object than a point; it is more clear which specific object is being indicated by a touch than a point." By touching each digit to branch off from the whole, Black signals that it warrants unique consideration as an individual item of evidence. He integrates repetition of the unfolding text with gestural rhythms to produce a semantic foregrounding affect (as mentioned earlier, conveying substantive information and performing a pragmatic function simultaneously), a persuasive oratory that may well tilt the balance of proof and put the defense case in the most favorable light.

That balance of proof poses important questions and problems in relation to the law. In the law, inconsistency is taken as a natural incongruity or juxtaposition among contradictory facts of evidence. However, as Black unfolds the digits to individuate items of evidence from the whole (and thus increase their size/weight), he conceals their "factual" status as a unity of similar, if not identical items, a multimodal ideology that naturalizes inconsistency in the mutual interplay of the fingers. Black's beats impart a natural "feel" to his verbal rhythms and inject them – and the inconsistencies – with a powerful sense of oratorical precision. *Rather than view inconsistency as a natural or objective incongruity between contradictory*

---

[2] Individuating the whole also displays a level of precision that confers authority on his words and shows the jury that Black considers all these items important enough to mention individually, and important enough to count off in gestural form. Moreover, notice that Black gazes at the little finger for the beginning beat progression. As Müller (2008: 236) mentions, "Directing the gaze at something ... indicates speaker's focal attention" and "turns the gesture into an interactively significant object" (see also, Streeck 1993: 286).

facts of evidence, we envision it as a contextually situated and multimodally emergent naturalizing process, emerging in part from the rhythmic integration of gesture and speech. Interdigital beats function to individuate, expand, and cumulate individual pieces of evidential significance through finger movements along the hand. In that process, counting may be viewed not as a static or given outcome of some mathematical operation, but as an active micro-technique of oratorical power: counting as a situated and multimodal accomplishment. In the previous example, the manual modality adds another dimension to meaning that is not as vividly captured through the oral modality alone.

Thus, our empirical investigation of the manual modality has yielded a rich vein of unexplored territory in the so-called "verbal" institution of the law, one that promises considerable payoff for further analysis of the rhetorical practices trial participants bring to bear on the construction of evidential significance and production of persuasive oratory. We have also delivered on the promissory note mentioned in the Introduction: that the study of multimodal conduct in the law makes distinct contributions to the study of the gesture-speech relationship. Looking at gestures in naturally occurring legal performance and in fine-grained detail reveals their multi-functionality – how they may, at certain moments, function both imagistically and rhythmically (or more generally, non-imagistically).

Of course, the strategic use of language and gesture to accomplish the speaker's persuasive goal goes back to ancient times. Writing in ancient Rome, Quintilian spoke of oratorical performance and the integration of language and gesture.

So there is no Proof – at least no Proof depending on the orator – which is so secure that it does not lose its force unless it is assisted by the assurance of the speaker. Again, all emotions inevitably languish unless they are kindled into flame by voice, face and the bearing of virtually the whole body [. . .] since words are very powerful by themselves, and the voice adds it own contribution to the content, and gestures and movements have a meaning, then, when they all come together the result must be perfection (Quintilian 2001, Book 11.3: 87–89).

By looking at the aesthetic dimensions of oratorical practice we have demonstrated how the interplay among speech, gesture, and other modalities furnishes powerful rhetorical resources for legal performance. We have shown not only how we "do things with words," but how we construct legal context through words and gesture – through multimodal conduct. While we can only speculate about their contribution to the final outcome of this case, we can still see how these emotions are "kindled into flame" from the poetic synchronization and integration of these communicative resources, a result that must be "perfection" in the art of legal persuasion.

References

Aijmer, K. (2002). *English Discourse Particles.* Amsterdam: John Benjamins.

Alibali, M., Heath, D., and Myers, H. (2001). Effects of visibility between speaker and listener on gesture production: Some gestures are meant to be seen. *Journal of Memory and Language,* 44 (2), 169–188.

Allerton, D. (2002). *Stretched Verb Constructions in English.* London: Routledge.

Aoki, H. (2011). Some Functions of Speaker Head Nods. In J. Streeck, C. Goodwin, and C. LeBaron (eds.) *Embodied Interaction: Language and the Body in the Material World.* New York: Cambridge University Press. pp. 93–105.

Archer, D. (2005). *Questions and Answers in the English Courtroom (1640–1760).* Amsterdam: John Benjamins.

Atkinson, J. M. (1984). *Our Master's Voices.* London: Routledge.

Atkinson, J. and Drew, P. (1979). *Order in Court.* New York: MacMillian.

Bakhtin, M. (1981). *The Dialogic Imagination: Four Essays.* Austin: University of Texas Press.

Bauman, R. (1986). *Story, Performance and Event.* New York: Cambridge University Press.

Bavelas, J. (1994). Gestures as part of speech: Methodological implications. *Research on Language and Social Interaction,* 27 (3), 201–221.

Bavelas, J., Chovil, N., Coates, L., and Roe, L. (1995). Gestures specialized for dialogue. *Personality and Social Psychology Bulletin,* 21 (4), 394–405.

Bavelas J., Gerwing, J., and Healing, S. (2014a). Hand and Facial Gestures in Conversational Interaction. In T. Holtgraves (ed.) *The Oxford Handbook of Language and Social Psychology.* New York: Oxford University Press. pp. 111–130.

(2014b). Including Facial Gestures in Gesture-Speech Ensembles. In M. Seyfeddinipur and M. Gullberg (eds.) *From Gesture in Conversation to Visible Action as Utterance: Essays in Honor of Adam Kendon.* Amsterdam: John Benjamins. pp. 15–34.

Bavelas, J., Nicole C., Douglas L., and Allan, W. (1992). Interactive gestures. *Discourse Processes,* 15 (4), 469–489.

Biber, D., Johansson, S., Leech, Geoffrey, Conrad, S., and Finegan, E. (1999). *Longman Grammar of Spoken and Written English.* New York: Longman.

Blommaert, J. (2010). *The Sociolinguistics of Globalization.* Cambridge: Cambridge University Press.

Broaders, S. and Goldin-Meadow, S. (2010). Truth is at hand: How gesture adds information during investigative interviews. *Psychology Science,* 21 (5), 623–628.

Bucholtz, M. and Hall, K. (2005). Identity and interaction: A sociocultural linguistic approach. *Discourse Studies*, 7 (4–5), 585–614.

Bulwer, J. (2003 [1644]). *Chirologia or the Natural Language of the Hand*. Whitefish, MT: Kessinger Publishing.

Calbris, G. (2011). *Elements of Meaning in Gesture*. Amsterdam: John Benjamins.

Cameron, D. (2003). Globalizing "Communication." In J. Aitchison and D. Lewis (eds.) *New Media Language*. London: Routledge. pp. 27–35.

Carr, E. S. (2010). Enactments of expertise. *Annual Review of Anthropology*, 17–32.

Carter, R. and McCarthy, M. (2006). *Cambridge Grammar of English*. Cambridge: Cambridge University Press.

Cassanto, D. and Jasmin, K. (2012). The hands of time: Temporal gestures in English speakers. *Cognitive Linguistics*, 23 (4), 643–674.

Cienki, A. (2008). Why Study Metaphor and Gesture? In A. Cienki and C. Muller (eds.) *Metaphor and Gesture*. Amsterdam: John Benjamins. pp. 5–26.

Cienki, A. and Müller, C. (2008). Metaphor, Gesture and Thought. In R. Gibbs (ed.) *The Cambridge Handbook of Metaphor and Thought*. New York: Cambridge University Press. pp. 483–501.

Conley, J. and O'Barr, W. (1990). *Rules versus Relationships*. Chicago: University of Chicago Press.

  (1998). *Just Words*. Chicago: University of Chicago Press.

Cotterill, J. (2003). *Language and Power in Court: A Linguistic Analysis of the O. J. Simpson Trial*. New York: Palgrave.

Crothers, C. (1987). *Robert K. Merton*. London: Tavistock.

de Jorio, A. (2000). Gesture in Naples and Gesture in Classical Antiquity. A translation of La Mimica Degli Antichi Investigata Nel Gestire Napoletano *(1832)*. Bloomington: Indiana University Press.

Deppermann, A. (2015). Positioning. In A. de Fina and A. Georgakopoulou (eds.) *The Handbook of Narrative Analysis*. New York: John Wiley & Sons. pp. 369–387.

Deppermann, A. and Streeck, J. (forthcoming). *Modalities and Temporalities*. Amsterdam: John Benjamins.

Drew, P. (1985). Analyzing the Use of Language in Courtroom Interaction. In T. van Dijk (ed.) *Handbook of Discourse Analysis*, vol. 3. New York: Academic Press. pp. 133–47.

  (1992). Contested Evidence in Courtroom Cross-Examination. In P. Drew and J. Heritage (eds.) *Talk at Work*. New York: Cambridge University Press. pp. 470–520.

Ehrlich, S. (2001). *Representing Rape*. New York: Routledge.

Ekman, P. and Friesen, W. (2003). *Unmasking the Face*. Cambridge, MA: Malor Books.

Enfield, N. J. (2001). Lip-Pointing: A discussion of form and function with reference to data from Laos. *Gesture*, 1, 185–212.

Fairclough, N. (2003). *Analysing Discourse*. New York: Routledge.

Ferré, G. (2011). Functions of three open-palm gestures. *Multimodal Communication*, 1 (1), 5–20.

  (2014). Multimodal hyperbole. *Multimodal Communication*, 3 (1), 25–50.

Fleming, L. and Lempert, M. (2014). Poetics and Performativity. In N. J. Enfield, P. Kockelman, and J. Sidnell (eds.) *The Cambridge Handbook of Linguistic Anthropology*. Cambridge: Cambridge University Press. pp. 485–515.

Friedman, L. (1977). *Law and Society: An Introduction*. Englewood Cliffs, NJ: Prentice Hall.

Fuller, J. (1993). Hearing between the lines: Style switching in a courtroom setting. *Pragmatics*, 3 (1), 29–43.

Gaines, P. (2016). *From Truth to Technique at Trial: A Discursive History of Advocacy Advice Texts*. New York: Oxford University Press.

Gibbons, J. (2003). *Forensic Linguistics*. Oxford: Blackwell.

Goffman, E. (1959). *The Presentation of Self in Everyday Life*. New York: Doubleday.

(1963). *Behavior in Public Places: Notes on the Social Organization of Gatherings*. New York: The Free Press.

(1967). *Interaction Ritual*. New York: Pantheon.

(1981). *Forms of Talk*. Philadelphia: University of Pennsylvania Press.

Goldin-Meadow, S. (2003). *Hearing Gesture*. Cambridge, MA: Harvard University Press.

(2015). Gesture in All Its Forms. In M. Seyfeddinipur and M. Gullberg (eds.) *From Gesture in Conversation to Visible Action as Utterance: Essays in Honor of Adam Kendon*. Amsterdam: John Benjamins. pp. 290–308.

Goode, W. (1960). A theory of role strain. *American Sociological Review*, 25, 483–496.

Goodwin, C. (1979). The Interactive Construction of a Sentence in Natural Conversation. In G. Psathas (ed.) *Everyday Language: Studies in Ethnomethodology*. New York: Irvington Publishers. pp. 97–121.

(1981). *Conversational Organization: Interaction between Speakers and Hearers*, New York: Academic Press.

(1987). Forgetfulness as an interactive resource. *Social Psychology Quarterly*, 50, 115–131.

(1994). Professional vision. *American Anthropologist*, 95 (3), 606–633.

(2000). Action and embodiment within situated human interaction. *Journal of Pragmatics*, 32, 1489–1522.

(2003). Pointing as Situated Practice. In S. Kita (ed.) *Pointing: Where Language, Culture, and Cognition Meet*. Mahwah: Lawrence Erlbaum. pp. 217–241.

(2007). Environmentally Coupled Gestures. In S. Duncan, J. Cassell, and E. Levy (eds.) *Gesture and the Dynamic Dimension of Language: Essays in Honor of David McNeill*. Amsterdam: John Benjamins. pp. 195–212.

Goodwin, C. and Goodwin, M. (1987). Concurrent operations on talk: Notes on the interactive organization of assessments. *IPrA Papers in Pragmatics*, 1 (1) 1–52.

(2004). Participation. In A. Duranti (ed.) *A Companion to Linguistic Anthropology*, Oxford: Blackwell. pp. 222–244.

Goodwin, M. (1990) *He-Said-She-Said*. Bloomington: Indiana University Press.

Hale, S. (1999). Interpreters' treatment of discourse markers in courtroom questions. *Forensic Linguistics*, 6 (1), 57–82.

Handel, W. (1979). Normative expectations and the emergence of meaning as solutions to problems: Convergence of structural and interactionist views. *American Journal of Sociology*, 84, 855–881.

Harris, S. (1984). Questions as a mode of control in magistrate's court. *International Journal of Sociology of Language*, 49, 5–27.

Haydock, R. and Sonsteng, J. (1990). *Trial Theories, Tactics and Techniques*. St. Paul, MN: West.

Heath, C. and Hindmarsh, J. (2002). Analyzing Interaction. In T. May (ed.) *Qualitative Research in Action*. London: Sage. pp. 99–121.

Heath, C., Hindmarsh, J., and Luff, P. (2010). *Video in Qualitative Research*. London: Sage.

Heffer, C. (2010). Narrative in the Trial: Constructing Crime Stories in Court. In M. Coulthard and A. Johnson (eds.) *The Routledge Handbook of Forensic Linguistics*. New York: Routledge. pp. 199–217.

Heritage, J. (2004). Conversational Analysis and Institutional Talk. In D. Silverman (ed.) *Qualitative Research: Theory, Method and Practice* (2nd edn), London: Sage. pp. 222–245.

Heritage, J. and Greatbatch, D. (1986). Generating applause: A study of rhetoric and response at party political conferences. *American Journal of Sociology*, 92 (1), 110–157.

Hester, S. and Francis, D. (2001). Is Institutional Talk a Phenomenon?: Reflections on Ethnomethodology and Applied Conversation Analysis. In A. McHoul and M. Rapley (eds.) *How to Analyze Talk in Institutional Settings*. London: Continuum. pp. 206–217.

Hilbert, R. (1990). Merton's Theory of Role-Sets and Status Sets. In J. Clark, C. Modgil, and S. Modgil (eds.) *Robert K. Merton*. New York: Falmer Press. pp. 177–186.

Hindmarsh, J. and Heath, C. (2000). Embodied reference: A study of deixis in workplace interaction. *Journal of Pragmatics*, 32, 1855–1878.

Hobbs, P. (2003). You must say it for him: Reformulating a witness' testimony on cross-examination at trial. *Text*, 23 (4), 477–511.

Hodges, A. (2016). Hunting for "racists": Tape fetishism and the intertextual enactment and reproduction of the dominant understanding of racism in US Society. *Journal of Linguistic Anthropology*, 26 (1), 26–40.

Hyland, K. (2002). Directive: Argument and engagement in academic writing. *Applied Linguistics*, 23 (2), 215–239.

Innes, B. (2010). "*Well* that's why I asked the question sir": *Well* as a discourse marker in court. *Language in Society*, 39 (1), 95–117.

Irvine, J. (1996). Shadow Conversations: The Indeterminacy of Participant Roles. In M. Silverstein and G. Urban (eds.) *Natural Histories of Discourse*. Chicago: University of Chicago Press. pp. 131–160

Jakobson, R. (1960). Closing Statement. In T. Sebeok (ed.) *Style in Language*. Cambridge, MA: MIT Press. pp. 398–429.

Jakobson, R. and Pomoska, K. (1988). *Dialogues*. Cambridge, MA: MIT Press.

Jaworski, A. (2000). Silence and Small Talk. In J. Coupland (ed.) *Small Talk*. New York: Longman. pp. 110–132.

Johnson, A. (2002). *So . . . ?*: Pragmatic Implications of *So*-Prefaced Questions in Formal Police Interviews. In J. Cotterill (ed.) *Language in the Legal Process*. New York: Palgrave Macmillan. pp. 91–110.

Johnstone, B. (2008). *Discourse Analysis* (2nd edn). Oxford: Blackwell.

Jones, S. and LeBaron, C. (2002). Research on the relationship between verbal and nonverbal communication: Emerging integrations. *Journal of Communication*, 52 (3), 499–521.

Kendon, A. (2002). Some uses of the head shake. *Gesture*, 2, 147–183.

   (2004). *Gesture: Visible Action as Utterance*. Cambridge: Cambridge University Press.

   (2017). Pragmatic functional gestures: Some observations on the history of their study and their nature. *Gesture*, 16, 157–177.

   (1990). *Conducting Interaction: Patterns of Behavior in Focused Encounters*. New York: Cambridge University Press.

Kita, S. (2003). Pointing: A Foundational Building Block of Human Communication. In S. Kita (ed.) *Pointing: Where Language, Culture, and Cognition Meet*. Mahwah: Lawrence Erlbaum. pp. 1–8.

Komter, M. (2000) The power of legal language: The significance of small activities for large problems. *Semiotica*, 131–3/4, 415–428.

   (2006). From talk to text: The interactional construction of a police record. *Research on Language and Social Interaction*, 39, 201–228.

Krahmer, E. and Swerts, M. (2007). The effects of visual beats on prosodic prominence: Accoustic analyses, auditory perception and visual perception. *Journal of Memory and Language*, 57, 396–414.

Labov, W. (1972). *Language in the Inner City*. Philadelphia: University of Pennsylvania Press.

Lakoff, G. and Johnson, M. (1980). *Metaphors We Live By*. Chicago: University of Chicago Press.

   (1999). *Philosophy in the Flesh: The Embodied Mind and Its Challenge to Western Thought*. New York: Basic.

Lempert, M. (2008). The poetics of stance: Text-metricality, epistemicity, interaction. *Language in Society*, 37, 569–592.

   (2011). Barack Obama, being sharp: Indexical order in the pragmatics of precision-grip gesture. *Gesture*, 11 (3), 241–270.

   (2012). Indirectness. In C. Paulston, S. Kiesling, and E. Rangel (eds.) *The Handbook of Intercultural Communication*. Oxford: Wiley-Blackwell. pp. 180–204.

   (2017) Uncommon resemblance: Pragmatic affinity in political gesture. Forthcoming in Gesture.

Lempert, M. and Silverstein, M. (2012). *Creatures of Politics*. Bloomington: Indiana University Press.

Luchjenbroers, J. and Aldridge, M. (2007). Conceptual manipulation by metaphors and frames: Dealing with rape victims in legal discourse. *Text and Talk*, 27 (3), 339–359.

Maricchiolo, F., Gnisci, A., Bonaiuto, M., and Ficca, G. A. (2009). Effects of different types of hand gestures in persuasive speech on receivers' evaluations. *Language and Cognitive Processes*, 24, 239–266.

Matoesian, G. (1993). *Reproducing Rape: Domination through Talk in the Courtroom*. Chicago: University of Chicago Press.

(2000). Intertextual authority in reported speech: Production media in the Kennedy Smith rape trial. *Journal of Pragmatics*, 32 (7), 879–914.

(2001) *Law and the Language of Identity*. Oxford: Oxford University Press.

(2005) Struck by speech revisited: Embodied stance in jurisdictional discourse. *Journal of Sociolinguistics*, 9 (2), 167–194.

Mauet, T. (1996) *Trial Techniques* (4th edn). Boston: Little, Brown and Company.

(2010). *Trial Techniques* (8th edn). New York: Aspen.

McClave, E. (2000). Linguistic functions of head movements in the context of speech. *Journal of Pragmatics*, 32, 855–878.

McNeill, D. (1992). *Hand and Mind: What Gestures Reveal about Thought*. Chicago: University of Chicago Press.

(2005). *Gesture and Thought*. Chicago: University of Chicago Press.

(2006). Gesture and Communication. In K. Brown (ed.) *Encyclopedia of Linguistics* (2nd edn). New York: Elsevier. pp. 58–67.

(2012). *How Language Began: Gesture and Speech in Human Evolution*. Cambridge: Cambridge University Press.

(2013). Gesture as a Window onto Mind and Brain. In C. Muller, A. Cienki, E. Fricke, S. Ladewig, D. McNeill, and J. Bressem (eds.) *Body – Language – Communication*, vol. 1. Berlin: De Gruyter Mouton. pp. 29–54.

(2016). *Why We Gesture*. Cambridge: Cambridge University Press.

Mendoza-Denton, N. (2002). Language and Identity. In J. Chambers, P. Trudgill, and N. Schilling-Estes (eds.) *The Handbook of Language Variation and Change*. Oxford: Blackwell. pp. 475–499.

Merton, R. (1957). The role set. *British Journal of Sociology*, 8, 106–120.

(1976). *Sociological Ambivalence and Other Essays*. New York: Free Press.

Mertz, E. (2007). *The Language of Law School*. New York: Oxford University Press.

Mondada, L. (2016). Challenges of multimodality: Language and the body in social interaction. *Journal of Sociolinguistics*, 20 (3), 336–366.

Morris, D. (1977). *Manwatching: A Field Guide to Human Behaviour*. London: Jonathan Cape.

Müller, C. (2008). What Gestures Reveal about the Nature of Metaphor. In A. Cienki and C. Muller (eds.) *Metaphor and Gesture*. Amsterdam: John Benjamins. pp. 219–245.

Müller, C., Cienki, A., Fricke, E., Ladewig, S., McNeill, D., and Bressem, J. (eds.) (2013). *Body – Language – Communication: Volume 1*. Berlin: DeGruyter Mouton.

(2014). *Body – Language – Communication: Volume 2*. Berlin: DeGruyter Mouton.

Nevile, M. (2015). The embodied turn in research on language and social interaction. *Research on Language and Social Interaction*, 48 (2), 121–151.

Norris, S. (2004). *Analyzing Multimodal Interaction: A Methodological Framework*. New York: Routledge.

O'Barr, W. (1981). *Linguistic Evidence*. New York: Academic Press.

O'Connor, P. E. (2000). *Speaking of Crime: Narrative of Prisoners*. Lincoln: University of Nebraska Press.

Ochs, E. (1996). Linguistic Resources for Socializing Humanity. In J. Gumperz and S. Levinson (eds.) *Rethinking Linguistic Relativity*. New York: Cambridge University Press. pp. 407–437.

Ochs, E. and Capps, L. (1996). Narrating the self. *Annual Review of Anthropology*, 25, 19–43.

Pascal, E. (2006). Questions in legal monologues: Fictive interaction as argumentative strategy in a murder trial. *Text and Talk*, 26 (3), 383–402.

Perrin, T., Caldwell, M., and Chase, C. (2003). *The Art and Science of Trial Advocacy*. Cincinnati, OH: Anderson.

Philips, S. (1972). Participant Structures and Communicative Competence: Warm Springs Children in Community and Classroom. In C. Cazden, V. John, and D. Hymes (eds.) *Functions of Language in the Classroom*. New York: Columbia Teachers Press. pp. 370–394

  (1987). On the Use of wh-Questions in American Courtroom Discourse: A Study on the Relation between Language Form and Language Function. In L. Kedar (ed.) *Power Through Language*. Norwood, NJ: Ablex. pp. 83–112.

  (1998). *Language in the Ideology of Judges*. New York: Oxford University Press.

Precht, K. (2003). Stance moods in spoken English: Evidentiality and affect in British and American conversation. *Text*, 23 (2), 239–257.

Quintilian. (2001). *The Orator's Education*, trans. D. A. Russell. Cambridge, MA: Harvard University Press.

Raymond, G. (2006). Questions at Work: Yes/No Type Interrogatives in Institutional Contexts. In P. Drew, G. Raymond, and D. Weinberg (eds.) *Talk and Interaction in Social Research Methods*. London: Sage. pp. 115–134.

Rosulek, L. (2008). Legitimation and the Heteroglossic Nature of Closing Argument. In D. Schiffrin, A. De Fina, and A. Nylund (eds.) *Telling Stories: Language, Narrative and Social Life*. Washington, DC: Georgetown University Press. pp. 181–194.

  (2010). Prosecution and Defense Closing Speeches: The Creation of Contrastive Closing Arguments. In M. Coulthard and A. Johnson (eds.) *The Routledge Handbook of Forensic Linguistics*. New York: Routledge. pp. 218–230.

  (2015). *Dueling Discourses*. New York: Oxford University Press.

Rozin, P., Lowery, L., and Ebert, R. (1994). Varieties of disgust faces and the structure of disgust. *Journal of Personality and Social Psychology*, 66 (5), 870–881.

Sacks, H. (1992). *Lectures on Conversation, Volumes I and II*. Oxford: Blackwell.

Saks, M. and Faigman, D. (2005). Expert evidence after Daubert. *Annual Review of Law and Social Science*, 1, 105–130.

Sacks, H. and Schegloff, E. (2002) Home position. *Gesture*, 2, 133–146.

Sasaki, Y. (1991). An analysis of sentences with nonreferential *there* in spoken American English. *Word*, 42 (2), 157–178.

Schegloff, E. (1988/9). From interview to confrontation: Observations on the Bush/Rather encounter. *Research on Language and Social Interaction*, 22, 215–240.

  (1998). Body torque. *Social Research*, 65 (3), 535–596.

  (2000). Overlapping talk and the organization of turn-taking for conversation. *Language in Society*, 29, 1–63.

Schiffrin, D. (1987). *Discourse Markers*. New York: Cambridge University Press.

Siewierska, A. (2004). *Person*. Cambridge: Cambridge University Press.

Silverstein, M. (1979). Language Structure and Linguistic Ideology. In P. Cline, W. Hanks, and C. Hofbauer (eds.) *The Elements: A Parasession on Linguistic Units and Levels*. Chicago: University of Chicago Press. pp. 193–247.

(1985). On the Pragmatic "Poetry" of Prose: Parallelism, Repetition, and Cohesive Structure in the Time Course of Dyadic Conversation. In D. Schiffrin (ed.) *Meaning, Form, and Use in Context: Linguistic Applications*. Washington, DC: Georgetown University Press. pp. 181–198.

(1993). Metapragmatic Discourse and the Metapragmatic Function. In J. Lucy (ed.) *Reflexive Language*. New York: Cambridge University Press. pp. 33–58.

(1998). The Improvisational Performance of Culture in Realtime Discursive Practice. In R. K. Sawyer (ed.) *Creativity in Performance*. Greenwich, CT: Ablex. pp. 265–312.

(2005). Axes of evils: Token versus type interdiscursivity. *Journal of Linguistic Anthropology*, 15 (1), 6–22.

(2014). Denotation and the Pragmatics of Language. In N. J. Enfield, P. Kockelman, and J. Sidnell (eds.) *Handbook of Linguistic Anthropology*. Cambridge: Cambridge University Press. pp. 128–157.

Simpson, A. (1988). *Invitation to Law*. Oxford: Blackwell.

Streeck, J. (1993). Gesture as communication: Its coordination with gaze and speech. *Communication Monographs*, 60, 275–299.

(1996). How to do things with things: Objets trouves and symbolization. *Human Studies*, 19, 365–384.

(2008). Gesture in political communication: A case study of the democratic presidential candidates during the 2004 primary campaign. *Research on Language and Social Interaction*, 41 (2), 154–186.

(2009). *Gesturecraft: The Manu-facture of Meaning*. Amsterdam: John Benjamins.

Streeck, J. and Hartege, U. (1992). Previews: Gestures at the Transition Place. In P. Auer and A. Di Luzio (eds.) *The Contextualization of Language* Amsterdam: John Benjamins. pp. 35–57.

Tanford, J. (1983). *The Trial Process: Law, Tactics and Ethics*. Charlottesville, VA: Michie.

Tannen, D. (1987). Repetition in conversation: Toward a poetics of talk. *Language*, 63, 574–605.

(1989). *Talking Voices*. New York: Cambridge University Press.

Taslitz, A. (1999). *Rape and the Culture of the Courtroom*. New York: New York University Press.

Tebendorf, S. (2014). Pragmatic and Metaphoric – Combining Functional with Cognitive Approaches in the Analysis of the "Brushing Aside Gesture." In C. Muller, A. Cienki, E. Fricke, S. Ladewig, D. McNeill, and J. Bressem (eds.). *Body – Language – Communication, Volume 2*. Berlin: De Gruyter Mouton. pp. 1540–1558.

Tiersma, P. (1999). *Legal Language*. Chicago: University of Chicago Press.

Thompson, G. and Hunston, S. (2000). Evaluation: An Introduction. In S. Hunston and G. Thompson (eds.) *Evaluation in Text*. New York: Oxford University Press. pp. 1–27.

Tsu, A. (1991). The pragmatic functions of *I don't know*. *Text*, 11 (4), 607–622.

van der Houwen, F. (2013). Reported writing in court: Putting evidence "on record." *Text and Talk*, 33 (6), 747–769.

van der Houwen, F. and Sneijder, P. (2014). From text to talk in criminal court: Prosecuting, defending, and examining the evidence. *Language & Communication*, 33 (2), 37–52.

Volosinov, V. N. (1973). *Marxism and the Philosophy of Language*. Cambridge, MA: Harvard University Press.

Walker, A. (1987). Linguistic Manipulation, Power, and the Legal Setting. In L. Kedar (ed.) *Power through Language*. Norwood, NJ: Ablex. pp. 55–76.

Weber, M. (1976). *The Protestant Ethic and the Spirit of Capitalism*. New York: Charles Scribner's Sons.

(1978). *Economy and Society, Volume 2*. Berkeley: University of California Press.

Wittgenstein, L. (1953). *Philosophical Investigations* (3rd edn). New York: MacMillian Publishing.

Wollock, J. (2002). John Bulwer (1606–1656) and the significance of gesture in the 17th century. *Gesture*, 2 (2), 227–258.

Woolard, K. (1998). Introduction: Language Ideology as a Field of Inquiry. In B. Schieffelin, K. Woolard, and P. Kroskrity (eds.) *Language Ideologies*. New York: Oxford University Press. pp. 3–47.

Wortham, S. (2001). *Narratives in Action*. New York: Teachers College Press.

Index